Justice Delayed, Justice Denied

Betty Boles Ellison

Copyright © 2008 by Betty Boles Ellison

All rights reserved. No part of this book shall be reproduced or transmitted in any form or by any means, electronic, mechanical, magnetic, photographic including photocopying, recording or by any information storage and retrieval system, without prior written permission of the publisher. No patent liability is assumed with respect to the use of the information contained herein. Although every precaution has been taken in the preparation of this book, the publisher and author assume no responsibility for errors or omissions. Neither is any liability assumed for damages resulting from the use of the information contained herein.

ISBN 0-7414-5064-X

Published by:
INFINITY
PUBLISHING.COM
1094 New DeHaven Street, Suite 100
West Conshohocken, PA 19428-2713
Info@buybooksontheweb.com
www.buybooksontheweb.com
Toll-free (877) BUY BOOK
Local Phone (610) 941-9999
Fax (610) 941-9959

Printed in the United States of America
Printed on Recycled Paper
Published November 2008

Table of Contents

Dedication i

Introduction iii

Betty Gail Brown 1

Mary Marrs Swinebroad Cawein 57

Carlton Elliott Ray 151

Rebecca Anne Moore 209

Cynthia Carol Baker-Harold Daniel Sheppard 239

Jean Michel Gambet 267

About the Author 335

Justice Delayed, Justice Denied

is dedicated to

Mary Grace and Charlie Wills,

who always loved a good mystery.

Introduction

Unsolved murders are, without a doubt, the most fascinating type of non-fiction. Their stories include the scene of the crime, the position of the body, the method at hand, the reports of the investigators, the backgrounds of the victim and their suspects. Each story could go down so many different roads. It's the utmost gamble in life, to kill someone, followed by the utmost effort by society, technology and human investigative impulse to find the killer, who will probably face the maximum our penal system will allow.

To watch Betty Boles Ellison work is to materialize every non-writer's vision of what a writer's world looks like: a room full of writer's accolades on the walls, large poster-size versions of the covers of her previous endeavors, file cabinets everywhere and stacks and stacks of research file folders.

A notorious and diligent researcher, Ellison delved into the world of corrupt athletic administration to pen *Kentucky's Domain of Power, Greed and Corruption* detailing the long history of mismanagement in University of Kentucky athletics. Her other books are *Illegal Odyssey, 200 Years of Kentucky Moonshine* and *A Man Seen But Once*, a biography of Cassius Marcellus Clay.

Ellison also wrote several of the cover stories for *Snitch Magazine*, of which I was co-owner and publisher. Ellison's stories of yesteryear, involving unsolved murders, were popular, controversial and good old-fashioned "can't put it down page turners."

Her investigative style and writing talents were of tremendous human interest in the world of crime due to her unusual style. Many writers stick strictly to the facts, and though Ellison bases everything on facts and interviews, her writing style is entertaining as her grandmotherly and insinuating tone demands constant thought and reflection by the reader. She inserts a little sarcasm here, a little innuendo there and a talent to ask readers question that should have been asked years before, when the crimes took place.

Ellison has chosen to pen *Justice Delayed, Justice Denied* based on seven of the more deliciously controversial murder investigations of the twentieth century in Lexington.

The cases include Betty Gail Brown, who was strangled with her bra on the Transylvania campus in 1961; Marrs Cawein, a socialite and doctor's wife, who was found in her bedroom with carbolic acid in her stomach in 1965; Elliott Ray, a young physician, was assassinated at Merrick Place in 1977, only weeks after Melanie Flynn disappeared never to be seen again; Rebecca Anne Moore, a beautiful art student mysteriously vanished in 1980, and her body surfaced in the Kentucky River six months later; Cindy Baker and Danny Sheppard, who authorities decided stabbed each other in the bloody bathroom of their home in the summer of 1981, and Jean Michel Gambet, a French horseman who was found shot in his burning BMW just before Christmas in 1982.

There are many more that she has sidestepped, perhaps in the event of a sequel, I ask with an Ellison-esque questioning tone and simultaneous raised eyebrow smirk?

Our friendship has been a unique one. I was a thirty-four-year-old bachelor when we met and she was a 60-something widow. But we have one thing in common, a desire to entertain and intrigue our readers and a devotion of keeping hope alive that the publicity from these cases will continue to publicize their uncertainly in the legal community and cause no stone to be left unturned.

I am sure you will find *Justice Delayed, Justice Denied* to be just as much of a page-turner as I will.

Tim Woodburn
woodburnky@aol.com

Justice Delayed,

Justice Denied

Betty Gail Brown

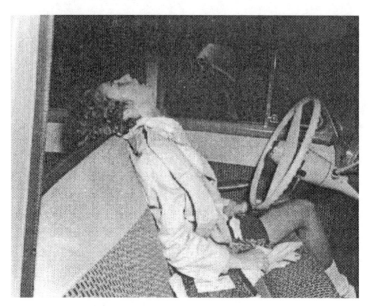

Betty Gail Brown inside her car.
(Lexington Division of Police)

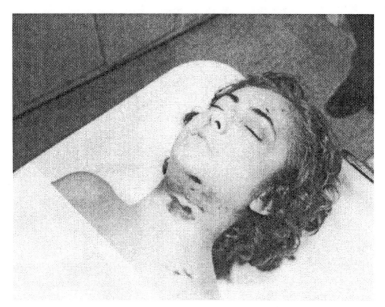

Wounds on Brown's neck and face.
(Lexington Division of Police)

Excitement in the Air

It was one of those nippy, frosty October evenings with just enough bite in the air for Transylvania College coeds to bring out the fresh, new fall clothes they had been collecting since summer. The rusts, reds, oranges and browns corresponded with the changing colors of leaves on the small tree-studded campus on the north side of Lexington, Kentucky.

There was something else in the air: excitement about the school's big annual autumn event, Rafinesque Week, held the last week in October.

There must have been some anticipation of the coming weekend as Betty Gail Brown, a beautiful, petite sophomore casually dressed for the season, drove from her south Lexington home back to the campus on Thursday evening, October 26, 1961, for a study session in Forrer Hall for a biology test the next day. A popular student, she planned to join the festivities, which included parties, a bonfire on the campus and competition where four students were selected to spend the night around the crypt of famed botanist and Transylvania professor, Constantine Rafinesque, in the basement of Morrison Chapel, the school's signatory structure.

The fact that Rafinesque's body probably was not in the crypt failed to dampen the excitement of the continuing tradition.

From 1819 to 1826, Rafinesque taught botany and modern languages when he could remember to return from his extended field trips in time to meet his classes. The Smithsonian Institution, which has many of his notebooks, described him as being chiefly interested in botany and ichthyology. "Despite a peculiar personality that alienated many colleagues, he contributed significantly to nineteenth century scientific thought," according to the Smithsonian.

It was that bizarre behavior, which led Transylvania president Horace Holley to have Rafinesque's belongings packed, his rooms cleared out and, when he returned from one of his over-extended field trips, booted him off the campus.

Outraged at such treatment, Rafinesque told Holley, "Damn thee and thy school as I place curses on you." A year later, Holley, who had built Transylvania on a par with Harvard and Yale, suffered a similar fate. Gov. Joseph Desha decided his progressive educational ideas were far too advanced for Kentucky. Holley, who was soundly castigated for attending horse races on Sundays, was fired and died a year later of yellow fever. Then, in 1829, the school's large administration/classroom building burned to the ground.

A century later, college officials decided Rafinesque, after becoming quite famous posthumously, had been treated unfairly by the school. Charles Darwin reportedly used some of Rafinesque's theories and ideas in his book, *On the Origin of Species*. The officials probably reasoned some of the botanist's fame could be transferred to the college by rescuing his remains from a pauper's cemetery in Philadelphia.

It was not Rafinesque's body but that of Mary Passimore, Charles Boewe wrote in *The Kentucky Encyclopedia*, that was unearthed. According to Boewe, cemetery workers failed to dig deep enough into the gravesite to retrieve the botanist.

The remains were unearthed and shipped back to Lexington to be placed in a special crypt built in the basement of Morrison Chapel, a Greek Revival styled structure with six massive Doric columns which replaced the building that burned in 1829. The top of his crypt was inscribed, "Honor to Whom Honor Is Overdue."

At Transylvania, it was considered an honor for a student to be selected to spend a night beside the crypt built for Rafinesque in Morrison Chapel during the autumn festival in his honor.

Morrison Chapel's massive Doric columns were probably the last things Betty Gail Brown saw that early Friday morning as an assailant squeezed the life out of her as the young woman's bra cut into her throat. Brown's Simca car was parked in a semi-circular drive in front of the building, whose façade was illuminated with floodlights.

Brown's body was stylishly clad in the colors of the season. She had on a beige silk blouse tucked into buttoned-up brown and black tweed Bermuda shorts topped with a tan shag cardigan and a short brown raincoat. She was fashionably and appropriately dressed for the cool autumn evening except for the torn bra draped over her left shoulder.

Solving the young woman's murder could be compared with botanist's leaving. A solution to Brown's murder and Rafinesque's tenure appeared expendable when compared to the reputation of the institution. Although Transylvania's standing declined after Holley left, Lexingtonians, over the decades, developed an elitist and possessive attitude toward the school that was established in 1780, the first college west of the Allegheny Mountains.

In 1961, protecting the college's reputation seemed to be much more important than solving the murder of one of its students, especially if prominent family names were involved in the investigation. That impression manifested itself in a number of way in the Brown murder investigation from the active involvement of the school's president in the investigation to a more public voice emerging from the local newspaper's editorials.

Irving Lunger, president of Transylvania when Brown was killed, inserted himself into the inquiry and, apparently, no one suggested he leave the investigation of the murder case to the professionals. Lunger insisted on interviewing male Transylvania students in his office about the murder. He was frequently included in briefings with law enforcement officials. Nothing was found in the Lexington Police Department's case file to indicate Lunger contributed anything of value to the investigation. No research was found to indicate that Lunger, or any other college official, interviewed any of the women students in their offices or anywhere else. A central figure in the murder investigation was a mysterious young woman who was never identified and could have been a current or former Transylvania student.

The local newspaper mirrored the attitude of many Lexingtonians that Transylvania's reputation was the principal concern. *Herald* editor Herndon J. Evans, in a November 2, 1961, editorial addressing outside interference in the investigation, expressed concern that the school's reputation which might be damaged by efforts to solve the young woman's murder.

"Transylvania is entitled to the best possible treatment during this trying time," Evans wrote. "Transylvania College has already suffered more than most of us ever will realize because of this tragedy."

Hargus T. and Quincy Brown's suffering the loss of their only child certainly eclipsed that of Transylvania's anguish at sustaining a dent in its reputation.

Evans and the newspaper were concerned about the manner in which some of Transylvania's students were questioned by investigators. "Several students have been shunned and scorned because some unfortunate rumors originated from routine questions by the authorities," the editorial continued.

The editorial did say college students' hurt feelings were of lesser concern than authorities solving this strange murder.

Evans' editorial attitude made it apparent he would have preferred to have the city's movers and shakers, not authorities, have total control of the manner in which the murder investigation was conducted. Had that been the case the word, sex, would probably not have ever been mentioned publicly.

Brown was killed at the beginning of a decade when young people were openly exploring the expansion of sexual freedoms and she could have been into or on the fringe of that movement.

Yet, Evans' newspaper attempted to convince their readers the death had nothing to do with sex. The *Herald*, in an October 29, article about the murder, emphasized that Brown's murder was not a "Sex slaying." The next day, another article stated, "The motive for the killing remains a mystery. Police said that, although the girl had been strangled with her own brassiere, there was no evidence of a sex attack and no robbery."

The police case file indicated that sex, regardless of the newspaper's denials, was an integral part of the murder investigation. The fact that Betty Gail Brown was not raped nor sexually assaulted did not mean sexual activities played no role in the murder investigation.

In addition to the newspaper, authorities were hampered in their investigation by the victim's mother, who insisted on being involved in the search for her daughter's killer. Qunicy Brown was quite often outspoken and required a great deal of the investigators' time. As a result, there was a public perception that she was somehow involved in the crime.

Quincy Brown, an unsuccessful candidate for the "Mrs. Kentucky" title in the 1956 "Mrs. America" beauty contest, interfered in the investigation of her daughter's murder to the extent of interviewing and attempting to intimidate a witness and allegedly offering the unidentified woman, whom she thought was with her daughter that evening, a bribe to tell her story.

There was no indication in the case file that Quincy Brown ever shared with detectives the identity of the woman she thought was with her daughter the evening she was killed.

According to the case file, an anonymous caller accused Quincy Brown of killing her daughter. When she reported the incident, investigators put a tap on the Browns' telephone line but it returned no results. A local man walked into police headquarters and told detectives he had a strong feeling Mrs. Brown was deeply involved in the case and might possibly have killed her daughter.

Female students at Transylvania bombarded investigators with numerous, frivolous ideas about who killed the young woman.

The murder case reached near cult status and even unofficial investigators reportedly became involved in trying to solve it. Evans, in yet another editorial, wrote "But things are going too far when students are called from their rooms in the early morning hours and confronted by would-be-detectives who have no official connection with the investigation into this unfortunate tragedy.

"Students who have had no connection with the case have been subjected to unauthorized questioning, which often implies that the questioner knows something about the case which would involve the person being interviewed," Evans wrote.

If Evans' editorial was an accurate description of events, two important questions were raised. Why did Lunger and other college officials not intervene and put a stop to such activities? If Evans knew about such activities, then Lunger most likely also knew about them. As college president, he certainly had the authority to control his own campus. There was no mention of any unauthorized questioning of students in the case file.

The newspapers and the victim's mother were probably in a dead heat for first in a contest for increasing detectives' work by interfering in the murder investigation.

Many people believed Betty Gail Brown's murderer would never be brought to justice because they saw the suspected involvement of young members of wealthy, politically powerful Lexington families as being the obstacle detectives were unable to overcome. After the murder, some parents, determined to protect their children, reportedly quickly shipped their off-springs out of town, sent them away to visit relatives or enrolled them in colleges out of state so they would not be tainted by rampant rumors of suspected sexual improprieties or marked by being questioned by the detectives working the murder case.

Transylvania was a small college and Betty Gail Brown knew most of the students and was, perhaps, friends with many of them. However, neither she nor her parents traveled in Lexington's elite social circle and they lacked the wealth that translated into political power and influence.

From all indications, the petite brunette was popular with her peers and enjoyed partying with them. Ron Ware, from Winchester, who attended junior high school with her, said his last meal, before moving to Ironton, Ohio, was with the Browns. "In 1958, when Ironton High School played Lafayette in Lexington, Betty Gail had three of her friends over to her house and three of my friends and I had a party at her house," Ware recalled.

Photogenic, with classic features, Betty Gail Brown was featured in a photograph on the front page of the local newspaper at Transylvania's Sadie Hawkins Day celebration, a short time before her death. Ware said, on the night of her death, his father mailed an envelope containing the clipping to him in Turkey, where he was stationed with the U. S. Air Force.

Some of the friends Brown made at Transylvania, such as Brenda Mattox who conducted the biology study session in Forrer Hall the night the coed was killed, have waged a four-decades effort to find her murderer. Mattox, in an email to the author, said she hoped to interest a Lexington detective in meeting with a psychic to further the search for Brown's killer.

Mattox said she spoke to a friend, Dennis McDougal in Los Angeles, concerning his writing a book about Betty Gail Brown's murder in hopes of calling attention to the unsolved murder that could possibly result in the killer being identified. Quincy Brown, who was then living in Florida, was opposed to the idea and Mattox honored her wishes.

Mattox called her friend's death "A heartbreaking experience in a lot of people's lives."

Brown's Last Day

Betty Gail Brown's last day began with the usual preparations for attending her Thursday classes at Transylvania. She returned home from campus and had dinner with her parents, Qunicy Brown, 39, and Hargus Brown, 43, at their home, on Lackawana Road, in a middle-class south Lexington neighborhood.

The Browns were, understandably, proud of their only child. She was an honor student at both Lafayette High School and Transylvania, a Sunday School teacher, belonged to Phi Mu social sorority, sang in school choirs and at Central Christian Church. In her senior year at Lafayette, she was awarded the Good Citizen Award by the Bryan Station Chapter of the Daughters of the American Revolution.

The Browns asked her to go to a drive-in movie with them after she finished washing the dinner dishes. She declined saying she was going to Forrer Hall dormitory, on the Transylvania campus, to study with friends for a biology test the next day and would be home around 10:30 or 11:00 p.m.

Hargus Brown, an insurance agent with Metropolitan Life Insurance Company, went to bed with a headache after he and his wife returned from the movie. Quincy Brown, a bookkeeper and decorator for painting contractor Davis C. Atkins, decided to stay up and wait for their daughter to return.

Lurking just beneath the surface, resulting from her actions after the murder, was the notion that Quincy Brown suspected her daughter might be engaged in questionable social activities with her college friends, although she bragged Betty Gail told her everything that was going on in her life.

Her apprehensions were soon realized.

On October 28, 1961, when midnight came and her daughter still had not returned home, Quincy Brown waited another twenty minutes and called Forrer Hall. She inquired of Mrs. John Combs, the dormitory housemother, if her daughter was still there. Mrs. Combs told Quincy Brown her daughter left a half-hour earlier, at 11:50 p.m.

Quincy Brown decided to drive the route her daughter normally followed to the Transylvania College campus, expecting they would meet along the way. Even with Lexington's expansive growth since the murder, it was still possible to drive from where the Browns lived on Lackawanna to the Transylvania campus in fifteen minutes, or less, depending on the volume of traffic.

She probably took her time on the drive to look carefully at each automobile she met but there was no sign of either her daughter or the four-door Simca automobile she was driving. Mother and daughter shared the Simca, a French vehicle, manufactured by Fiat. Returning home, she expected to find her daughter and the car there but there was no sign of either.

Deciding against awakening her husband, Quincy Brown made a second trip to the campus, which she estimated to be between 1:00 and 1:30 a.m. That time frame was later determined to be the approximate time of her daughter's murder.

According to the case file, Quincy Brown, on her second trip, said she considered turning into the half-circle Morrison Chapel driveway as she drove down Third Street past the campus landmark. Instead, she apparently drove past the entrance. The high hedges, along the drive, might have somewhat obscured her view of that portion of the campus but there appeared to be more than adequate lighting to see the parked Simca just to the east of Morrison Chapel's steps.

Had Quincy Brown turned off Third Street into the semi-circular Morrison Chapel drive, she might have witnessed her daughter's murder or even frightened the killer away. That knowledge must have been an unbearable burden for the mother to carry the rest of her life.

Investigators repeatedly referred to the high hedges, which were later removed, on either side of the half circle drive in front of Morrison Chapel as possibly concealing the location of Betty Gail Brown's car.

Yet, the October 29, *Lexington Herald* described the site differently. "The slaying occurred in a driveway which served Morrison Chapel on the south, or Third Street, side of the campus. The area is brightly lit and easily visible from Third Street."

The *Courier-Journal*, of the same date, reported that Betty Gail Brown's car was within twenty-five feet of a brilliant overhead light and almost directly opposite a floodlight used to illuminate the Doric columned façade of Morrison Chapel.

No evidence was found, other than her statement, that Quincy Brown did not turn into the campus drive off Third Street.

There was nearly an hour of unaccounted for time, by Quincy Brown's own admission, between her second and third nocturnal trips to the campus.

Case file notes indicated Quincy Brown said she returned from her second trip to the campus about 1:45 a.m. She said she then awakened her husband and told him their daughter was missing. Hargus Brown called hospitals and the police. The case file indicated his call to Lexington Police came in at 2:51 a.m. Four minutes later, an "All Units Alert" went out on the student.

What happened in the more than an hour after Brown said she returned home and the time her husband called the police was never clear. Did it take them over an hour to call authorities? At that time Lexington had both city and county police departments and four hospitals, which involved only six telephone calls. The Browns already knew their daughter had left the Transylvania dorm. Did they attempt to call any of her friends who lived in town? Or, did they already know she was dead?

There was a theory that Quincy Brown night have found her daughter, on the second trip to campus, already dead and arranged her clothes to make her more presentable. However, that would not account for the bra draped around Betty Gail Brown's shoulder. A caring and protective mother of Quincy Brown's generation, would never have left her daughter's intimate apparel in plain view. On the other hand, in her agitated state of mind, she could have been mistaken about the time frame she gave investigators.

Another explanation was that students, celebrating Rafinesque Week in and around Morrison, could have been responsible for manner in which the victim's clothing was arranged had they found her already dead. Or, perhaps not realizing she was already dead someone draped the bra over her shoulder as some sort of macabre prank. After all, the murder did occur during Rafinesque Week.

No mention was found in the case file nor media accounts of the kind of security Transylvania used for the campus during the hours of darkness. During Rafinesque week, one would have expected the administration would have been extra vigilant with security measures. Yet, Betty Gail Brown appeared to breeze in and out of the campus with her car at will that evening as if it was a regular occurrence.

Responding to the "All Units Alert," officer Donald Duckworth found the Simca, covered with frost at 3:05 a.m., parked just to the east of the Morrison Chapel's steps. Inside the car was a young woman, sitting behind the steering wheel, who appeared to be asleep but was soon identified as the missing student.

Duckworth's flashlight tapping on the driver's side window failed to elicit a response. Upon closer inspection, he saw blood on her forehead, according to the case file. The young woman was neatly dressed with a bra hanging over her left shoulder. The bra's torn clasp end, still fastened, was in her lap.

Duckworth said he did not attempt to enter the car but called headquarters and asked that a detective be sent to what he correctly assumed was a homicide scene.

Quincy Brown, meanwhile, had made a third trip to the campus leaving her husband at home to handle any questions authorities might have and to answer the telephone if police called with news of their daughter. She parked in another semi-circular campus drive, off Broadway in front of Haupe Hall and across the street from Forrer Hall, where her daughter had parked earlier in the evening.

Seeing the housemother and a group of sobbing girls in the Forrer Hall doorway, Quincy Brown crossed the street and asked if they knew anything about her daughter.

Quincy Brown described events that followed to the November 3, *Lexington Herald* in a somewhat detached manner. She was quoted as saying, "They were in complete shock but they took my arm and said, 'come in, the police will be here soon.' I felt something was wrong; I jerked loose. I got in my car and saw a policeman come by. When I looked at his face it was very compassionate. I knew that something was badly wrong. He said, 'get in Mrs. Brown.' Have you found her I asked? 'Yes, we've found her,' he replied. His chin was trembling. Is she alive, I asked? 'No Ma'am you daughter is dead,' he said. Don't tell me any more. Let's go home."

The fact that Quincy Brown, from all available information, did not request to see her daughter at that time, ask where she was found or how she died was a possible indication that she may have already known the worst. She was an obsessive mother who, according to some of her daughter's friends, read her dairy and kept a close watch on her only child. Yet, she apparently left the campus without making the normal inquiries about the circumstances surrounding her daughter's death.

Perhaps she was in shock. She may have been taken to view her daughter's body but there was nothing in the case file, in her statements or detectives' memos to indicate that occurred.

Detectives certainly considered her behavior unusual. An unsigned note in the case file suggested investigating to see if Quincy Brown had ever been in a mental hospital. However, there was no indication in the file that the suggestion led to any inquiries.

When Capt. Gilbert Cravens arrived on the campus, in response to officer Duckworth's request for a detective, he found the crime scene had been secured. Cravens, according to the case file, found the Simca's doors locked except for the right front and all four windows were closed. Betty Gail Brown was sitting behind the steering wheel, head thrown back against the head rest, one hand was in her lap and the other by her side.

The bloody wounds on her head corresponded with blood on the car's right dashboard. Those wounds along with scrapes on her forehead, nose and cheek were signs a death struggle had earlier occurred inside the automobile. There were brutal-looking bruises and abrasions on her neck.

Brown's keys were on the floor behind the driver's seat. Textbooks were in disarray on the front passenger seat. She had left her biology textbook in Becky Huie's room in Forrer Hall, where Brenda Mattox conducted the biology study session.

Capt. Bryan Henry was in charge of fingerprinting the crime scene. He later admitted that he failed to fingerprint the victim. "I was working by myself that day and I had so many things to do," he was quoted as saying in the October 4, 1965, *Herald*, "That's one thing I overlooked."

Detectives ruled out robbery as a motive in Brown's death. Her jewelry and purse, with money and other items, were intact.

A broken fingernail indicated that she possibly resisted her attacker. Betty Gail Brown was a small woman, 4'1" tall, weighing only ninety pounds. She would have had difficulty defending her self against any assailant, man or woman.

Coroner Chester Hager said the laceration on the top of Brown's head looked like someone had grabbed her by the hair and yanked it back. He found no wounds below the abrasions on her neck. Hager pronounced her dead at 3:40 a.m., which was the time he arrived on the scene. "But," he added at a later court hearing, "she'd been dead some four hours prior to that."

Hager's time frame was puzzling. Officer Duckworth found Brown's body at 3:05 a.m., according to the case file. The dormitory housemother said she left Forrer Hall at 11:50 p.m. To accept the coroner's time frame, Brown would have been killed before she left Forrer Hall.

The coroner's involvement in this murder case investigation was another aspect of the bizarre twists that occurred.

After Cravens finished his crime scene investigation, officers accompanied Brown's automobile to the impound lot. Hager removed the body to the coroner's office at his Whitehall Funeral Home, on North Limestone Street, near the campus. He began the embalming process without performing an autopsy, which according to Kentucky law in questionable deaths, is the coroner's decision. Brown's death was unquestionably a homicide; she obviously had not strangled herself.

Hager proceeded as far in the embalming process as draining the blood from the body, which he later maintained was standard procedure. The embalming process was halted but how that came about was never clear. Brown's body was moved from Hager' establishment to Kerr Brothers Funeral Home, on East Main Street before the autopsy was performed.

Hager later claimed he ordered an autopsy of Brown's body. If the coroner ordered an autopsy, why did he begin the embalming process first?

An autopsy was performed by University of Kentucky pathologists, Drs. James D. McClellan and Randolph Mueling. They listed the cause of death as suffocation by strangulation from external forces applied to the neck by unknown person(s). Brown's bra was the death weapon. McClellan and Mueling, part of a newly formed forensic pathology team at the recently opened University of Kentucky Medical Center, estimated that Brown's death occurred between 1:00 and 1:30 a.m. The autopsy revealed that Brown had not been vaginally raped. Her death might have been accidental if it resulted from her seeking sexual gratification from oral sex or autoerotic behavior. There was a lipstick smear on her left forearm, which could have been hers if she struggled with the killer or could have belonged to the girl she was seen with that evening if they had engaged in mutual sexual activity.

Hager later testified that the contents of Brown's stomach indicated she had eaten six to eight hours prior to her death.

Investigators said Betty Gail Brown ate nothing while studying with friends in the dormitory. The newspaper reported, "Rumors that she had been seen eating at various Lexington restaurants that night remain unverified."

The town was filled with rumors about the murder and much of the responsibility for that came from the newspaper, which, at the same time, complained about the college's reputation being damaged by such gossip. The October 29th *Herald* speculated that a Transylvania maintenance employee might have been connected to the murder.

"The most persistent of the rumors concerned the arrest and disappearance of a Transylvania maintenance employee. No arrests have been made in the case (Brown's murder) and police are aware of no such disappearances they said last night. Officers added that about 30 reports of hitchhikers seen in and around Lexington at about the time of the slaying have been checked out with no concrete results."

Reasons to Be Concerned

Quincy Brown, it appeared, had reasons to be concerned about her daughter's social activities on the night of her death.

Between the time Betty Gail Brown left Forrer Hall at 11:50 p.m., and her death less than two hours later, she had an extremely active social life. Her car was a virtual revolving door of passengers.

According to the case file, Gay Brock, a waitress at Asher's Drive-In, on New Circle Road, said she served Betty Gail Brown and a female companion hot chocolate and hot tea at the restaurant around midnight. Brown paid the twenty-five cent ticket and the pair left. Asher's was a favorite gathering place for Transylvania students.

Brock described Brown's companion as being twenty or twenty-one, 5'2", 115 pounds with short, curly brown hair, slightly built, almost skinny, and wearing beige slacks and a white shirt. Two Transylvania students, Roy Bennett and Sammy Lynn, Jr., who knew the murdered student, were in the restaurant at the same time. They told detectives they did not see her there. Detectives later found Brock's cash ticket for an order of hot chocolate and hot tea showed the time of service to be 10:30 p.m.

It was possible the waitress, rushing to complete orders from a restaurant full of customers, could have written the wrong time on her cash ticket. Or, she could have served more than one order of hot tea and chocolate during the chilly October evening.

Two Lexington newspaper circulation deliverymen, P. C. Nunnelly and Franklin Davis, saw Brown in her car with different companions at separate locations that evening after she left Forrer Hall, according to the case file.

Nunnelly told investigators he saw a man, at the corner of Third and Market streets get into a vehicle similar to the Simca with a woman driving. He heard the man call the driver, "Betty," and saw them turn into the Morrison Chapel drive off Third Street. Nunnelly said earlier in the evening he saw the same car, or one similar to the Simca, with two women inside at the Greyhound Bus station on North Limestone, only a couple of blocks from the campus.

In 1961, the Greyhound Bus Station was on the perimeter of the campus in an area of Lexington known as the "Red Light District."

Franklin Davis told investigators he also saw a man at the corner of Third and Market get into a small foreign car. Davis could not identify the driver but he said the car turned into the Morrison Chapel drive.

Gay Brock said a nurse, Nora Johnson, who worked with Brock's husband at the Veterans' Administration Hospital, on Leestown Pike, saw a young, blond woman running down Broadway between 1:00 and 1:30 a.m., as she was driving home from work the night Brown was killed. Was that the woman who left lipstick marks on Betty Gail Brown's left arm? Or, could the fleeing woman have been the murderer, since the time she was seen on Broadway was near the estimated time of Brown's death?

Those questions were never answered.

Quincy Brown appeared desperate to keep her dead daughter's reputation intact and her actions indicated she knew something she apparently did not share with detectives.

She confronted the waitress three days after her daughter's body was found. An October 30th entry in the case file indicated Mrs. Brown went to Asher's Drive-In, sought out Gay Brock, asked her why she said what she did about her daughter, demanded to know who paid her off and accused her of lying.

From all indications, Quincy Brown knew one of the girls with her daughter the night she was murdered.

Ron Ware said, when he returned from Turkey, he visited the Browns. "The story she (Quincy Brown) told me was there was a girl who was with Betty Gail that night but (that girl) changed her story. That is who Mrs. Brown told me she offered money to tell the truth," Ware recalled. He speculated Betty Gail's companion that night probably knew the murderer but kept quiet in fear something might happen to her.

There was nothing in the case file to indicate Quincy Brown told detectives that she knew the name of at least one of her daughter's companions the evening she was killed; nor that she told investigators of the alleged bribe while meeting with the girl.

Ware said Quincy Brown wrote him in Turkey telling him about Betty Gail's death. "She said," Ware recalled in a September 2004 email, "that she thought an English student had done it. At first, I didn't know if she meant a person majoring in English or from England."

Betty Gail Brown had also corresponded with Ware while he was in Turkey. He said, in one letter, she wrote of an English teacher taking a special interest in her. "This and the letter from her mom was the beginning of several possibilities that she may have had an affair with her teacher," he said.

Decades later, Ware said he was discussing her murder with a Lexington woman who attended the same church as the Brown family. "She told me that she believed the person who did it (killed Brown) was an English teacher's son who was not quite right and he wasn't seen much after that (Brown's death)," he wrote.

Investigators could have used Ware's input into the case had he been in Lexington when his friend was killed. However, they had no hesitation in asking for outside assistance in an attempt to solve the puzzling case.

Kentucky State Police (KSP), at the request of Lexington police, polygraphed a number of male Transylvania students in connection with the murder. The case file indicated the KSP examiner suspected Transylvania student Robert James Wright had not been truthful about meeting Betty Gail Brown that evening. The examiner, according to the case file, was of the opinion that Wright had met Brown secretly, gave her oral sex the night of the murder and tried to force her to perform oral sex on him. Was Wright the man Nunnelly and Davis saw with Brown in her car as it turned into the campus drive off Third Street?

Investigators worked overtime canvassing the neighborhoods around the college. Police chief E.C. Hale said his investigators were quite knowledgeable about events, which occurred around the college campus. He did not elaborate further but that part of town was known for prostitution arrests.

With all the manpower the police expended, there was every reason to believe they would solve the case if the town and the college cooperated.

Investigators often had to sift through too much information that was of little use. The case file indicated Transylvania students Cathy Shay, Shirley Frey, Ann Burke, Sue Ann Hawkins and Pat Bilker told detectives they might know who killed Betty Gail Brown. The names of their suspects were not mentioned in the case file.

Another student, Faith McCullock, told police she suspected a male student was the culprit because he had been rude to her. Investigators were less than impressed with McCullock's idea. She was described, in the file, as being highly emotional.

Still another student, Nancy Jo Kemper, was mentioned separately in the case file as being a close friend of Betty Gail Brown's. The November 1, 1961, *Courier-Journal* reported that investigators said there was nothing significant in the questioning of Kemper other than she was a close personal friend of Brown's.

Years later, according to Brenda Mattox, she and Kemper corresponded regarding their friend's murder. Mattox, in her email, said Kemper told her about a Lexington detective who was still interested in the Brown case.

Solving the murder hinged on identifying the mystery woman who was with Betty Gail Brown that night. From all indications, authorities searched in vain for her. Was she a member of a prominent, wealthy Lexington family? Did her family ship her out of state to avoid any further involvement in the murder case? There were rumors one of the Lexington newspapers was ready to print her identity but the article was pulled at the last minute before the press run.

In 1961, the Lexington newspapers were locally owned by the Stoll family and Fred Wachs, the publisher, was known to influence news coverage of events if investigative results might prove embarrassing to his friends or those in his social set. In another prominent murder, four years later, Wachs clamped down on news coverage of the investigation for weeks.

Despite authorities telling the October 31, *Lexington Herald* they expected to pick up the mystery woman for questioning, Brown's female companion remained unknown as detectives conducted house-to-house interviews around the college. License plates of cars parked on or near the school were checked. Occupants of the men's dormitories at Transylvania were fingerprinted, a process which took almost a week.

Police chief E. C. Hale, according to the November 1, *Herald*, said the fingerprinting was necessary because unidentified prints were found in and on Betty Gail Brown's car. By fingerprinting only the 223 male students, Hale said detectives were not ruling out the unknown woman being involved in the case. "This obviously has been gaining prominence hourly with the obvious reference of a mystery woman companion of Miss Brown to identify herself and cooperate with the police," he was quoted as saying.

Hale's statement raised, perhaps unintentionally, the question of why Transylvania's women students were not fingerprinted since witnesses described two females, one the brunette with Betty Gail Brown at the drive-in and the other a blond seen fleeing the vicinity of the murder scene.

Hale, in reference to the mysterious companion, told the November 1, 1961, *Courier-Journal*, "She may be fact and she might be fantasy. You guys can just forget about that for right now."

Hale soon decided all news releases concerning Brown's murder had to be approved by and come from his office. However, the police chief appeared to be the guilty party in issuing news releases which went first, one way and then another.

Detective Morris Carter stated that three sets of identifiable prints, those of Hargus and Quincy Brown and the mechanic who worked on the Simca, and numerous other sets of unidentifiable fingerprints were found on the car. No fingerprints were taken from Brown's body before she was buried.

Some of the unidentifiable fingerprints from the automobile obviously belonged to the victim and others were the fingerprints of those seen in the car with her at different times the night of her death. Her passengers certainly had to use the car's door handles to enter and exit the vehicle, unless they floated through an open window.

Betty Gail Brown was not fingerprinted either at the crime scene or at the autopsy.

The failure to fingerprint female Transylvania students left a gaping hole in the investigation of the case. What was to prevent college officials and investigators from working out a similar schedule for fingerprinting the women as they did for the men?

The Investigation Stalls

Gay Brock, the Asher's Drive-In Restaurant waitress, appeared to be the best asset detectives had in their attempts to solve Brown's homicide. The drive-in where she worked, on New Circle Road, was about a ten-minute drive from the Transylvania campus, perhaps less in the early morning hours, and was popular with college students.

Brock was the last known person to have seen the young woman alive. Despite the time difference on her cash receipt for hot chocolate and tea she served to Brown and her female companion, Brock identified Betty Gail Brown's body at Kerr Brothers Funeral Home. She correctly identified Brown's clothing, including the white socks, she was wearing in the restaurant the night of the murder.

Investigators had Brock observe Brown's classmates while they were being interviewed by detectives at police headquarters, according to the October 31 *Herald*. Teams of detectives, the article pointed out, were working around the clock on the case, some on their own time.

Brock was at the funeral home visitation for the murder victim, where investigators hoped she would recognize Brown's companion among the mourners. A classmate of Brown's, according to the newspaper, burst into tears upon viewing her friend's body. "I know who did it; I know who did it," she said sobbing inconsolably. When detectives questioned her, she responded, "I won't tell you who I think it is...If I'm right OK, if not, no one will ever know." Transylvania students were excused from Monday afternoon classes to attend Brown's funeral.

Dr. Leslie R. Smith, Central Christian Church's minister, told mourners at the funeral service, that the love of God would take away the bitterness of the bereaved and bring confession and forgiveness to the guilty. Smith had known the deceased for most of her life and taught her confirmation class. Survivors were her parents Hargus and Quincy Brown and her maternal grandfather S. H. Stanton.

Detectives accompanied Brock to the cemetery, hoping the waitress could identify Betty Gail Brown's companion from the restaurant. Brock was unable to identify anyone. A ring of Transylvania students encircled the Brown family and close friends, who were seated beside the gravesite, obscuring them from the view of several hundred other mourners in the back.

After Brown's funeral, detectives gathered some Transylvania students, a single man, six single women and a married male student, and interviewed them with negative results. Hargus and Quincy Brown and an unidentified woman spent forty-five minutes at police headquarters after the funeral service. The interview process extended into the early morning hours when two more male students were taken to police headquarters for questioning while Brock looked on.

According to the case file, Brock was unsuccessful in identifying, from Transylvania year books, the woman with Brown at the drive-in. Whether or not Brock examined University of Kentucky and Lafayette High School year books was not known.

Detectives had little success in questioning a young married man Brown had mentioned in her diary. The man's name was withheld by authorities. After about forty minutes, he was released. The November 4, 1961, *Herald* suggested the diary's clues were too plentiful. "The diary, it was understood, contained a detailed record of Miss Brown's goings-and-comings from early 1960 to the day before her death."

Betty Gail Brown was probably careful with her diary entries due to the high probability of her mother reading them. Ron Ware, her friend, said, "Were she seeing a married man, she would have been leery of putting a name in the diary for fear her mom might see it."

Neither Brown's diary, detectives' intense investigative work, nor a $3,000 reward brought forth any substantial information leading to solving the murder case. The reward, according to the October 28, *Herald*, contained donations from friends of the family, the Lafayette High School Student Council and the *Lexington Herald-Leader*. The next day's newspaper listed additional names to the reward fund: Second National Bank, Phi Mu sorority, the Transylvania College Choir, Jack Hagler and there were donors who preferred to remain anonymous.

The October 30, *Herald*, while appearing to shy away from the unidentified woman, provided other news about possible male suspects. "Other officers indicated a witness who reportedly saw a man in the vicinity of Morrison Chapel about the time of the killing had little definite information. Questioning indicated that a man had seen another man emerge from some bushes near Skillman Alley and proceeded in the direction of Morrison."

Since the newspaper appeared to be getting better information about the murder, a local radio station decided to scoop the publication. The station broadcasted a news bulletin, which turned out to be false, saying authorities had taken the suspected killer, a girl, into custody, she had made a full confession and was arrested, according to the November 1 *Herald*. The station retracted the bulletin but its announcement certainly drew even more attention to Brown's unknown companion.

Chief Hale, his investigators, commonwealth attorney Paul Mansfield, commonwealth detective Charles Calk, coroner Chester Hager, city manager Jack Cook and others held a three and one-half hour meeting behind closed doors to evaluate the evidence collected, which failed to provide a motive for the homicide. Mansfield told the newspaper, "Any motive that could apply to a murder case could apply to this one--whether a man or woman is involved."

Hale was dithering here and there about what information should be provided to the media and he was perhaps the worst offender in the not-well-thought-out statements he made to the newspapers.

Investigators learned she always locked her car when traveling alone, even during the day, and when she got out of the vehicle. When asked if he thought the killer was a stranger to Betty Gail Brown, Hale replied, "I don't want to give anything away on what I suspect." Actually, about all Hale had were suspicions and he was probably too vocal with many of them.

While the figure of the anonymous female companion hovered over the case, detectives concentrated on male suspects in their investigation.

On November 3, Virgil J. Rollins, a medical technology student at St. Joseph Hospital, was questioned in connection with Brown's murder. Rollins, according to the November 5, *Herald*, was in custody on the charges of detaining two University of Kentucky women students against their will. Hale was quoted as saying Rollins, who claimed he was home with his wife at the time of the Transylvania student's death, steadfastly denied any connection with the Brown case when he was questioned by shifts of detectives.

Witnesses who told police they saw a young man with Betty Gail Brown the night of her murder, the article continued, observed Rollins being questioned. Since Rollins was not charged, he obviously was not the man that witnesses saw in her car.

Until November 3, day and night shift detectives had been working the murder case on a semi-independent basis, the newspaper reported. Police major Joe Modica was given overall charge of the Brown murder investigation. The failure to fingerprint Brown, before she was buried, again arose. Modica, according to the article, pointed out that fingerprint specialists would undoubtedly be able to establish which prints belonged to the victim.

Modica announced that investigators were beginning to eliminate the less likely leads and concentrate on those which were the more promising. "He indicated that he was still optimistic that the slayer will be found," the article concluded.

Although authorities attempted to keep her parents current with their investigation, Quincy Brown continued to be outspoken. Less than ten days after her daughter's death, she told the November 3 *Herald* that she did not believe in capital punishment and would not want the killer electrocuted if caught and convicted. "There was absolutely no reason for this on earth," she said. "We know of no one that would have or could have done it."

Publicly silent most of the time, Hargus Brown said he wanted the law to take its course. "Even if he is never found, he will be punished by his conscience but I want to see him caught," he added.

The case file notes indicated that on November 15, Hargus and Quincy Brown took a lie detector test and passed.

Night police chief William Davis told the November 5, *Herald* that six Transylvania male students had been lie detector tests in Frankfort and the results indicated all of them were telling the truth. Among those students was Charles Risdon, III, who spoke with Betty Gail Brown as each of them was driving out of the parking lot, across the street from Forrer Hall, on the night of her death.

However, the case file contained a November 12, 1961, entry about the lie detector tests. The KSP examiner determined that another Transylvania student, Robert James Wright, failed the test. Hale did not mention Wright publicly or make any reference to the examiner's report concerning his test failure.

As the time passed, the murder case simmered like a festered boil in Lexington for four years. Then, in January 1965, Alex Arnold, an alcoholic drifter in a Kalmath Falls, Oregon, drunk tank and told jail officials he might have murdered a woman in Lexington, Kentucky. Oregon authorities called the Lexington Police.

Investigators thought they had their man.

Questionable Confession

A U.S. Army veteran, Arnold was of the age to have served during the Korean Conflict. Mae Hedges, of Lexington, an acquaintance of Arnold's, said when he was inebriated he talked about killing women and children when he was in Germany.

Being inebriated, which he was most of the time, was Arnold's chosen way for facing whatever personal demons he was fighting. Having been in the armed services, possibly in battlefield situations if he was in the Korean Conflict, Arnold could have been suffering from what is now called Post Traumatic Stress Syndrome.

In describing his addiction, Arnold said he drank, "Continuously, wine, whiskey, beer, anything that had alcohol in it; if there was enough available, I'd drink until I passed out, which was pretty often."

Consequently, jobs he held at International Business Machines, on Thoroughbred horse farms and in restaurants were short lived due to his alcoholism. After being jailed in Kentucky for numerous alcohol offenses, Arnold drifted across the country, finding menial jobs in Chicago, Omaha and Lincoln, Nebraska and Salt Lake City before going to Oregon.

In Kalmath Falls, Oregon, he lived in the Cozy Hotel, doing various odd jobs to pay for his room and his addiction. On January 17, 1965, he was arrested for public intoxication in the small central Oregon town near the California border.

After spending three days in the Kalmath Falls Jail on the charge of public intoxication, Arnold appeared to be hallucinating and suffering from delirium tremens (DTs) as a result of his body being deprived of the alcohol to which it was accustomed.

Kalmath Falls detective Sgt. Dennis Lilly said Arnold told him, on January 20, 1965, "He wasn't sure whether or not but that he was '90 percent sure I killed a woman in Lexington, Kentucky.'" The October 4, 1965 *Herald* quoted Lilly as saying, "After Arnold told him (Lilly) he strangled Miss Brown with her own brassiere he walked away from the car saying to himself: 'And all over a goddam match.'"

Somewhere, between the partial confession made to Lilly and the arrival of Lexington detectives in Oregon, Arnold was examined by Dr. Seth Kerron, a Kalmath County health officer. Kerron later testified that Arnold was not suffering from delirium tremens (DTs) at the time he examined him.

Since the transcript from Arnold's trial for the Betty Gail Brown murder at which Kerron testified has disappeared, there was no way to establish the time of Kerron's examination, which was important in determining how severe Arnold's DTs were. The author was unable to locate the trial transcript in the Fayette Circuit Court Clerk's office, the Commonwealth Attorney's office or in the Kentucky Department of Libraries and Archives (KDLA), in Frankfort, the official repository for such legal records. The only records, relating to Arnold, that the KDLA was able to locate were those of his preliminary hearing on March 24, 1965.

The unavailability of court documents, dealing with Arnold's trial, was unfortunate. Consequently, most accounts of Arnold's trial came from newspaper articles.

The severity of Arnold's DTs at the time of his confession became a major factor in his murder trial.

Dr. William Grossman, project medical director for the Department of Emergency Medicine at The Mount Sinai Hospital in New York City, in a 2003 paper on DTs, described symptoms which matched those Arnold apparently experienced in 1965. Grossman said DTs usually began within a 24-72 hour period after the cessation of alcohol use. Arnold had been in jail three days when he talked about his possible having killed a woman in Kentucky.

DT symptoms described by Grossman, matched those attributed to Arnold. They included altered mental status, severe agitation, delusions, excessive sweating and hallucinations.

Arnold said he heard what sounded like a public address announcer calling his name telling him his mother had been in an automobile accident and he should telephone her. He implored an officer, at the Oregon jail, to provide him with a telephone. Instead, he was placed in a cell in the women's drunk tank, where the duty officer was working and could watch him. Arnold said he strenuously objected to the move because there was a machine near that cell which could determine if he was telling the truth.

"I was screaming and hollering, talking to doors and spots on the wall and things that weren't there, talking to door handles, toilet tissue," he said. "I was out of my mind."

In 1965, all the treatment Arnold received was probably no more than a cursory examination by a county physician while being left to deal with his alcoholic demons.

In 203, Dr. Grossman described the treatment a patient such as Arnold would have received in an emergency room: isotonic saline solutions, cardiac monitor, oxygen, bedside glucose testing, thiamine administration and sedation.

Lexington detectives Morris Carter and Bryan Henry traveled to Oregon, in response to Sgt. Lilly's telephone call, to interview Arnold. Their description of visits with Arnold in the Oregon jail, at the suspect's preliminary hearing in Fayette Quarterly Court, indicated Arnold was still suffering from DTs as their descriptions matched that of Dr. Grossman's.

Carter described Arnold as "Noticeably trembling, he seemed easy to perspire and very nervous." On their first visit, the detectives took no statement from Arnold; they just talked with him. Carter's description of Arnold, after he had been examined by Kerron, appeared to contradict the Oregon physician's statement that the suspect was not suffering from the DTs.

Carter and Henry returned to the Kalmath Falls jail on the second day they were in Oregon, and Arnold was somewhat calmer, and talked with them for two hours. Although Arnold told them the same story, Carter said, but the detectives took no statement that day either. On the day of their third visit with Arnold, Carter, Bryant and Lilly witnessed his confession, which Carter wrote out in longhand. The confession was found the case file on the Brown murder.

At the preliminary hearing, Carter recalled that he advised Arnold of his rights on all three occasions he and detective Bryant visited the suspect in the Oregon jail. Carter included that advisory in his handwritten copy of Arnold's confession.

The Miranda Rule, coming from the Supreme Court decision in *Miranda v Arizona*, became standard operational police procedure after the 1966 decision was handed down, a year after Arnold made his confession to Brown's murder.

Carter's statements to Arnold, however, included the main points of Miranda: the right to remain silent; anything Arnold said could be used against him in a court of law; the right to an attorney before questioning, and, if indigent, an attorney would be appointed to represent him. Arnold chose to waive those privileges.

The confession was signed by Arnold, the three officers in attendance and their signatures were notarized. Arnold's attorneys later questioned whether he had sufficiently recovered from the DTs to give a statement at that time. Carter had the suspect initial each page and each correction but Arnold did not read the final confession document when given an opportunity.

According to Arnold's January 26, 1965, confession, Carter advised him of his rights, inquired if he understood those rights and asked him to tell them all about the Brown case. Arnold confidently replied, "Sure, that's why I had you all come all the way out here."

Arnold said he was thirty-three years old and lived in the Cozy Hotel in Kalmath Falls. "On the night of October

27, 1961, having gotten drunk in the vicinity of Short and Broadway in Lexington, Kentucky, and looking for a place to sleep it off. I went up Broadway to Second Street and down Second Street to Mill, Up Mill through Gratz Park. There was a couple sitting in Gratz Park where I intended to lie down. (Gratz Park was directly across Third Street from Morrison Chapel on the Transylvania campus.) Beings they were there I crossed Third Street and went into Transylvania College (the campus) and laid down and went to sleep."

Arnold said he slept for about an hour until the cold night air woke him up. He finished off the quarter of a bottle of wine he had with him and wanted a cigarette. He started back toward Short and Broadway. "Upon passing a car in the driveway of the campus," he said, "I seen what looked like two women making love. They were hugging and kissing each other. As I passed the car, I asked them for a match as I had cigarettes and no matches. They begin to cuss me. I said, pardon me and started on for Short and Broadway."

Arnold said the women continued to curse him as he walked away and, on the spur of the moment, he turned back to the car, jerked open the driver's side door and grabbed the driver as she was leaning away from him. The other girl got out of the car and ran away.

"Hitting the girl's head against the dash board I either knocked her out or she fainted," he continued. "Jerking her back against the seat by her hair and shoulder I realized she was out. Getting scared and being drunk, I opened the back door and got in the back seat. Picking up her brasier (bra) that was laying in against the back of the seat I hung it around her neck and strangled her by putting my hands on each end of the brasier (bra) and putting my knee against the back of the seat for leverage. I held it there for about a minute and a half. The only thing she did was just quiver a little bit. I throwed the (word marked out and initialed by Arnold) brasier (bra) on the front seat and reached and closed the front door. I noticed that the blouse was open all the way down. I climbed in the front seat to button it up because I thought if she was found that way they would think I had tried to rape her thinking sure I would be caught."

"As I buttoned up the blouse from the bottom up and being crazy drunk I thought what a cute little son of a bitch you are and kissed her lightly on the top of the breast. Then I climbed over in the back seat wiping my prints off of the dashboard. I locked the door beside the girl, wiped the rear door and the left rear door as I got out of the car. Noticing the left front window was half open I put my hands on the glass and forced it closed."

Arnold's confession, at that point, raised several red flags.

Most of what Arnold told detectives had been in the newspapers, such as Brown being with another young woman at the drive-in restaurant. However, the mention of a young woman seen running down Broadway between 1:00 and 1:30 a. m., came from the case file, not from the newspapers the author examined. In his confession, Arnold said he exited Brown's car by the left rear door. That door was locked when Brown's body was found.

A particularly troubling portion in the confession was his description of climbing, "Over in the back seat and wiped my prints off the dash board." Why not wipe his fingerprints off the dash when he was in the front seat? When he talked about being in the vehicle's front seat, he made no mention of the textbooks in the passenger seat.

If Arnold actually killed Betty Gail Brown, as he described in his confession, his fingerprints would probably have been all over her car especially on the driver's side window. His fingerprints were readily available as Arnold was already in an Oregon correctional facility and had previously been in jails in Kentucky. In addition, Arnold had served in the military, which made his fingerprints available for a law enforcement background check.

Details about the location of her car were not clear in Arnold's statement. Either he did not know the automobile's exact location or Carter erred in writing down Arnold's description of where he said the car was while writing the confession. Possibly he confused the semi-circular driveway in front of Morrison Chapel, with the entrance and exit off Third Street, with a similar driveway off North Broadway, across from Forrer Hall.

Arnold said he left the car and body and went down Market Street to the apartment of May Hedges, a friend of his. "I told her I had just killed a woman," he continued. "She asked where and I said down on Broadway. Not believing me she said, 'Oh!' and ignored me. I then laid down on her couch and passed out."

The murder did not occur on Broadway.

Carter wrote, "I have (word marked out and initialed by Arnold) read this statement and it is true to the best of my knowledge and belief and is all that I know about this case. I have been asked by Lt. Carter and Capt. Henry if I wish to add or take anything from this statement and (words marked and initialed) I do not. I have not been threatened nor has anyone made any promised to me before, during or after the taking of this statement. I have been treated (word marked out and initialed) with nothing but kindness and respect by both the Kalmath Falls police and the Lexington police. Signed Alex Arnold Jr. Transcribed by Lt. A. M. Carter, witnessed by Capt. Bryan Henry, witnessed by Dennis W. Kelly."

Based on his confession Alex Arnold was returned to Lexington, and a preliminary hearing was held in Fayette Quarterly Court, with Judge L.T. Grant presiding. Arnold appeared thin and wan as he entered the courtroom. At the hearing, on March 24, 1965, Armand Angelucci represented the people as commonwealth attorney. Two exceptionally well qualified court appointed attorneys, Amos Eblen, a former State Court of Appeals judge, and Robert Lawson, who later became dean of the University of Kentucky College of Law and the principal drafter of the *Kentucky Penal Code* and *Kentucky Rules of Evidence*, were appointed to represented Arnold.

Captain of detectives Gilbert Cravens testified that he was called to the crime scene five minutes after patrolman

Duckworth found the body. Cravens described the shrubbery as being five to six feet high on the inside and outside of the semi-circular drive in front of Morrison Chapel. Duckworth testified he waited for Cravens before opening the Simca's doors. Although it was a cold frosty morning, Duckworth said they did not look for footprints around Brown's car.

That could have been a mistake as those conditions might have made footprints more easily detectible.

Cravens also said he found no evidence of another girl having been in Betty Gail Brown's car in front of Morrison Chapel.

The name of Gay Brock, the waitress who was believed to be the last known person to see the victim alive, eluded detective Morris Carter at the preliminary hearing. Carter said he might have the waitress' name somewhere in his notes.

It was Brock who investigators considered their best lead and the one witness who could identify Betty Gail Brown's companion at the restaurant. Yet, the detective could not remember her name in court.

Carter admitted that none of the three sets of identifiable fingerprints found on the car were Arnold's. The commonwealth, despite Arnold's confession, was unable to produce any physical evidence connecting the accused to the murder. Prosecutors only had Arnold's questionable confession.

Coroner Hager testified that that the deceased student had a 1 1/2 inch laceration on the top of her head that appeared to indicate someone had grabbed her hair and yanked it back. Hager said he found the imprint of the Simca logo on the left side of her forehead. The logo was located on the right dashboard.

Arnold was indicted for Betty Gail Brown's murder by a grand jury on the basis of his confession. On March 30, 1965, his bail was set at $50,000, and Fayette Circuit Court Judge Joseph J. Bradley refused defense attorneys' request to reduce it to $15,000.

However, Arnold and/or his family had substantial financial connections, according to his preliminary hearing file. Several people were willing to pledge their homes and land for his bail. Edward and Martha Ethington used their Traveler Road property, in an affluent development on the city's west side, as surety for his bail. The Ethingtons were possibly maternal relatives of Arnold. His mother name was Betty Ethington Jackson. Arnold had three stepbrothers, Roger, Raymond and Luther Jackson.

Betty E. and Luther M. Jackson, Arnold's mother and stepfather, pledged a house and lot on High Street for his bail. Don H. Mitchell put up western Kentucky real estate in McCracken County worth $398,250. Finally, the Johnson Bonding Company picked up Arnold's bail.

Arnold's preliminary hearing file also contained the deposition of Mae Hedges taken June 4, 1965. Mrs. Hedges, despite meeting three times with prosecutor Angelucci and detective Cravens in preparation for her testimony, was adamant that Arnold did not come to her apartment the night of Brown's murder and tell her that he had killed the woman.

The Trial Begins

Jury selection in Arnold's trial for the murder of Betty Gail Brown began October 2, 1965, as prospective jurors were dismissed in wholesale lots due to objections to the death penalty. Prosecutor Donald Moloney indicated he would probably seek capital punishment. Amos Eblen, one of Arnold's attorneys, questioned prospective jurors about any connections they might have to Transylvania College. That further depleted the jury pool.

One prospective juror, according to the Lexington newspaper, said Arnold had worked for him for six months ten years previously and, because of that, it might be painful for him to sit on the jury. Two other possible jurors told judge Joseph Bradley they had expressed opinions on the case. Another said he had personal problems that would prevent him from being on the jury for the long period of time the trial was expected to take. Finally, a jury, with one alternate, was seated.

The jury, for the most part, was made up of professional individuals, some of whom lived in the south Lexington area where the Betty Gail Brown had grown up. Four of the jurors had ties to IBM, where Arnold once worked and two were in the insurance business as was Hargus Brown.

When Alex Arnold, Jr., was photographed by the *Herald* being escorted into the Fayette County Courthouse on October 2, 1965, the opening day of his trial for the murder of Betty Gail Brown, he was neatly dressed and groomed. He appeared in much better physical shape than he was at his March preliminary hearing. He certainly looked much better than he did when Carter and Bryant talked with him in Oregon the preceding January.

Arnold entered a plea of not guilty in the murder of Betty Gail Brown.

In his opening statement, commonwealth attorney Donald Moloney told the jurors that Arnold, who used aliases Don Ringo and Don Eagle had been indicted for the murder of Betty Gail Brown, who was killed on October 27, 1961, according to the *Herald*. He told the jury the prosecution would show that Arnold used the back of the front seat of Brown's car for leverage to literally squeeze the breath of life out of her with her own bra.

Moloney then introduced into evidence the confession Arnold made in Oregon.

His attorneys, Amos Eblen and Robert Lawson, asked judge Bradley to suppress his confession to Brown's murder on the grounds that he was not competent to understand what he was doing or his right to have an attorney present when the confession was taken. They pointed out he was suffering from the DTs, caused by prolong consumption of alcohol, after spending three days in the Kalmath jail on a charge of public intoxication.

Commonwealth attorney Moloney objected saying that Arnold indicated he had understood his rights and refused to read the confession before signing the document.

Judge Bradley excused the jury and spent four hours, according to the October 7, *Courier-Journal*, hearing the defense's problems with the confession as written by Carter and the prosecution's defense of the document. The October 7, *Herald* reported that Arnold told the judge he was suffering from the delirium tremors when he signed the confession. He recounted his hallucinations, hearing voices, talking to spots on the walls and thinking there was a "truth machine" near his cell in the Kalmath Falls Jail.

Sgt. Dennis Lilly and Dr. Seth Kerron, from Kalmath Falls told the judge they were observing Arnold at that time and the defendant displayed none of the symptoms he described, according to the article. Lilly said Arnold objected to talking with him in the women's drunk tank because "He said there was a machine near his cell that could tell whether he was telling the truth."

Lilly's statements appeared at odds with each other. If Arnold displayed none of the symptoms he described, how could Lilly account for his statement about the so-called truth machine near his cell?

Detective Bryan Henry admitted that Arnold was nervous, looked bad and was restless during his confession. "His speech was low and his voice would quiver at times," Henry was quoted by the newspaper as saying. Arnold acknowledged that, off and on, he would think that he could not have killed Brown and, later, would sometimes think he did.

Arnold conceded that he was offered an attorney before he signed his confession in Oregon and waived the right to have one present. He also said that afterwards, he told the Lexington detectives that he felt like a 500-pound weight had been lifted off each shoulder.

Arnold said he was working in a Lexington restaurant when Betty Gail Brown was murdered and that one of the waitresses there read him the newspaper accounts of the homicide, according to the *Courier-Journal*. When asked by Eblen if thoughts occurred to him at that time that he had had killed Brown, Arnold replied, "Absolutely none whatsoever."

Arnold also recalled discussions he had in 1963, with a cellmate in the State Reformatory, at LaGrange, Kentucky, about the Brown murder. According to the Louisville newspaper, Arnold said, "I got to thinking I'd had something like a dream" following those conversations. Several months later, while in the Fayette County Jail, Arnold said he accumulated a lot of information about the Brown murder from other inmates. In accounting for his jail sentences, Arnold said he drank constantly.

In defending the taking of Arnold's confession at their third meeting with him, detectives Carter and Henry were quoted in the Louisville newspaper as saying his state of mind improved after his confession. If that was the case, then his state of mind at the time of his confession could have been as questionable as his attorneys maintained.

Eblen and Lawson, according to the October 8, *Courier-Journal* noted errors (previously mentioned) in the confession, which they maintained Carter and Henry knew were false. The detectives insisted their role was to take down the statement as Arnold made it and not to attempt to influence him.

In an attempt to explain his confession to the murder, Arnold was quoted in the Lexington newspaper as saying, "I knew that now we'd get to the bottom of it and I'd know for sure." Arnold candidly answered the judge's questions about the confession he made to Carter and Henry the previous January.

Judge Bradley overruled the defense's objection to admitting Arnold's confession into evidence and asked the jury to return to the courtroom to hear Sgt. Lilly read Arnold's confession as written by Carter and witnessed by Henry and Lilly.

Why Lilly read the confession instead of Carter, who wrote the document, was never clear.

Moloney then called Quincy Brown to the stand. She was described by the *Herald* as being remarkably composed. She told the jury about her three trips to the Transylvania campus to look for her daughter when she failed to return home after midnight. The victim mother's said she only glanced at the drive into the campus off Third Street and "Saw nothing there."

The media devoted little coverage to the testimony of Hargus Brown.

Mrs. John Combs, the Forrer Hall housemother, testified that Betty Gail Brown left the dormitory at 11:50 p.m., the night she was killed. At the time of the trial, Mrs. Combs was working at Bell Haven College in Jackson, Mississippi.

Former Transylvania student, Charles Risdon, III, from Huntington Woods, Michigan, told the jury of the contact he had with the victim after she left the dormitory.

Risdon, according to the *Herald*, was leaving the parking lot, off Broadway, after returning his date to Forrer Hall, when he stopped to talk to Betty Gail Brown. Risdon said he, "Didn't believe anyone was in the car with her," as he drove up along side the Simca. Brown, he said, slid across the front seat, rolled down the passenger side window and chatted briefly with him before they left the parking lot. Risdon said both cars turned off Broadway on to Fourth Street and on to Upper. He said he pulled into a parking lot behind the men's dormitory while Brown's car continued south on Upper toward town and he never saw her alive again.

Under cross-examination, Risdon said he saw no one walking around the campus when he took his date to Forrer Hall and returned to the parking lot across the street.

Detective Henry testified that Arnold seemed relieved after his confession and talked about things he experienced as a youngster. He remembered when a little girl squeezed his pet duck too hard and it died.

The subject of the victim's fingerprints, or the absence thereof, again came into the case. Henry admitted the mistake of not fingerprinting the young woman before she was buried, according to the article. He said only three identifiable sets of fingerprints were found on the automobile: those of Robert Hamilton, the mechanic who worked on the Simca and Quincy and Hargis Brown. The fingerprints on the door handles, windows and other areas of the car were smeared, Henry said. His admission that Arnold's fingerprints were not found anywhere on Brown's car was a blow to the prosecution's case.

Henry also recalled, during his and Carter's conversation with Arnold before making his confession, the defendant described the girl in the car with Betty Gail Brown as being blond and wearing glasses. No such description was included in Carter's handwritten account of Arnold's confession. That portion of the confession read, "I seen what looked like two women making love, they were hugging and kissing each other."

There must have been a reason the detectives left that important description out since the so-called mystery woman was at the heart of the murder case.

The October 9, *Herald* related Henry's description of the murder scene to the jury. "At the scene to the slaying he (Henry) had someone open the car doors but didn't know who opened them or how they were opened. I had been called out of bed at 3 a.m., in the morning and I was still half asleep when I arrived there."

Officer Duckworth, who found Brown's body at 3:05 a.m., testified that the Simca was parked, "Opposite the corner of the end of the steps of Morrison Chapel." The car, he said, was covered with frost, all the doors and windows were closed, the victim was seated behind the steering wheel her head thrown back with one hand in her lap and the other on the seat beside her.

However, Sgt. Joe Brown, according to the *Herald*, said he opened both front doors without using a key. Brown took the first pictures of the crime scene but the time of his arrival there was not clear.

Drs. James T. McClellan and Rudolph Mueling, pathologists who performed the autopsy on Betty Gail Brown, told the jury the procedure was performed seven hours after her body was found.

McClellan, the articled continued, said she was "Strangled to death with a ligature, something other than human hands placed around her neck and tightened." Such actions, he added, fractured cartilage in her neck. There were bruises on her neck and forehead, scrapes on her nose, left chin and neck, and a torn place on the top of her head, he said. The pathologists also found ink on Brown's hands and fingers and a lipstick smear on her left arm.

The next day, Wednesday, the jury spent about half a day dealing with items that never mentioned Arnold but were clearly designed to back up the confession he made in Oregon. They carefully examined Brown's blouse and bra during testimony of coroner Chester Hager. Quincy Brown came near to losing her composure at the sight of her dead daughter's clothing, according to the *Herald*.

Hager told the court, "That Miss Brown probably died between midnight and 1:00 a.m., said an autopsy, which he ordered, showed death was caused by suffocation by strangulation from external force applied to the neck," according to the article.

Hager demonstrated how the bra was draped across Betty Gail Brown's shoulder when her body was found. The back section, with elastic and fastening hooks, had been ripped loose on the left side and pulled out of the stitching on the right end; the hooks were still fastened. Photographs from the crime scene showed the bra draped across Brown's left shoulder with part of it lying in her lap.

Hager, according to the *Herald*, told the jury her silk blouse was standing open at the neck leaving the tops of her breasts visible. "The top four buttons on the blouse were unbuttoned," he was quoted as saying. "Although the jurors were given Miss Brown's raincoat and sweater as well as the blouse and brassiere," the newspaper article continued, "they focused their attention on the latter two garments, even examining the buttons and buttonholes on the blouse to see if they were ripped. They were not."

When cross-examined by the defense, Hager defended commencing the embalming process before the autopsy began. "The blood had nothing to do with her injuries...the fracture of cartilage in her neck." he was quoted as saying.

Charles Risdon, III, then living in Huntington Woods, Michigan, told the jury of his brief conversation with Betty Gail Brown as both were leaving the campus parking area across Broadway from Forrer Hall. Upon cross-examination Risdon repeated that he saw no one walking around the campus when he returned his date to the dorm or when he and Brown left the parking lot.

Officer Duckworth testified that Brown's car was parked opposite the east end of the steps to Morrison Chapel when he found the body. He said the six-foot hedge along either side of the drive could have hidden the car from the view of someone traveling along Third Street. The officer said all of the doors and windows in Brown's car were shut when he found the frost covered vehicle and none were opened until Capt. Cravens arrived on the scene. Duckworth said he helped search the area near the car and, after daylight, conducted a wider search pattern on the campus but found nothing relating to the crime.

A notation if the case file, dated November 11, 1961, listed a ladies' gold watch was found in the grass in front of Haupe Humanities Building, which stood between Morrison Chapel and Broadway. There was nothing in the file to indicate the watch was connected to the Brown murder. However, detectives searched the campus grounds for two weeks after Brown's body was found.

Documents in the Department of Libraries and Archives, in Frankfort, revealed that Arnold had been treated at the Veteran's Hospital, in Lexington, in 1962. Details of the ailment or diagnosis were unknown. The hospital's medical director, Dr. Albert Mason, was subpoenaed to appear in court on October 6, with all of Arnold's medical records. No mention of his testimony was found in media accounts of the trial.

Before Arnold took the witness stand in the defense portion of the case, juror Charles Brown told Judge Bradley and attorneys from both sides that he received a call the previous evening from a woman who wanted to discuss the Betty Gail Brown murder case with him. The October 8, *Herald* quoted Brown as saying, "When he realized what the woman wanted to discuss he told her he could not discuss the case and would have to report her call to the judge. When she continued talking he held the receiver away from his ear and told his wife to tell her he had gone out or something." Charles Brown was unable to identify the woman's voice.

The judge ruled no harm had occurred and the trial continued.

The Defense's Turn

Amos Eblen, in his opening remarks, told the jury about discrepancies in his client's confession, which was the only evidence against him, and fallacies raised by the prosecution. "There's not one factual statement in that confession that was not circulated in the press," Eblen told the jury according to the October 8 *Herald*. "He doesn't honestly know whether he did it or not."

The prosecution would later use the defense attorney's statement, about media coverage of the murder, against his client.

Eblen said he intended to establish that Arnold, the night Betty Gail Brown was murdered, was at his aunt's home. Seemingly, that would give Arnold an impeccable alibi.

When Arnold took the stand, Eblen asked him his recollections of the night the college student was killed. Arnold, according to the newspaper, replied "At one time I thought I'd murdered a girl. I know now that I didn't do it." Arnold said he had spent the night at the home of an aunt not at Mae Hedges' as he previously stated.

Eblen used his client's witness stand statements to attack testimonies of prosecution witnesses point by point, pertaining to the location of Brown's car; how the car doors locked; his mental condition when he first talked to Sgt. Lilly in Oregon; his description of the murder scene, and the location of the girl's bra.

Arnold said he told Carter and Henry he found the car, with Betty Gail Brown and her alleged companion inside, parked near Broadway in a horseshoe-shaped driveway even before he made his signed confession. Arnold's signed confession on that point read, "Upon passing a car in a driveway on the campus..." Eblen pointed out such a description could be either the semi-circular driveway off Broadway or a similar one off Third Street in front of Morrison Chapel, where Brown's car and body were found.

The defense attorney had another problem with Arnold's confession concerning the door locks on the Simca. Arnold recounted in court he told Carter and Henry that he pushed down the lock buttons upon leaving the car but it was not included in his signed confession. On that point, his confession stated, "I locked the door beside the girl (the) right front and the left rear as I got out of the car." The Simca's doors did not have push down button-type locks. Investigators found that the car's doors could only be locked from the inside by pulling the door handles up.

In his confession, Arnold said he used his hands to push up the driver's door window. Robert Hamilton, the mechanic who serviced the Simca, testified the car's windows were working properly, according to the October 12, 1965 *Herald*. Hamilton added that the windows could not be manually pushed more than a half an inch.

Since there was no indication that Arnold wore gloves that night, if he had pushed up the car door window, he would have left his fingerprints.

Dr. Kerron, Arnold said, had taken his pulse and temperature when he examined him in the Kalmath Falls' jail. Kerron said he did not perform those functions, further indicating he probably gave Arnold no more than a cursory examination. Kerron earlier testified that Arnold told him about the slaying and that he did it "Because she made me so damn mad I couldn't help myself."

Kalmath Falls patrolman James Pratt's testified that Arnold's arrest card was marked, "Watch-possible DTs," which seemed to refute both Lilly and Kerron's statements that he was not suffering from DTs.

Betty Gail Brown's bra was found draped around her left shoulder, not in the back seat of her car as Arnold described in his confession.

Then, there was the mystery woman Arnold said was in the car with victim the night of the murder. Arnold said he described her to detectives Henry and Carter before he made his confession but it was not included in the document.

Eblen pointed out that Arnold admitted that he obtained information about the murder from his Fayette County Jail cellmate, Linwood Green, while they were incarcerated there at the same time. While he was in jail, he said, the idea that he might have killed Brown began to trouble him. "I began to think about it, so sure I'd done it, yet I wasn't (sure) that I thought I'd find out for sure and get it over with," he told the jury. "Never being sure almost drove me crazy."

Arnold said he first began to doubt that he was guilty of murdering Betty Gail Brown after his attorneys talked with Mae Hedges and his aunt.

In cross examining Arnold, Moloney attempted to validate his confession as he walked him through the document step by step, according to the October 9 *Herald*. Following the newspaper's earlier editorial statement that the student's death was not sexual related, the *Herald's* account of Arnold's testimony was quite different from his confession, in which he described two women making love in the automobile. After waking up and finding he had no matches to light a cigarette, "He started back for Broadway, he said, and came upon a car with two women in it. He asked them for a match and they began to curse him and he walked away."

Moloney asked Arnold a series of questions, which the Lexington newspapers would either have to leave out of their articles or by including them admit there was a sexual side to the case. The publication quoted Moloney as saying, "Did you read anywhere about the murderer walking through Gratz Park, a wine bottle, people hugging and kissing in a car, a match, a bra on the seat, a body quivering or a kiss?"

Eblen objected but was overruled by the judge. Moloney told the jury Arnold's negative answers disproved the defense's statement there was nothing in his confession that had not been in the newspapers.

Other factors entered into the Moloney's questions, which he told the jury were not reported in the newspapers. Gratz Park was directly across Third Street from the Transylvania campus and the semi-circular drive into Morrison Chapel. Hundreds of people probably walked through Gratz Park every day as the public library was located on the south end of the park. In the evening, lovers were known to sit in the park. The Morrison Chapel portion of the campus was another gathering place for those with romantic notions.

The school was celebrating the revelry of Rafinesque Week and finding empty wine bottles, as well as beer and whiskey containers, could be expected under shrubbery on both the campus and Gratz Park.

Lexington newspaper accounts of the co-ed's murder gave her bra prominent coverage as it was a most unusual death weapon. But, those articles also undermined the publication's contention that her death had no connection to sex.

Arnold, although he maintained his innocence, said that the detectives failed to correctly record his description of locking the doors on the Simca. He insisted that he pushed the door lock buttons down on all four doors, including the right rear when he exited the vehicle. Judge Bradley, in a blow to the defense, refused to allow Eblen and Lawson to take the jurors to examine the Simca's door locks, according to the October 12 *Courier-Journal*. Such an examination would have certainly refuted a portion of Arnold's confession.

The newspaper's account indicated Arnold was rather dramatic in demonstrating how he strangled Betty Gail Brown with her bra by using his knee and the back of the driver's seat for leverage, pulling back on the bra ends to saw into her neck and throwing the garment in the back seat. He said he buttoned up her blouse because he did not want anyone to think he had raped her. Yet, investigators found the blouse's four top buttons unfastened and the tops of her breasts visible. Arnold had difficulty deciding whether he kissed the top of her right or left breast.

His description of how he left the campus and went to Mae Hedge's apartment on Third Street was hazy. He appeared confused about which semi-circular campus drive he crossed, the one off Broadway or the one off Third Street. Moloney asked him why he did not go to his mother's home on West High Street as he usually did instead of sleeping on the ground. "I've often wondered that myself," Arnold was quoted as saying.

Mae Hedges, a witness the prosecution had spent a lot of time with and who Arnold identified in his confession as the person in whose home he spent the rest of the night after the murder, followed him on the witness stand and testified he did not come to her apartment that evening, according to the October 9 *Herald*. Mrs. Hedges said she knew the defendant as Don Arnold. Her brother, Albert Kendig, who was living with her in October 1961, told jurors he had never seen Arnold before the trial and he was certain the defendant did not come to their home on the evening in question.

Hedges was the proverbial witness from hell for the prosecution since she denied Arnold's statement in his confession that he came to her home the night of the murder. In her June 4, 1965, deposition, she detailed three meetings with Armand Angelucci, the commonwealth attorney, and detective Cravens as they prepared her to testify. She flatly refused to back up Arnold's confession that he spent the remainder of the night at her home saying her brother would not have let him in the door. Brought into the courtroom in a wheel chair and placed facing the jury box, the crusty lady brought laughter from the spectators during her questioning by Moloney, according to the October 9, *Herald*. After the prosecutor asked her the same question three times and she gave him the same answer three times, Hedge's asked caustically, "Isn't that clear?" Judge Bradley cautioned spectators about their decorum and the room settled down.

Imogene Marshall, Arnold's aunt, said she visited him in jail after his mother told her he had no memory of where he spent the night of October 26, 1961.

Arnold's mother did not figure prominently in the case. Mae Hedges described the woman in her June 1965, deposition as being a nurse whose last name she thought was Johnson and who worked at the narcotics hospital, the United States Public Health Service facility, on Leestown Road.

Imogene Marshall testified that Arnold brought her husband Johnny Marshall home drunk that evening. He was drinking at the Black Cup Restaurant, near Short Street and Broadway, where Arnold was then working. "When his uncle became drunk," the article continued, "Arnold said they took a taxi to a small bar in the 300 block of North Limestone. They stayed there a short time and then he took his uncle home before the bars closed so it must have been around midnight."

She also testified she remembered well the night in question because she asked Arnold to stay with her husband, who had been sick after he went to bed. Arnold, she said, remained with him the next day while she took her children to the Fayette County Health Department for their shots. Johnny Marshall was admitted to the Veterans Administration Hospital three days later.

Marshall's statements were verified by health department and hospital officials.

A witness was located who saw a man the Lexington newspaper earlier described as seen coming from the bushes at the corner of Broadway and Third Street the night of Brown's murder, according to the October 12, *Courier-Journal*. Gillespie Hall, from Nicholasville, testified he was driving home from work about 1:30 a.m. the night Betty Gail Brown was murdered. The man he saw was not Arnold, Hall said, but was taller, well over six feet, slim, with brown wavy hair, wore glasses and had a long sharp nose. Arnold was six feet, weighted 205 pounds, had brown eyes and hair and a straight nose and did not wear glasses.

Hargus and Quincy Brown were again called to testify, the October 12 *Herald* reported. "Both answered no, when asked if their daughter was physically attracted to other girls." Qunicy Brown pointed out the date book, found in her daughter's purse after her death containing the names of the boys she dated, was not introduced into evidence when the handbag was. There must have been a reason for the commonwealth attorney's decision to withhold those names.

Judge Bradley issued a court order, agreed to by both parties, allowing the Browns to remain in the courtroom after they had testified. They could, he wrote, "Remain in the court room during the remainder of the trial with the right of both parties to recall said witnesses, or either of them, if necessary, after they have testified."

The Rev. Leslie R. Smith, the Browns' minister, Mrs. Pete Waldrop, a sorority sister of the victim's, and Brenda Mattox, from New Haven Connecticut, attested to Betty Gail Brown's good character. Mattox was then a student at Yale Divinity School as was Brown's good friend, Nancy Jo Kemper. There was no indication that Kemper testified. Apparently, the commonwealth attorney felt the need to refute rumors of sexual activity between Brown and another woman.

Commonwealth attorney Moloney, in his summation, told the jury, "Only a relative and a friend first shook his 99 percent sureness of his confession," according to the October 12, *Herald*. Moloney accused Arnold of blurring the confession, made in Oregon, from the witness stand. He derided the defendant's search for his "inner memory" and what he termed Arnold's futile attempts to recall details. Moloney also questioned the accuracy of the testimonies of Mae Hedges and Imogene Marshall. He plainly thought Hedges was less than truthful and said if Marshall thought her nephew was innocent she should not have waited two weeks to tell authorities what she knew.

Moloney maintained that Arnold's account of two girls hugging and kissing in the Transylvania driveway was a guilty man's justification of his act and intimidating his victim made it easier for him to confess.

Eblen, who referred to the trial as a six-day search for the truth, maintained that "Arnold's only crime was excessive drinking deteriorating his brain to the point of imagined guilt," according to the October 12, *Herald*. Convicting Arnold, he told the jury, would be the same as convicting Betty Gail Brown of immoral practices. Eblen then launched into an attack on the Lexington Police. "If I had botched this case they way they did, I'd want to get rid of it." He said he was glad to be "Defending Alex Arnold rather than the Lexington Police Department." The attorney scorned the investigation for lack of fingerprints. Arnold's confession, he said, was the "Only evidence without one little bit of supporting evidence-not an iota in all that time (referring to the four years since the murder)."

The Verdict

Judge Bradley instructed jurors to consider either a murder verdict, if they decided Arnold killed Brown with malice aforethought, or an involuntary manslaughter verdict if they concluded he committed the crime in a fit of passion.

The jury began deliberations at 3:12 p.m., on October 12, and returned with the verdict at 9:55 p.m., the Lexington newspaper reported, to say they were hopelessly deadlocked. After five votes, all producing the same results, seven for acquittal and five for conviction, jury foreman John W. Barker reported to the judge that further deliberations were unlikely to change anybody's mind.

There was no physical evidence pointing to Arnold as the killer. His fingerprints were not found on or in Betty Gail Brown's car. Only his confession, made in an alcoholic haze, possibly connected Arnold to the crime. Yet, it was amazing that five of the twelve jurors voted for his conviction.

Three days after the jury's verdict, Arnold's bail was reduced from $50,000 to $15,000, according to judge Bradley's orders. The court order noted that the commonwealth attorney objected. Arnold was free on the bonded amount because of the hung jury and the possibility of a new trial.

The indictment on the murder charge, however, loomed over Arnold for an astounding eight years after the trial jury rendered their deadlocked decision. Another indictment was never sought and there was not another trial.

In the meantime, Moloney died and Patrick Molloy became commonwealth attorney. A January 30, 1973, letter from Molloy to Lexington police chief James L. Shaffer, relating to the dismissal of charges against Arnold, was found in the Department of Library and Archives, in Frankfort. "It is my opinion," Molloy wrote, "based on a review of the case files and upon the recommendation of assistant chief (Morris) Carter that it would be virtually impossible to reconstruct the case for presentation to a jury."

Molloy was quoted in the February 5, 1973, *Herald* as saying the same murder charge could not be reinstated but it was possible that Arnold could be indicted again if new additional evidence was found.

Finally the murder charge against Arnold was quietly dismissed in 1973, in the chambers of Fayette circuit judge N. Mitchell Meade. In his dismissal order, judge Meade stated that Hargus and Quincy Brown concurred with the action. The Browns later praised the prosecution's handling of the Arnold trial.

Herald reporter Tom Carter, in a 1973, article about the case wrote, "The fact that Arnold did frequently drink to excess-together with numerous confessions received by the police from other sources-contributed to his defense in the later trial."

There was no mention in the case file of any confessions other than Arnold's or in newspaper accounts from the murder investigation or the trial. The unavailability of the murder trial transcript left many questions unanswered.

Ron Ware description of the Browns' life after their daughter's death was poignant. He said Quincy Brown told him their lives were ruined. "She told me how there had been accusations that she had done it and about all the stories about Betty Gail. She told me that as long as they were a suspect they could never adopt a child. She said they offered free rent to any student that needed a place to stay and no one would do it.

"She said there were pistols in the rooms of the house because people would even look in their windows." Ware added that Hargus Brown, an officer in the Army Reserves at the Lexington Army Depot, was no longer able to make door-to-door insurance collections after his daughter's murder.

Hargus Brown died before Quincy Brown's death in the 1980s. In the interim, she had move to Florida.

Hopefully, she found some peace there away from the scene of her daughter's death.

Alex Arnold, Jr., died in the V. A. Hospital, in Lexington, in June 1980, after an extended illness. He was 49, and lived at 330 South Upper Street. His funeral was held in coroner Chester Hager's Whitehall Funeral Home and he was buried in the Versailles Cemetery. In addition to his mother and three brothers, Arnold was also survived by a sister Shirley Combs.

Lexington's Division of Police, in June 2006, was still attempting to solve the murder of Betty Gail Brown. Sgt. Paul Williams, according to the *Herald-Leader*, said detectives were using funds from a $112,500 state cold case grant to conduct DNA touch-testing of Brown's clothing from the night of her murder as skin cells were sometime left behind on items touched by an individual.

Williams was quoted as saying, "There are a lot of possibilities that could result if there is reliable, testable DNA."

There could be more DNA possibilities than expected since the twelve-member jury carefully examined Brown's clothing, specifically her bra and blouse, during Alex Arnold's trial for her murder.

It has been nearly half a century since Betty Gail Brown's murder shocked Lexington and only a few are left to clamor for the justice that has long been denied their friend.

Mary

Marrs

Swinebroad

Cawein

Marrs Swinebroad Cawein
Photograph courtesy *1947 Kentuckian* Yearbook, University Archives and Records Program, Division of Special Collections and Digital Programs, University of Kentucky.

Caweins' bedroom washstand drawer showing needles/vials.
(Lexington Division of Police)

The Blue Chair

Mary Marrs Swinebroad Cawein, in a full slip and bra, probably nestled in the blue damask chair in her bedroom enjoying the refreshing air conditioning in the July 4, 1965, hot weather as she admired her newly painted toenails. At thirty-nine, she was still a vibrant, tall, attractive woman.

Ever the optimist, perhaps she was thinking there was still a small chance she could hold on to her wayward husband, Madison J. Cawein III, forty, a prominent medical researcher at the University of Kentucky's A. B. Chandler Medical Center, in Lexington, Kentucky. On the other hand, if she gave him his freedom, her life would certainly be less complicated.

The socialite/real estate agent's thoughts possibly turned to the new home she planned to build or buy, even if she had to accomplish the feat as a single parent. The three-bedroom dwelling at 326 Chinoe Road, in Lexington, Kentucky, she and her husband purchased in 1959, had been adequate then. With a fifteen-year-old son, Madison J. Cawein IV, who was called, "Skip," and a nine year-old daughter, Elizabeth, known as "Betsy," the family had outgrown their modest brick cottage.

The blue damask chair, the only one in the master bedroom, was one of Marrs Cawein's favorite placed to read and relax. She had no idea she would be found dead in the same chair hours later, with carbolic acid in her stomach.

Her macabre murder, thanks to wealthy, politically powerful Lexingtonians, some of whom claimed to be her friends, would never be solved. Instead of helping to solve her murder, they lawyered up because they were scared-down to the toes of their wing tips and high heeled shoes, that their own reputations might suffer during the investigation of her murder.

Marrs, as her friends and family called her, knew she had to finish dressing and join her husband and Betty and Sam Strother for the big Independence Day party at the Idle Hour County Club, on Richmond Road.

Possibly chuckling at the idea of her philandering husband waiting for her in their hot living room, she took her time dressing. Small victories, like that, were important to Marrs Cawein, a woman verbally abused and brow beaten first by her father, the internationally famous Thoroughbred auctioneer George Swinebroad, and later by her husband.

She had also been subjected to periodical physical attacks by first one and then another of her husband's mistresses. Russell Lutes, an antique dealer favored by the social set, told investigators that the day before Marrs Cawein died she had "A pretty good sized fight with one of her husband's paramours, who had known (Madison) Cawein for years and who insisted they still loved each other."

Nettie Duvall, her long time hairdresser, told detectives when Marrs Cawein kept her regular 11:00 a.m., appointment on July 2, she noticed several bruises on both her arms and legs and some hair missing at the crown of her head. Duvall said she had never seen any bruises on her in the past six years she had been doing her hair.

Marrs Cawein' sense of self worth was at such a low level that she was excited that a strange man actually engaged her in conversation at a New York art gallery a couple of years earlier. That elation continued when the man wrote her after she returned to Lexington. Her friend, Betty Strother, said she did not think a relationship grew out of the casual meeting. Strother said she felt that her friend, with her ego so beaten down, latched on to it and built it into something that it was not.

Obviously, Marrs Cawein was a woman who was a stranger to friendly masculine attention, which brought no confrontations or violence to her and her children.

There was probably a lot on her mind that evening. Her husband was having yet another affair. This time, he chose a young doctor's wife who, if rumors were correct, he had impregnated. Cawein told his wife he was really in loved this time and had asked her for a divorce.

She first refused to give him the divorce. Then, she threatened to take everything he had or would ever accumulate. In Lexington, she had the clout, through her father, to do just that. Marrs Cawein told her mother and some friends she was tempted to give him the divorce just to get rid of all the problems he brought into her life.

Unsure of what steps to take, she frantically attempted to get in touch with her father-in-law Madison J. Cawein II, but was unsuccessful. She wanted to ask for his advice in dealing with vast number of personal problems his son had brought into her life.

She used her contacts in New York in an effort to reach the elder Cawein. She contacted her stepbrother, Allen Woods, a New York stockbroker. Mrs. John Merrit, a friend who lived on Moreland Drive, told investigators that Marrs Cawein called her and asked for her brother's number in New York, "In a frantic attempt to get hold of Madison Cawein."

The fact that Marrs Cawein sought advice from her father-in-law rather than her father, who was also her business partner, was telling of the relationship, which existed between Swinebroad and his only child. When detectives asked Betty Strother if Marrs Cawein got along with her father, she waffled in her reply. "They got along, they didn't see that much of each other; didn't have a lot in common," she said. "They had never been too close but the only problem Marrs would have had with her father would be him getting mad about some little thing."

Searching for something to occupy her time, after her children were older, Marrs Cawein found a successful career in real estate. "She adored it and she was good at it," Betty Strother said. "I really think Marrs was happier since she had gone into it. She was so proud when Mr. Swinebroad asked her to go into an office with him." Marrs' father's successful auctioneering and real estate firm was then known as Swinebroad, Denton & Cawein.

In retrospect, Marrs Cawein knew she made a mistake in including her husband's name on her stock portfolio. In 1959, she inherited $49,000, equal to more than $330,000 in 2008 dollars. She invested $30,000, of the inheritance, with her stepbrother Allen West's firm, Goodbody & Company, in New York, in her own name. After much harassing from Madison Cawein, she relented and made it a joint account.

There was no doubt that Madison Cawein would demand his portion of her stock portfolio in a divorce action. The physician was investing his salary in his own stock portfolio leaving her to pay the family's bills out of her real estate sales commissions.

Her personal financial records indicated the chasm between her income and expenses was growing wider each month.

If her husband divorced her and left town, he had been offered a position at the prestigious Mayo Clinic, in Rochester, Minnesota, she might have to postpone building or buying a new home. She seemed to be operating on the premise that a divorce was inevitable and had already listed their Chinoe Road home for sale in the newspaper.

Marrs Cawein was not blind to the problems both she and her husband brought into their family life. It was doubtful if either of them admitted they had an alcohol problem. Her children were growing up in a dysfunctional family atmosphere. She was married to a man who publicly boasted of his sexual prowess, often in her presence, to their friends. Marrs Cawein had to be tired of hearing her husband's cruel rhetoric, in addition to having his lovers pull her hair out, inflict bruise on her body, break her china, overturn her furniture and look in her bedroom window.

Regardless of the verbal and physical abuse and embarrassment he brought into her life, she said she still loved him.

Eventually, the elegant woman, whose sparkling brown eyes were often dulled from the pain she allowed the men in her life to inflict, arose from comfortable security of her blue chair. Marrs Cawein stepped into a pristine yellow and black cocktail dress, with a black cummerbund and put on a pair of black strappy patent leather dress shoes, showing off her newly painted toenails. She probably took another look in the mirror to see if any bruises were showing, slipped on her rings and bracelets, fluffed up her short brown hair, picked up a small black purse and marched into the living room to join her husband. They were riding to the country club with Betty and Sam Strothers, who planned to buy their new home from Marrs Cawein.

She told Phoebe Edwards, the baby sitter, there was ground beef for hamburgers for her, Betsy, and the two Strother girls, Mary Pryor, five and Elizabeth, seven, and two cans of food for the cats. Skip Cawein was spending the weekend with a friend, Tommy Merrit, at his family's retreat on Herrington Lake.

Windows in the second floor bedrooms, where the girls would sleep, would have to be left open and the curtains pulled back, Marrs Cawein told Edwards, because the air conditioner for the second floor was not working.

Originally, Betty Strother said plans for the evening called for the sitter to keep the girls at their home on Bristol Road. However, she explained, her daughters always thought they had more fun at the Cawein home when their parents were out.

The two couples got into the Strothers' gray and black Chevrolet Impala convertible and breezed off for the short drive to the Idle Hour Country Club.

Like many of their friends, the Caweins and Strothers lived in an enclave around the country club in residences with addresses on Richmond Road, Fairway, Kingsway, Chinoe, Bristol, Henry Clay Boulevard and other nearby streets. For some the club was the center of their seemingly exclusive, but sometimes secret, lives.

Idle Hour Country Club, the haughtiest social establishment in town, admitted no Blacks and few if any Jews or foreigners. The sitting governor was accorded a membership for the length of his term and, if he met their criteria, might be permitted to join after his term ended.

The club was incorporated in 1947, after Thoroughbred horsemen Louie A. Beard and Leslie Combs II, of Lexington; A. B. "Bull" Hancock, of Paris, and Lexington businessman A. B. Gay purchased the Ashland Golf Course from the estate of Colonel E. R. Bradley. Known for his flamboyance, Bradley was a famous Thoroughbred breeder and owner as well as a professional gambler and bookmaker, who boldly offered to make wagers on horses' racing careers before they were foaled. The club was named for Bradley's Idle Hour Stock Farm, which was located on Old Frankfort Pike, but he had kept horses at the Richmond Road location at one time.

One of Bradley's great fillies, Busher, was Horse of the Year in 1945, when the distaff side seldom won that honor. Busher was purchased from Bradley's estate by Louis B. Mayer, one of the owners of MGM movie studios in Hollywood. The ownership of Busher, whose sire Fair Play was a son of the great Man O' War, was an example of the tight knit group which, much like the Idle Hour enclave, made up the Thoroughbred business in the 1940s, 1950s and 1960s.

The filly was sold again in 1948, at Swinebroad's auction of the dispersal of Mayer's stable. She was purchased by cosmetic mogul Elizabeth Arden, whose real name was Florence Nightingale Graham, for her 746-acre Lexington Farm, Main Chance. Arden's colt, Jet Pilot, also auctioned by Swinebroad, won the 1947 Kentucky Derby. After Arden's death in 1966, Swinebroad auctioned her farm on Newtown Pike, which was purchased by the University of Kentucky amid protests by her heirs, Lexington horsemen and mayor Joe Johnson.

Many prominent horsemen from Lexington as well as Midway, Versailles and Paris belonged to the Idle Hour.

Thoroughbred horse deals and syndications of stallion shares were reportedly made at the club amid a décor of Thoroughbred prints and hunt scenes, Queen Ann and Chippendale reproductions and chintz upholstered wicker furniture.

Other deals, of a more personal nature, were engaged in by some of the Idle Hour members, according to rumors. Allegedly, women threw their house keys in a pile and each woman spent the night with the man who drew her key from the stack. A few prominent divorces were said to have resulted from the mate swapping activity. Called the key club it was one of Lexington's worse kept secrets.

Lexington, in 1965, was a small gossipy town of 75,000. Subtract the students at the University of Kentucky, Transylvania College and the College of the Bible and the base population was around 50,000. Many of Lexington's old families were still adjusting to the infusion of new businesses and out-of-state employees brought about by the arrival of International Business Machines (IBM) a decade earlier and the new Albert B. Chandler Medical Center at the University of Kentucky (UK). While some of those who came with IBM and the Medical Center bought houses from real estate firms like that of Marrs Cawein and her father, only a few were admitted to their social set.

The Lexington establishment, socially as well as in business and politics, was ruled by a combination of the *Lexington Herald-Leader*, owned by the Stoll families and managed by Fred Wachs; Kentucky Utilities; First Security National Bank and Trust Company; the law firm of Stoll, Kennon and Park and the University of Kentucky. The power brokers who headed those entities were also Idle Hour members and some attended the July 4 dinner at the club.

Participants and their friends did not broadcast their social activities, such as the key club, but others did. Maids, hairdressers, seamstresses, caters, housekeepers and baby sitters had no compulsions to refrain from gossiping about the juicy details of their employers' personal lives.

Whether the Caweins and Strothers belonged to the key club was not known. Cawein's extra martial affairs were common gossip and he appeared to relish the notoriety. There was an allegation, during the investigation of her murder, that Marrs Cawein might have had some sort of relationship with Sam Strother but that was doubtful.

The Caweins and Strothers arrived at Idle Hour between 6:30 and 7:00 p.m. They headed for the nearly empty bar, ordered drinks and then walked out on the terrace. "Sam walked over to talk with Mary Jo and Billy Holton and Marrs was talking with Sarah Knuckles," Betty Strother later recalled in an interview with detectives. "It was hot and there was no place to sit down and Madison and I went back inside and sat down in the bar."

Billy Holton was also in real estate and Strother was the secretary-treasurer of Bluegrass Mortgage. Sarah Knuckles, whose husband Alfred was a major Thoroughbred breeder and owner in Midway, was a childhood friend of Marrs. Strother and Marrs Cawein returned to the bar, joined their spouses, began chatting with Ed Parker, who was the First Security listing agent for the Richmond Road house Marrs planned to show the Strothers the next day.

Obviously, the Strothers could have purchased the house directly from Parker but, knowing her marital situation, the couple said they wanted to give Marrs Cawein the commission.

Marrs Cawein's interaction with her Idle Hour friends was something of a subliminal message to her husband that they were on her turf that evening. From all indications, Madison Cawein spent most of his time drinking and talking with Betty Strother while they were at the club.

"Bob, the headwaiter, came to tell us we had better come to the dining room," Betty Strother said. "I suggested we not have another drink and go eat dinner. They all wanted one; so they had one and I didn't."

After dinner, she said, the two couples returned to the bar where they chatted with Carrie and Bennett Robinson, he was also in real estate, and Ann and Haden Kirkpatrick, he was the publisher of *The Thoroughbred Record.* "We talked and enjoyed ourselves; just had a real pleasant evening and were the last to leave the club," she said.

Sam Strother told detectives that he noticed an undercurrent of tension between the Caweins that evening at the Idle Hour. After Madison Cawein came back from a trip to the restroom and rejoined the party, Strother said Marrs Cawein looked at her husband and said, "It is a good thing that I love you because you have no physique at all. However, you are brilliant and fair looking." Photographs depicted Cawein as being tall and slender, with wavy steel gray hair, sharp facial features and wearing horn-rimmed glasses. Regardless of his looks, Cawein, from all indications, chased anything in skirts that struck his fancy and caught most of them.

Idle Hour bartender Avery D. Martin told detectives he overheard Cawein on the telephone that evening saying, "I can't get away." Robert K. Lewis, manager of the club, said he heard Cawein on the telephone saying, "I can't see you tonight...my wife is with me..." Ruth Bledsoe, a waitress at the club, also heard a portion of the same conversation.

Phoebe Edwards, the babysitter, said a woman called the Cawein home that evening and asked for the doctor. Edwards told her he had gone to the Idle Hour Country Club.

The caller was Barbara Leapman, a doctor's wife who was being treated by Madison Cawein for lymphoma. They were also having an affair. Barbara Leapman later told detectives she called the country club around 7:00 p.m., and talked with Cawein about her illness. Cawein told her he would call her back. "Dr. Cawein called back and seemed to be very drunk," according to the detective's report of her conversation. "Dr. Cawein wanted to know if it would be all right for him to come over to her apartment but she refused. The conversation ended around 11:00 p.m., and she went to bed."

Martin, the bartender, said he observed Sam Strother making a pass at Marrs Cawein. "Mr. Strother and Mrs.

Cawein went to the piano (in the bar) and Mr. Cawein and Mrs. Strother stayed at the table and talked. I saw Mr. Strother make a pass at Mrs. Cawein by feeling her buttocks. Mrs. Cawein reacted by looking around to see if anyone was watching, she then separated herself and went back to the table and Mr. Strother went to the restroom."

In his lengthy interview with detectives, a few days after Marrs Cawein's death, Strother failed to mention the pass he made toward her at the country club. It was possible he actually did not remember.

Both couples, according to their individual bar tabs, consumed thirty-nine drinks that evening. The Caweins' nineteen drinks included Scotch, Bourbon and water and old fashions. Their tab was $20.00. The Strothers consumed twenty orders of beer, Scotch, rum and Vodka and tonic. Their tab was $19.00.

Martin, the bartender, described Marrs Cawein and Sam Strother as being drunk but said Madison Cawein and Betty Strother were less intoxicated. However, club manager Robert Lewis, faithfully protecting club members, told investigators Marrs Cawein was just in a happy and jovial mood.

Lewis, a tall imposing man, who could have passed for a bouncer, was well compensated for his work. A former Idle Hour waitress, who preferred to remain anonymous, said every Christmas, as guests filed into the dining, they handed Lewis fat envelopes as he stood at the door. He smiled knowingly, accepted each gratuity, stowed the envelope inside his jacket, acted as if the transactions had never occurred, and waited the next member to enter the dining room.

There was little that occurred at Idle House that Lewis did not know about but he was unable to protect the club from the public attention it received after that Fourth of July evening.

Before the night was over, there was an explosion in the lives of the Caweins, Strothers and their friends that would change them forever.

Somewhere around 1:00 a.m., the Caweins and Strothers left the Idle Hour and went to the Strothers' home on Bristol Road and continued drinking, except for Marrs Cawein. Coroner Chester Hager's report later stated, "They went into the Strother house and immediately after entering, Mrs. Cawein stated to the party that she thought she ought to go home. She was tight and did not feel like any other activity at this time."

Marrs Cawein had something else on her mind as she declined to have any additional drinks. Betty Strother, while preparing drinks in her kitchen, said she made a rather blunt statement about her husband.

"How it came up, I don't know the context," she recalled. "I don't remember how it was said. But out of the blue Marrs made a statement I had heard her say it quite a few times before, that there were only two women in the world that Madison truly loved and this was his grandmother, Mrs. Walker, and little Betsy. Then Marrs announced she wanted to go home."

Cawein wanted to stay at the Strothers and continue drinking.

Sam Strother volunteered to drive Marrs Cawein home and they arrived at the Cawein residence between 1:30 and 1:45 a.m. Instead of driving the baby sitter home, perhaps he was too impaired, Strother decided to call a taxi for her.

Either Strother gave taxi company the wrong address or the dispatcher wrote down the incorrect house number. After waiting about a half an hour, Strother called the taxi again and the cab finally arrived.

Marrs Cawein told Phoebe Edwards, who was the regular maid for the family of her business partner, J. T. Denton, that she would pay her the next day as she was going to the Dentons' home for lunch and swimming.

Strother said he paid Edwards. The baby sitter said nobody paid her and that she got home just before 2:00 a.m.

"Neither of them acted like they had anything at all to drink," Edwards told investigators. "Mrs. Cawein talked like she always does and she wasn't drinking. Mrs. Cawein didn't have any stocking(s) or socks on, just them pretty patent leather shoes. She was a real good woman."

Detectives and experts on alcoholism pointed out that alcoholics, such as the Caweins and their friends appeared to be, could consume enormous amounts of alcohol and appear to carry on perfectly normal conversations to the untrained eye. Edwards stoutly maintained that Marrs Cawein was not drunk that evening when she came home and that she talked about the new home she was going to build while they waited for the taxi.

After Edwards left, the two continued drinking. Strother fixed Marrs Cawein another drink, Bourbon and water, and opened a beer for himself. He said they left the living room because it was such a hot night and went into the master bedroom, the only downstairs room with air conditioning.

Strother told investigators his conversation with Marrs Cawein in her bedroom was of a general nature. They talked about the house on Richmond Road she was going to show them the next day. The Strothers, who apparently had sold their home on Bristol Road, had only a short time to find a new house He was unable to remember whether there was a light on in the bedroom or if he sat on the bed or stood up while they were talking.

He did remember saying goodnight to Marrs Cawein, who was still sitting in the blue damask chair in the same dress she wore to the party. Strother said he left the room, closed the door, went out the front door and drove home.

Strother told detectives he was sure the Caweins' front porch light was on when he left the driveway.

If Strother left her alive, then Marrs Cawein had another visitor, or visitors, who, in the early morning hours, took her life in a most diabolical manner.

When Strother returned to his home, two and a half blocks from the Cawein residence, Betty Strother and Madison Cawein were still talking and drinking in the living room. Sam Strother joined them and a short time later his wife went to bed. He and Cawein continued talking and drinking until they decided to retire, which, according to Strother, was around 3:00 a.m.

Strother asked Cawein if he wanted to spend the night instead of walking home. The doctor accepted and Strother said he assisted Cawein in undressing in the family room, helped him to his daughter's room where he put him to bed. Strother said he then went into his bedroom and went to bed.

Cawein later maintained he undressed himself in the bedroom. However, Betty Strother said she found his clothes in the family room, when she went into the kitchen to make coffee the next morning, and took them to the bathroom across the hall from the bedroom where he was sleeping.

Apparently, all four of them, the Caweins and the Strothers, were so drunk they had little recollection of their actions.

Sam Strother's reconstructed time line of the evening later baffled authorities. Phoebe Edwards, the baby sitter, said it was around 2:00 a.m., when she got home from the Cawein house. Strother said he and Marrs Cawein drank and talked for a half hour or more before he returned to his home.

So, it was 2:30 a.m., before he left Marrs in her bedroom.

Strother later said he and Cawein talked and drank for another hour before going to bed. That put the end of their revelry at around 3:30 a.m.

If Strother and Cawein were telling the truth and went to bed when they claimed, then whose car were parked in the Caweins' driveway at 3:30 a.m., when the newspaper carrier delivered their paper? Was there an explanation for one of the vehicle, which looked like Strother's convertible, in the driveway? Did the car belong to one of Madison Cawein's lovers?

Strother told detectives, when he took Marrs Cawein home in the early morning hour of July 5, he parked in the driveway behind the Caweins' two cars. Madison Cawein, he said, drove an MG. Marrs Cawein, Strother said, drove a

1964 Chevrolet convertible, which he thought was either tan or green in color. Strother said he did not notice any other cars nearby.

The newspaper carrier for the *Lexington Leader*, George Ferrel, said he delivered the combined holiday edition to the Cawein's house around 3:30 a.m. Ferrell, noticing several lights were on inside the house, threw the paper on the porch. The paper came open and he had to go to the porch and refold it. He said there was a black sports car parked in the driveway, a Chevrolet convertible behind it and a strange car behind that which took up part of the sidewalk.

Steve and Doug Watkins, newspaper carriers for the *Lexington Herald*, came by the Cawein's house around 6:00 a.m., and saw the newspaper was already on their porch. The Watkins, who lived at 230 Chinoe Road, noticed a hall light was on but no other lights were on in the house. Familiar with the Caweins' automobiles, they describe the cars parked at the house in a different location from Ferrell's description. Steve Watkins said a black sports car was parked in front of the house and the Chevrolet convertible was in the middle of the driveway.

Who were her mysterious late night visitor(s)?

Neither this question nor other pressing inquiries about Marrs Cawein's mysterious death were ever answered. Detectives worked hard to solve the puzzling murder. Their efforts were foiled by her family and friends, who prized their reputations more than seeking justice for Marrs Cawein.

Their attitudes seemed to say that it was her fault that she had the bad graces to get herself killed.

Old Money, Horses, Brains and Society

The marriage of Mary Marrs Swinebroad and Madison J. Cawein III, brought together families with deep but different roots in the commonwealth. The match joined old money, German traditions, Thoroughbreds, real estate, society, power brokers and intellectuals.

His grandfather, Madison J. Cawein, was the son of a German immigrant confectioner and herbalist in Louisville and a spiritualist mother. Cawein was one of Kentucky Poet Laureate. Joyce Kilmer called Cawein the "Greatest nature poet of his time." Others referred to him as the John James Audubon of nature poetry. Cawein's poetry was published in *Atlantic Monthly*, *Century* and *New England* periodicals. Cawein published more than thirty volumes of the poetry he wrote at night while working at the Newmarket Pool Room in Louisville.

In 1903, Cawein married the former Gertrude F. McKelvey and they had one son, Preston Hamilton. At some point the son's name was changed to Madison Julius Cawein II.

After her husband's death in 1914, Gertrude F. Cawein, with the famous Irish dramatist, Lady Augusta Gregory, embarked on a national tour, which included New York, Philadelphia and Lexington. Cawein's widow read from his books of poetry, sang and also signed volumes of his poetry that she sold. Lady Gregory, who with William Butler Yeats established the Irish Literary Theatre, presented one of her famous one-act plays.

Their son, Madison J. Cawein III, became a highly respected hematologist with a national reputation. Mayo Clinic, in Rochester, Minnesota, had offered him a position. He also had an opportunity to establish a hematology department in a hospital in Ethiopia.

If Madison Cawein brought intellect to the marriage, Marrs Swinebroad's contributions were money, influence and powerful business, political and social connections.

Marrs Cawein's father not only belonged to the ruling equine regime in the commonwealth but he wielded influence in the international Thoroughbred world. George Swinebroad, who came from landed gentry in Garrard County, attended preparatory school in Tennessee and graduated from Centre College, in Danville, Kentucky, where he was a cheerleader. Swinebroad had decided to be an auctioneer when he was a college freshman and said he took singing lessons at Centre because an old auctioneer told him the key to successful auctioneering was learning how to breathe properly during the chant.

Swinebroad married the former Minerva Gordon, of Madisonville, Kentucky, and Marrs Cawein was their only child. They divorced when their daughter was young.

Said to be arrogant, egotistic and heavy-handed, Swinebroad used a singing chant to sell cattle, real estate and Standardbreds before becoming associated with Keeneland's Thoroughbred sales in 1944. Nine Kentucky Derby winners were sold under his gavel at Keeneland: Hoop Jr., (1945), Jet Pilot (1947), Count Fleet (1951), Dark Star (1953), Determined (1954), Venetian Way (1960), Majestic Prince (1969), Dust Commander (1970) and Canonero II (1971).

Swinebroad not only auctioned horses for Keeneland, he was a member of the sale company's selection committee. Each yearling, nominated for Keeneland's July Select Yearling Sale, had to pass his inspection for both confirmation and pedigree before the horse was accepted for the sale. He became Keeneland's sales director in 1947 and held that position the rest of his life.

Sports Illustrated, in their September 20, 1965, issue, called Swinebroad "The internationally famous horse auctioneer."

His auctioning of Thoroughbreds, in the dispersal sale of Hollywood movie mogul Louis B. Mayer's stable, was broadcasted over three nation-wide radio hook-ups in

1947. The Mayer auction, held at Santa Anita Race Track, in Arcadia, California, was attended by 7,000 Thoroughbred owners and breeders, actors and socialites in a glittering array of diamonds, furs, tuxedos and evening gowns.

Swinebroad's auctioning of Mayer's sixty horses in training brought the MGM studio co-owner $1.6 million in one evening, an outstanding sales figure for 1947.

When Walt Disney Productions came to Lexington in the early 1960s, Swinebroad, who was also a member of Idle Hour Country Club, was selected to play J. R. Rollins, a typical horse farm owner, in the full-length movie, "Tattoed Police Horse."

The Lexington auction and real estate firm he established included J T. Denton and Marrs Cawein. Denton was once the lead auctioneer for the Fasig-Tipton Sales Company, a rival to the Keeneland sales, and long time general manager of the Junior League Horse Show, in Lexington. Swinebroad, Denton and Cawein listed some of the most prominent and expensive farms and mansions in the Blue Grass. The firm, according to records in the Kentucky Secretary of State's office, was never incorporated.

One would have suspected that Marrs Cawein, with her father's deep connections in the horse business, would have been a Junior League member taking part in their famous annual horse show. According to the Junior League archives, she was not. However, her good friend, Betty Strothers, belonged.

Swinebroad removed his daughter's name from the firm after her death. In December 1966, Swinebroad and Denton's incorporation papers were filed in the Secretary of State's office by attorney Nathan Elliott Jr., a relative of the auctioneer's second wife Elizabeth West.

A child of divorce, young Marrs Swinebroad moved with her mother to Madisonville, Kentucky. She later lived in Frankfort with her mother and stepfather Wesley V. Perry, Jr., who was a wealthy malt beverage distributor.

Marrs Swinebroad Cawein told friends that she did not believe in divorce although the man she chose to marry was, in many ways, as domineering, verbally abusing and egocentric as her father.

Madison Julius Cawein III, was equally proud of his heritage. His mother Jane W. Cawein came from a prominent Woodford County family and his father was Madison Julius Cawein II, who grew up in Louisville. Young Cawein attended Woodbury Forest School, in Virginia, and came to Lexington in 1943 to attend the University of Kentucky, where he met, courted and married a popular young socialite, Mary Marrs Swinebroad.

Marrs Swinebroad, still living with her mother and stepfather in Frankfort, graduated from UK in 1947, with a business degree. She belonged to Kappa Kappa Gamma society and was president of the campus organization of the League of Women Voters and the Panhellenic Council.

They were married after her graduation and his returned from World War II.

After his stint in the Army, Cawein received an undergraduate degree from Harvard in 1949. Three years later he finished medical school at Tulane University, in New Orleans, and did a four-year residency at the Mayo Clinic, in Rochester, Minnesota. While at Mayo, he also earned a Master of Science degree from the University of Minnesota.

Cawein, after finishing his residency at Mayo Clinic, borrowed money from Woodford County Bank and Trust in 1958, to open a practice in Lexington. Two years later, he was among the first physicians recruited to research and teach at UK's new Albert B. Chandler Medical Center and College of Medicine. The facility was named for the former Major League Baseball commissioner and the two-time Kentucky governor, who appropriated funds for the facility during his second term, 1955-1959.

Jane W. Cawein, at the time of her daughter-in-law's death, lived just down Elm Street from Gov. and Mrs. Chandler in Versailles. When Marrs Cawein attempted to get in touch with her father-in-law, he was in New Jersey or

New York, which gave the indication her in-laws were possibly divorced or separated.

Cawein belonged to numerous medical societies and organizations including the Society of Nuclear Medicine. At the time of his wife's death, he had published eight medical treatises, including two on hematology in Thoroughbred horses.

Cawein received accolades for the research he and his associate and alleged mistress, Dr. Emma J. Lappat, did in helping to develop L-dopa to treat Parkinson's disease. The two also did ground-breaking research on sickle cell anemia, cloning and cancer. Their findings were published in respected medical research publications such as *The New England Journal of Medicine, Journal of Internal Medicine, Annals of Internal Medicine* and the *British Journal of Hematology*.

The blue-blooded Cawein solved the century old mystery of the "Blue People" of Troublesome Creek, in the eastern Kentucky mountains, who actually had blue-colored skin as the result of a genetic blood disorder.

Cathy Trost wrote about Cawein and the "Blue People" in the November 1982, issue of *Science*. "Madison Cawein began hearing rumors about the blue people when he went to work at the University of Kentucky's Lexington medical clinic in 1960," Trost wrote. "I'm a hematologist, so something like that perks up my ears, Cawein says sipping on whiskey sours and letting his mind slip back to the summer he spent 'tromping around the hills looking for blue people.'"

Cawein became interested in hematology while he was an Army medical technician in World War II. He told Trost that blood cells always looked beautiful to him. Cawein met a nurse, Ruth Pendergrass, who worked in a Hazard, Kentucky, clinic and who assisted him in locating the blue people. Trudging up and down the hollows, Trost wrote, and fending off the two mean dogs that everyone had in their front yard, the doctor and nurse would spot someone at the top of a hill who looked blue and take off in wild pursuit. "By the time they'd get to the top, the person would be gone. Finally, one day, when the frustrated doctor was idling inside the Hazard clinic, Patrick and Rachel Ritchie walked in.

"Cawein remembers the pain that showed on the Ritchie brother and sister's faces. 'They were really embarrassed about being blue,' he said. 'Patrick was all hunched down in the hall. Rachel was leaning against the wall. They wouldn't come into the waiting room. You could tell how much it bothered them to be blue.'"

After drawing blood from the Ritchies and Fugate families, who also had blue skin, Cawein rushed back to Lexington to test for abnormal hemoglobin. All the results were negative. He remembered, he told Trost, a medical journal article he had read about an Alaskan physician who discovered hereditary methmoglobinemia, the absence of the enzyme diaphoreses, among the Alaskan Eskimos and Indians, who were also blue. This profile seemed to match the blue people in Kentucky.

"So I brought back new blood and set up my enzyme assay," Cawein told Trost, "and, by God, they didn't have the enzyme diaphoreses. I looked at other enzymes and nothing was wrong with them. So I knew we had the defect defined." The hematologist knew, from previous studies that the body had an alternative method of converting methmoglobin back to normal, which required adding to the blood a substance that acted as electron donor, methylene blue.

"Some of the blue people," Trost continued, "thought the doctor was slightly addled for suggesting that a blue dye could turn them pink." When Cawein injected Patrick and Rachel Ritchie with 100 milligrams of methylene blue, everybody waited. "Within a few minutes, the blue color was gone from their skin," Cawein said. "For the first time in their lives they were pink. They were delighted."

In 1964, Cawein published an article on the blue people of Troublesome Creek and their hereditary deficiencies of diaphoreses in the *Archives of Internal*

Medicine. Lappat assisted him in the research, as did Drs. C. H. Behlen and E. J. Cohn, in the various other journal articles they wrote on the subject.

"The doctor was recently approached by the producers of the television show, "That's Incredible," Trost wrote. "They wanted to parade the blue people across the screen in their weekly display of human oddities. Cawein would have no part of it and he related with glee at the news that a film crew, sent to Kentucky from Hollywood, fled the 'two mean dogs in every front yard' without any film."

The Caweins' careers were flourishing but their personal and family lives were in shambles.

The Doctor and his Demons

Whatever demons inhabited the brilliant mind of Madison Cawein, he attempted to exorcise them with sex and alcohol. The hematologist made no secret of his dalliances and bragged openly about his affairs. His family and friends strongly suggested he mend his ways.

Cawein's ego was such that he ignored, not only that advice, but also the possible influence his swinging lifestyle might have on his children, especially his impressionable fifteen-year-old son.

From all indications, neither of the Caweins dealt effectively with their son Skip. Investigators, looking into Marrs Cawein's death, were interested in why Cawein confiscated his son's chemistry set prior to his mother's death but never determined the reason.

Skip Cawein was an exceptionally bright but troubled youngster according to Don Hollingsworth, headmaster of Sayre School, the private institution Skip Cawein attended with his sister in Lexington. Hollingsworth told detectives that Skip Cawein had no integrity, no sense of honor and did not know the meaning of self-discipline or responsibility.

When Skip was eleven, Hollingsworth said, he had an intelligent quotient of 170, which occurred only once in several million people. "His mind is so quick that he can usually think beyond your line of conversation," Hollingsworth said. "Even in sports he seems to be able to contemplate the moves of others before they are made." In the eleventh grade, he said, the student was capable of doing university work. Hollingsworth said in the fall the Caweins planned to send Skip to the Andover School, which was established in Andover, Massachusetts, in 1778.

For all his brilliance, Madison Cawein attempted to avoid the problems in his life, many of which he created.

Cawein appeared anxious to leave Lexington and talked about talking a leave of absence from the Medical Center to establish a department of hematology at a hospital in Ethiopia. Mayo Clinic, according to some accounts, wanted to bring him back to Minnesota.

Since the early 1960s, Cawein had allegedly been having an affair with his UK research associate, Dr. Emma J. Lappat, an equally brilliant physician. He was not monogamous in either his relationships or his marriage. While seeing Lappat, Cawein engaged in other affairs. Lappat, however, was the exception. She latched on to him like a leach and refused to be replaced.

While Cawein appeared equally desirous of the personal relationship in the beginning, he was never really able to get away from the woman from Tonopah, Nevada, until the death of his wife.

Lappat, tall, slender with light brown hair and an engaging smile, apparently feared nothing and no one. She was determined to have Cawein at all costs. Lappat once told Marrs Cawein that she had no business hanging on to her husband when he really belonged with her. If Madison Cawein had any idea of just how dangerous Lappat could be, he gave no indication. Later, detectives, investigating Marrs Cawein's death, pursued a deep interest in the clever Lappat.

Lappat graduated in 1947 from the Northwestern University School of Nursing, in Chicago. Four years later, she graduated summa cum laude from Colorado College, in Colorado Springs, with a degree in zoology and a Phi Beta Kappa key. A year earlier, she married geologist James F. Gilkerson, from Bellview, Washington. Whether Lappat ever divorced Gilkerson was not known. In 1955, Lappat graduated ninth in a class of seventy-three with a medical degree from the University of Colorado. For two years, while in medical school, she was awarded the coveted Boettcher Foundation Scholarships. She interned at Denver General Hospital.

When working as the town doctor in Silverton, Colorado, she lived in the dilapidated San Juan County Hospital built during the 1909 silver boom. When an avalanche roared down Red Mountain and buried a car with a Dallas, Texas, woman and her niece inside, Emma Lappat dug them out and saved their lives. She left Silverton in 1957, to work at the National Jewish Hospital in Denver.

From Denver, Lappat's career followed a route, which left a trail of troubling questions from Buenos Aires, Argentina, to Oak Ridge, Tennessee, to Lexington, Kentucky.

Lappat worked at the Institute de Ivestigacitones Medica, in Buenos Aires, from December 1958 until January 1961, according to her resume. What she did at the Institute was not known. While in Buenos Aires, she lived with Dr. J. G. Martinez, who she claimed was her husband. While in Argentina, she attended a medical meeting, where Dr. Charles Congdon, from the Oak Ridge National Laboratories, in Oak Ridge, Tennessee, was the guest speaker. Congdon recruited her to work at Oak Ridge. For some reason, Lappat arrived at Oak Ridge early and was given temporary employment for a month.

Lappat could have arrived in Oak Ridge early for a meeting of ORINS (Oak Ridge Institute for Nuclear Scientists). ORINS was chartered in 1946 by the state of Tennessee and fourteen southern universities to share technology developed at Oak Ridge during World War II as part of the Manhatten Project. A January 1961, meeting of ORINS showed Lappat and Madison Cawein sitting together in a photograph.

Her time at Oak Ridge was shortened for two reasons. One was her involvement with another doctor and his wife. The other was that Lappat lied about being married to Martinez during her background check and was denied a permanent position there.

During Emma Lappat's four months in Oak Ridge, a doctor's wife, whom she volunteered to care for during a hospital stay, died under mysterious circumstances.

Dr. Ralph Kinseley and his wife Helen befriended Lappat and sought to alleviate her being in a strange town and knowing no one by offering her friendship. Kinseley vigorously denied having an affair with Emma Lappat.

Helen Kinseley was hospitalized on May 11, 1961, for a tubal ligation and an appendectomy. Lappat, a registered nurse as well as a physician, offered to stay with the woman after she returned to her room from the surgery at 12:45 p.m.

UK pathologist Wilmier M. Talbert, Jr., at the request of Lexington detectives investigating Marrs Cawein's death, contacted Oak Ridge pathologist, William Nelson, for an abstract on Lappat's involvement in the Kinseley case. Lappat, according to the abstract, was in Helen Kinseley's room for several hours, beginning at 1:00 p.m. No one appeared to know how long she was there as no written records were maintained by the hospital of when or how often she left Kinseley's room.

According to the abstract, a nurse at 7:00 p.m., noticed Helen Kinseley lying comfortably on her side. An hour later, Dr. Kinseley found his wife to be without a pulse or respiration and began mouth-to-mouth resuscitation. With the assistance of the hospital staff, Kinseley opened his wife's rib cage and began heart massage without success. She was pronounced dead at 9:15 p.m. An autopsy, begun less than an hour later by pathologist William Nelson, revealed Kinseley's body had chocolate brown, un-clotted blood. Three separate lab reports found the amount of methemoglobin varied from nineteen to forty percent.

In a 2007, paper on Methemoglobinemia, Dr. David C. Lee, research director in the New York University Medical School's department of emergency medicine, wrote, "When hemoglobin becomes oxidized, it is converted to the ferrous state or methemoglobin. Methemoglobin lacks the element that is needed to form a bond with oxygen and, thus, is incapable of oxygen transport. Oxidation of iron to the ferric state reduces the oxygen-carrying capacity of hemoglobin and produces a functional anemia."

Lee pointed out that organs with high oxygen demand, such as the cardio vascular system, were usually the first systems to manifest toxicity. "Oxygenated blood is red, deoxygenated blood is blue and blood carrying methemoglobin is a dark reddish brown," he wrote.

Nelson, according to Lexington detective Nolen Freeman's report, found that Helen Kinseley had died from a "Condition known as methemoglobinemia. The largest question in this case is that Dr. Lappat stated to Dr. Nelson that she knew nothing of methemoglobin at the time of the death."

There was no police investigation of Helen Kinseley's death because Nelson, the pathologist, notified the coroner who had just left office instead of the newly elected coroner. The mistake, for some reason, was never corrected. Freeman's report continued, "The police department in Oak Ridge are investigating the death at this time (September 1965) and are very disturbed over not having a report at the time Dr. Nelson suspected murder. Dr. Nelson stated that he suspected Dr. Lappat of causing the death but did not report this to the police."

Helen Kinseley died on May 11, 1961, and shortly thereafter that Lappat was working at the UK Medical Center as an instructor in medicine. Whether Madison Cawein obtained the position for Lappat was not known.

By November 1962, Lappat, Cawein and Dr. Charles H. Behien had prepared and presented a paper on methemoglobinemia to the prestigious American Society of Hematology in Columbus, Ohio.

Nobody becomes enough of an expert on such a complicated subject as methemoglobinemia that they can assist in the research and preparation of a scientific treatise in just a few months.

Lappat's connection to Helen Kinseley's death was not the only bad news she left behind in Oak Ridge. Dr. Charles Congdon, who brought Lappat to the facility, discovered that she was disliked by the people she worked with and that she had caused other trouble between her physician co-workers and their wives.

Regardless of her conduct in Tennessee, the medical community in Lexington closed ranks and temporarily protected Lappat. Talbert wrote "The conclusion of the above investigation in Lexington is that we have no records in our department that Dr. Lappat had expert knowledge of methemoglobin on or before May 12, 1961."

Of course, the UK Medical Center did not have any records of Lappat's research before that date because she had not begun work there. Nor did the abstract delve into just what work Lappat did in Argentina.

It was possible Lappat could have been working with Cawein on methemoglobinemia before she came to UK.

Cawein probably knew something about Lappat's background and, having a distaste for physical altercations, was afraid to end their affair. Emma Lappat's actions, prior to and directly after Marrs Cawein's death, raised questions about both her mental stability and her obsession with Madison Cawein.

Betty Strother described Pat Lappat, as Cawein and his friends called her, as being something of a voyeur. "I can remember Marrs telling me some story about Pat dragging a table over from Mrs. Fray's, next door, so she could stand on the top of the table and look over the air conditioner into their bedroom," Strother recalled. "I don't remember the context of how she discovered Pat had done this; I have a vague recollection that Pat came in to speak with them."

The previous Christmas, Lappat invaded the Cawein's family party with presents for Skip and Betsy Cawein. The uninvited situation allegedly resulting in Marrs Cawein knocking Lappat down before she left.

In the autumn of 1964, one of the Cawein's next door neighbors witnessed a physical confrontation between Marrs Cawein and Lappat while Madison Cawein watched. Rosa Beard, who lived next door at 328 Chinoe, said the pushing and shoving was between the two women. Beard heard Lappat tell Marrs Cawein that she had no business interfering in her relationship with Madison Cawein. She told Lappat to leave her husband alone.

Finally, Beard said, Marrs Cawein became tired of the entire disgusting spectacle and threw both Lappat and Cawein out of the house saying she had to get to bed in order to get up the next morning and take her children to school.

Beard told detective Frank Fryman that the Caweins had lots of parties lasting through all hours of the mornings. Beard also mentioned affairs between Cawein and other women.

Betty Strother said she never asked Marrs Cawein about the fight with Lappat and she never told her. "My sister-in-law," she recalled, "who is friends with the girl across the street told me about it. It was last summer or summer before last. Pat and Marrs evidently had a real fight over there. There were plates broken and Marrs was badly bruised. Elizabeth Swinebroad (Marr's stepmother) knew about it. Elizabeth said something to me about it at the time of the funeral when I was running some of my errands with her.

"They evidently had screamed and hollered and broken all kinds of dishes and then Madison had drove off in the car with Pat."

Kentucky Post reporters, who were canvassing the Caweins' neighborhood after Marrs Cawein's death looking for information, found another person who also witnessed the violent confrontation between the two women.

The newspaper described a woman, who drove up to the brick bungalow, as a blond, of medium build who wore slacks. Actually, any number of women with whom Cawein was involved matched that general description.

The unidentified witness told reporters that the woman walked up to the Cawein's front door, turned away, retraced her steps and walked through the unlocked front door. "Right away there was a lot of yelling and screaming," the witness said. "I don't remember hearing a man's voice. There was a lot of other noise too, like furniture being moved, glass breaking, crashing and banging. The two Cawein children were yelling and screaming. I could see two women, through the open front door, they were pushing and scuffling back and forth. Lights were coming on all over the neighborhood. I don't see how anyone could have slept through it. It must have lasted a half hour. Then, the woman in slacks left, drove away in a car."

The witness, who watched the fight from forty or fifty yards away, had no knowledge what the fight was about and said the women's words were indistinguishable. Usually, there was only one reason for two women to have such a confrontation, the man they both had in common.

It appeared Lappat not only stalked the women in Cawein's life but the physician himself. Lappat appeared uninvited at a 1962, birthday party for Martha. Kieckhefer, the heiress to a hardware fortune, in the garden of her mansion on Tates Creek Road. Martha Kieckhefer told detective Nolen Freeman, during the investigation of Marrs Cawein's death, that Cawein needed ice for his drink and she went back into the house to get some ice. "She walked back out on the garden patio to find Dr. Cawein," Freeman's report stated. "She hollowed the Drs. Name and saw (beside him) a woman with a bandana over her head, tall and with pants on. The woman didn't speak but when Mrs. Kieckhefer walked up to the person she squirted something from a plastic bottle or bag into Mrs. Kieckhefer's face. Mrs. Kieckhefer stated that the liquid burned a little so she went into the bathroom and washed it out."

The detective's report continued to say that Cawein, when his hostess asked him to do something about the woman, just stood there and did nothing. Martha Kieckhefer told the detective that a friend, Mrs. John Merrit, told her that Marrs Cawein, who was also at the party, identified the woman as Lappat.

Betty Strother told detectives about finding Lappat lurking outside the Cawein home early one morning. "It was pretty creepy," she said.

"I guess it was about three years ago, three summers ago," she said. "Marrs and Madison, Sam and I, Dick DeCamp, Helen and Bob Mayes and Phoebe and Doug Root had all gotten in our station wagon and gone to Shakertown for supper." DeCamp was then an account executive with WKYT-TV, in Lexington, Mayes, who had married into the Stoll family, was a building contractor, and Root was a researcher at the Medical Center.

Shakertown, a restored Shaker village south of Lexington in Mercer County, is noted for the delicious but simple foods they serve family style.

"We'd all had a real good time," Strother continued, "and (when) we got home it was about 1:30 or 2:00 in the morning. Our cars were all over there (at the Caweins') and so we decided we would go in and have a nightcap before we went home.

"Marrs had a teenage babysitter and she was worried about the babysitter seeing us all because we were all tight. She asked us to wait in the front yard while she paid the babysitter so the sitter wouldn't have to run in to us all. Down one side of Marrs and Madison's house is the driveway. Down the other side of the house is a very little used (path). I've never maybe once or twice looking for a stray child, I haven't been down that side of the house but I knew you could walk down through there and it would put you by the back door where the terrace is; the kitchen and den are the only rooms on that left side of the house.

"I thought, well instead of standing here in the front yard, I'll just walk around the house and go in the back into the kitchen. I was walking down there in the dark. I don't see very well in the first place and I was looking down at the ground watching where I was going and all of a sudden I saw these feet!"

Laughing, Betty Strother said she looked up and saw Lappat, who had flattened herself against the side of the house. "We had a very civil conversation," she recalled. "I said, 'hello, Pat.' She said, 'hello Betty.' I said, 'won't you come in?' She said, 'no thank you.' I said, 'well, see you around.'"

Strother said Dick DeCamp, who in 2008, retired as a Lexington Fayette Urban County Government councilman, saw Lappat running through the front yard while he was there.

"Anyway, I went in and said guess who I found in the back yard? Marrs wasn't mad at Pat or Madison but she was furious at me because I'd told all those people. Madison disappeared ten or fifteen minutes later. It was really right funny. The funniest part of the whole thing was that Marrs always tried so hard to protect Igger." Igger was a childhood nickname for Cawein.

'Do you know of any other instances involving this Pat Lappat and Madison or Marrs?" detective Carter asked.

"What kind of instances do you mean?" Betty Strother asked. "Things come to mind, all kinds of stories; I could sit here and gossip."

She turned to Don Sturgill, who was acting as the Strothers' attorney, and asked, "Weren't you at their (the Caweins) house the Sunday afternoon, six months or so ago when Marrs called me and asked me to drive her around to look for Madison's car?"

Sturgill was heard muttering something like a disclaimer on the tape.

The doctor's car, a flashy MG, would not have been difficult to find.

"BB was there but we drove by--I keep thinking I am gossiping," she said, "will anybody get hold of this?"

Sturgill advised, "Tell them where you found the car."

"Well, we drove by one house looking for it before we drove out to Pat Lappat's and found it," Betty Strother said. Emma Lappat lived on Pine Meadow Drive across town from the east end where the Strothers, Caweins and their friends lived.

"The car," she continued, "was parked, not in front of her house but down and kind of in the next block." She added that Marrs Cawein had told her in the last two or three months that, "It was all over between Madison and Pat; that they had a real falling out and Madison was having nothing further to do with her."

Detectives were very interested in Lappat. In his interview with Betty Strother, Carter asked, "Is she (Lappat) the kind of person who could have come into the house that night and gained entrance to Marrs' bedroom?"

"It is hard for me to imagine but maybe so," she replied.

Cawein's short-lived affair with a married Cincinnati woman was so brief that Lappat probably had no chance to intervene. The husband did that. Crauthers Coleman, Jr., a Lexington architect and a lifelong friend of Marrs Cawein, told detectives that Madison Cawein had an affair with his sister-in-law, who lived in Cincinnati, two years earlier. The affair was brief, he said and ended when his brother Pope Coleman had a face-to- face confrontation with Cawein.

For all his bragging and bravado, Cawein appeared to avoid physical confrontations with men as well as women.

The short-lived relationship, however, had no impact on their social lives. Crauthers Coleman entertained the Caweins and the Strothers on his boat at the lake (probably Herrington Lake, just south of Lexington) the third week in June. Coleman told detectives the gathering was quite cordial.

Even when it was obvious Cawein's affections for Lappat might have been waning, she inserted herself into his relationships with other women.

Both Coleman and antiques dealer Russell Lutes told detectives about an alleged affair between Cawein and Betty Gay Lewis, from a wealthy Lexington family. Coleman said he had only hearsay information about them. Lutes, in his interview with detectives, said Lewis and Marrs had a "Pretty good sized fight" the night before Cawein's wife was murdered.

Lewis, who dated Cawein when they were teenagers, was divorced from W. B. Lewis II, from South Carolina, and had moved back to Lexington several years earlier. She lived on the same street as the Caweins, belonged to Idle Hour Country Club and said she attended some of the same social events. Lewis told detectives that, for some reason, she thought Marrs Cawein did not like her. Lewis added that, on numerous occasions, Madison Cawein threw up to his wife in public that he had and did love her (Lewis). Lewis told detectives she had not seen Cawein since April.

When Lewis was overcome with smoke inhalation in a fire that consumed her home, she had the hospital call Madison Cawein because she knew he would come to her aid, regardless of the hour. After she was released from the hospital, Lewis told detectives that Cawein visited her at the Center Motel, on South Limestone, where she lived while her house was being rebuilt. She said they just talked during his visits and denied rekindling her affair with him. Lewis told detectives that a woman doctor, who worked with Cawein at the Medical Center, was following him when he visited her at the motel and made inquires about her at the motel desk.

Without a doubt, the Medical Center was one swinging place in those days.

Old timers, who worked at the Chandler Medical Center, in the 1960s, still talk about the Play Room, which was located in a vacant area on the fifth floor. The Play Room was where some of the staff doctors and nurses engaged in sexual fun and games. It was rumored that many young nurses, new to the staff, were initiated in the Play Room. None of the old timers, who spoke with the author agreed to be identified, but they all said that Cawein was an active participant in the Play Room.

Cawein affair with a young doctor's wife, Barbara Leapman, who was also his patient, began in the spring of 1965, according to detectives' reports. Cawein was treating her for Hodgkin's disease. According to the National Institutes of Health, Hodgkin's disease is a type of lympthoma, which attacks lympth nodes, spleen, liver and bone marrow and which, if diagnosed early, can often be cured.

Leapman and Cawein, according to the case file, each planned to get a divorce so they could marry. The Leapmans' divorce, they were already separated at the time, was supposed to be a simple matter. His divorce was more complicated since Marrs Cawein refused to cooperate. In addition, Madison Cawein was under considerable pressure from his family and friends to either abandon his lovers or get a divorce.

Barbara Leapman confided details of her affair to a close friend, Judith Weech, whose husband was a physiatrist at the United States Public Health Hospital, on Leestown Road, where Dr. Herschell R. Leapman also worked. Leapman, Weech told detectives, had caught his wife and Cawein in a tryst at the Cawein home and they separated. Barbara Leapman had custody of their children and was working at the Continental Inn, on new Circle Road, to supplement the support provided by her husband.

Evidently, Madison Cawein was not helping Barbara Leapman financially.

Barbara Leapman described her husband, to Weech, as being very provocative and hostile and seemed to enjoy seeing her have a rough time. "Barbara Leapman felt she could end this and write her own ticket by living with Dr. Cawein as he had made this offer to her," Weech told investigators.

Marrs Cawein told some of her friends that her husband had not only asked for but demanded a divorce because he was in love with Barbara Leapman.

Betty Strother said Cawein told her about his new love interest. "He said her name was Barbara," she recalled, "and that she wanted him to call her Barbie and he thought that sounded like a 'Barbie Doll.' He said she just walked into his office one day and threw herself at him."

Whatever personal qualities Cawein lacked, conceit was not one of them.

If Cawein thought he was through with Emma Lapatt, he was sadly mistaken. When Lappat caught Cawein out of town, she asked Barbara Leapman to meet her at the Medical Center for coffee. Lappat offered to get Leapman a better job in Berea, thirty miles south of Lexington, or somewhere in the mountains, if she would get out of town and leave Cawein alone.

Lappat and Cawein shared an office in the Medical Center and she told the secretaries that none of Leapman's calls were to be put through to Cawein.

In order to avoid their spouses and Emma Lappat, Madison Cawein and Barbara Leapman moved their trysts from Lexington to Frankfort, according to the case file. Lappat, however, was not deterred and began calling the Leapman home and asking the maid or babysitter about the family's activities. She kept calling Herschell Leapman at the hospital until she convinced him to meet her at the Medical Center.

When he met her, Lappat must have intimidated him to no end.

Lappat told Leapman, according to the case file, if he did not stop the affair between his wife and Cawein, she would take drastic action and something terrible would happen. Lappat was so convincing and Leapman appeared to be so scared of her that he began seeing a psychiatrist and retained an attorney, according to the case file.

Meanwhile, Barbara Leapman was concerned that Cawein would not perform a legal abortion on her. She told Judith Weech that an abortion was necessary due to her Hodgkin's disease. Cawein ordered medical tests performed on her to gauge the advancement or decline of her disease. When the test results came back to his office, Cawein was out of the office . Lappat saw the tests results and called Leapman and told her the Hodgkin's disease was spreading and she needed to come in immediately for treatment. Since Cawein was not available, Lappat said she would take over her care and begin treatments with nitrogen mustard at once.

Nitrogen mustard, according to the Centers for Disease Control, is a potential chemical warfare weapon agent, which can cause blindness, fluid in the lungs, second and third degree burns where it touches the skin and brain tumors.

Barbara Leapman was smart enough to refuse to allow the woman to treat her. She contacted Cawein the next day and told him what had transpired with Lappat, according to the case file. Cawein was upset over the situation but, even then, he attempted to protect Lappat. He told Leapman that Lappat had read the test reports wrong and pointed out that both he and the neurologist agreed that she needed no further treatment at that time for the disease.

Did that mean they could go ahead with the abortion? The old timers at the Medical Center thought so.

The more Madison Cawein pressed for a divorce, the more apparent it became to Marrs Cawein that she had little choice. She told her stepbrother Allen W. Woods that the situation between Cawein and herself were getting worse and was coming to an end. She was going to have to give him a divorce. She told Woods that Cawein was at the point where he hated and disliked her and she could not take him flaunting his affairs in front of her and her friends any longer.

Woods said Marrs was periodically withdrawing a thousand to fifteen hundred dollars from her account to pay household bills since Cawein refused to pay them. Marrs, in a June 26, telephone conversation with Woods, confirmed that Cawein was investing his salary check so he would have some money when he left the country or divorced her. Above all, Marrs wanted to get her stock portfolio back into her name.

Marrs Cawein used the Strothers for sounding boards for her personal problems. Betty Strother said Marrs Cawein confided in her constantly about her husband's affairs. "It just got so a few years ago, that Sam and I couldn't run our own lives and take care of our stuff and have her telling us all this stuff all the time because it was so upsetting," she said. "I said to her a few years ago, Marrs, I just cannot have you coming over here telling me all this stuff because it upsets me too much and I have my own problems; I just can't take it."

Sam Strother agreed with his wife and added that the Caweins' drinking had also been a factor in their not seeing them much until recently.

"We used to see a lot of the Caweins four or five years ago," he said. "Then they were having all this trouble and he was running around and so forth. Marrs would come over and talk to Betty about it. I told Marrs the only thing you can do is get yourself a lawyer and get a divorce. I can't tell you any more than that because he apparently isn't going to stop. He'd leave, maybe take off after they came in and wouldn't come home. Maybe leave Friday night and come home Sunday afternoon or something like that.

"I told Betty we had our own problems and we couldn't get messed up in theirs. For the last three or four years, we haven't seen as much of them. Then we started seeing a little more of them in the last six months."

It was a resumption of a relationship that Betty and Sam Strother ultimately regretted. They found themselves in a real mess--a mysterious murder in which they appeared to be accessories after the fact.

She Might Not Be Alive

Apparently, Betty Strother found Marrs Cawein dead in the blue chair in her bedroom on the morning of July 5. When she found her and under what circumstances was never clear because Betty Strother told detectives one story. She told her friends, Priscilla Johnson and Frances Hillenmeyer, another version and then called them the next day with a different story.

Another friend, Mrs. John Merrit, told detectives she heard that that young Elizabeth Strother called her mother and said they (her sister and Betsy Cawein) found Marrs Cawein in her bedroom and that she was sick.

Betty Strother got up around 8:00 a.m. on July 5, while her husband and Madison Cawein were still in bed, to prepare breakfast and get ready to take her older daughter, Elizabeth, to swimming practice at Idle Hour Country Club at 10:00 a.m. Betty Strother's time frame, for the rest of that day, was exceedingly difficult to follow.

"I held up on calling over there (the Cawein home) because Marrs liked to sleep late mornings; not Sunday School mornings (but) where she didn't have to get up to go to work or a school morning," Betty Strother told detective Morris Carter four days after Marrs Cawein died. The interviews of the Strothers, which took place in the office of their attorney, Don Sturgill, occurred on July 9, and coroner Chester Hager had not made an official determination as to the cause and manner of Marrs Cawein's death although he had known for four days, as a result of the autopsy report, that poison was found in her body and that she had not died a natural death.

It would be almost a month before the coroner, up for reelection four in November, would finally rule her death a homicide. Until authorities had a legal ruling that an unnatural death had occurred, their investigation was limited. Detectives could attempt to question those who they knew had pertinent information but they were unable to expand the investigation into other areas, such as search warrants and financial records, because they were unable to obtain court orders.

When Betty Strother called the Cawein house, around 9:15 a.m., on July 5, she said Betsy answered the phone. "I said, Betsy, is your mother up yet?

"She said, no.

"I said you all run upstairs and get your bathing suits on real fast and Sam will run over and pick you up so you can have some breakfast before you go to swimming practice. I remember I didn't have time to fry bacon but I scrambled some eggs and made toast."

Sam Strother, in his interview with detectives, said he went over to the Cawein's house to pick up the girls. "The porch light was on and the door was open so I just walked in," he said. "We've been close enough with them that we never bother to knock. The children's bags and things were upstairs. The door to Marrs and Madison's bedroom was shut. I didn't look in; just went upstairs to get the children's things and brought them back down and took the children over to our home for breakfast."

During breakfast, Madison Cawein, according to the Strothers, was still asleep.

After they ate, Betty Strother said she put the three girls in the car and took them to the country club. There was some question in the case file about why she took Betsy Cawein with her when she was not on the swim team.

"We got over there and I chatted with the lifeguard for a few minutes because there weren't very many people there," she told Morris Carter. "I decided since things were not moving very fast and Sam was at home, I would take Mary Pryor, my four-year-old back home with me and I could leave Elizabeth and Betsy over there as long as the lifeguard was there and they were going to be doing the swimming practice.

"When I came in, Sam said Madison was up and maybe I should call Marrs again. She was going to show us this house; we were going to look at it and maybe do something about it. Sam said he called and she didn't answer the phone. I remember Sam laughing and saying, 'it's a hell of a note when you want to buy a house and you can't get your real estate agent out of bed.' I think I yelled back through the hall to Madison and said, 'Sam said something funny; it's a hell of a note when you want to buy a house and can't get your real estate agent out of bed.'"

Madison Cawein told detectives that he got up around 9:00 a.m., and went in the bathroom to shave, using Sam Strother's razor, and to dress. Detective Frank Fryman's report quotes Cawein as saying he was sober that morning and knew what he was doing at that time. "He states," the report continued, "that after they called the Cawein home and got no answer, Mrs. Strother, who had returned from Idle Hour, went over to wake Mrs. Cawein as she was to show them some houses that day. Later, Mrs. Strother called and told them to come over that she thought that Mrs. Cawein was dead."

Betty Strother said they tried calling Marrs Cawein again, let the telephone ring and ring but she still did not answer. "I said it didn't seem right that Marrs didn't answer the phone because if Marrs had something to attend to, she got up and did it," she recalled. "Lord, she would be up real late at night and get up and take those children to school in the morning; they were never late for school in their lives. It didn't make sense to me that she wasn't answering the telephone."

She told Carter that she then drove over to the Cawein house, leaving her husband and Cawein at her house.

It seemed strange that Cawein was not concerned enough about his wife's failure to answer the telephone to drive over to his house with Betty Strother.

"I walked into the bedroom," she continued, "opened the door, she wasn't in the bed; my gaze swung around and she was sitting there in the chair. She looked funny. I ran over to her and touched her on the arm and it was cold."

Carter asked her to describe the position in which she found Marrs Cawein's body.

"The chair is kind of a club chair, an overstuffed, comfortable chair with low arms," she replied. "She was just sitting there, her right arm was lying beside her, palm up and the veins looked awfully blue. Her left arm was on the arm of the chair. Her head was to the right and forward and her mouth was to the right. She looked yellowish but that could have been because I had my sunglasses on."

She said she called her husband, "Sam, I think Marrs is dead. You and Madison get over here right away and I ran out the front door like I was trying to run away from it all. After I got into the front yard, I realized if they were leaving to come over here, my four-year-old Mary Pryor was at home by herself. I was glad to have an excuse to leave anyway; jumped into the car and passed them (her husband and Cawein) as I was going back."

When she got home, Betty Strother began looking for her daughter, who had wandered away. 'I was hysterical," she said, "running up and down the street screaming; then I started ringing doorbells and I found her at the Greens. At Frances Hillenmeyers, I rang the doorbell to see if Mary Pryor was there. She came to the door and said, 'Betty what in the world is wrong?'

"I said, Frances, I don't know Marrs is sick, dead or something. She called little Walter to get his clothes on and sent him out with me to find Mary Pryor. Then, I went back home--you know you just can't accept things—and I kept calling the Caweins because I needed somebody to tell me if what I knew was really right or not. The line was busy, busy, busy. Finally, I ran across the street to the Hillenmeyers to get a cigarette; couldn't find one at home. I told Frances what had happened. I finally got a line through and Sam answered the phone. He said, 'Betty, Marrs is dead.''

The Hillenmeyers also belonged to Idle Hour Country Club. Walter Hillenmeyer was president of First Security

Bank and Trust Company and sat on the board of the Federal Reserve Bank in Cleveland. His family established one of Lexington's earliest businesses, a nursery, on Sandersville Road.

"After that," Betty Strother continued in her interview, "I realized that Elizabeth and Betsy were over at the swimming pool and I didn't want this to get out and have somebody tell Betsy, nine going on ten, anything until her father could tell her in the right way. So, I went back over there, took Mary Pryor; I think I took Mary Pryor, I may have left her at the Hillenmeyers. I don't remember. I went back over to the swimming pool to get Betsy and Elizabeth, had to wait a few minutes for them and then we went back to my house. I called over to Marrs' (house) again and Bill Winternitz answered the phone and, I think, I asked to speak to Sam."

William Winternitz was a physician friend from the Medical Center who Cawein called when his wife was unresponsive. Winternitz initially told Cawein she died from a heart attack.

Betty Strother continued her recollections, "Sam said, 'Betty would please come back over here.' So, I got Harriett Hillenmeyer to come over and stay with the children. I went back over there and was there for the rest of the day practically. I was there when they were telling George and Elizabeth (Swinebroad) and all the family was contacted."

Frances Hillenmeyer later told detectives that she kept the three children while Betty Strother retuned to the Cawein residence.

Detective Carter asked Betty Strother, "When you went back over to Idle Hour to pick up the kids did you mention this (Marrs Cawein's death) to anyone?"

"Yes, I did," she replied. "I mentioned it to Pricilla Johnson. There was this business about this thing and I called Pricilla later and matter of fact I said the same thing to Frances (Hillenmeyer). George (Swinebroad) came and we got all mixed up on some of the details because of trying to help the family out a little bit. When Madison sat him down in a chair to tell him about his daughter, he just went all to pieces.

"The first thing he kept saying was, 'Madison did she kill herself?' Madison said, 'no George, there was nothing in the house she could take; there was no way she could have killed herself.' Then he (Swinebroad) started saying, 'Madison was she drunk?' I really don't know how drunk Marrs was—I've seen her much drunker; I've seen her when she was incapable. Yet, that night she'd had an awfully lot to drink and she was loaded but Marrs was dead and so we all just said she was tight, that we had all been drinking. She was not drunk.

"Then he (Swinebroad) said, 'Madison was she just asleep in the bed and just died?' Sam, Madison and I looked at each other and it seemed like the kindest thing to do, we just said yes. Then I had to tell Priscilla Johnson and Frances Hillenmeyer not to say anything (about what she had told them earlier) because it was just getting messy."

Betty Strother's comment about things beginning to get messy turned out to be a gross understatement. According to the taped interview, detective Morris Carter asked her no further questions about either the multiple stories she told of finding Marrs Cawein nor the timeline of her actions. In fact, Carter appeared to avoid asking her pertinent questions.

When detective Frank Fryman interviewed Joe and Priscilla Johnson (he was the Fayette County judge) on August 16, he got a different time scenario about Betty Strother's movements and conversations on the day Marrs Cawein was found dead.

Fryman was unable to resolve the discrepancies in the Strothers' statements.

Priscilla Johnson told Fryman she arrived at Idle Hour with her children for swimming practice just before 10: a.m., and Betty Strother was already there. Her statement to detective Carter indicated she was among the first to arrive at the country club that morning.

"Mrs. Johnson noticed her," Fryman wrote in a lengthy report to Captain Gilbert Cravens, "because she didn't appear to be herself, seemed worried, preoccupied, and wasn't speaking to anyone. At this time Mrs. Johnson went over to her and asked her what was wrong. Mrs. Strother took her to the patio where no one else was around and told her that she had found Mrs. Cawein dead a short time ago. This talk took place around 10:30 a.m.

"Mrs. Johnson states that Mrs. Strother told her that she had gone over to the Cawein home to pick up the children for the practice at the club at 10:00 a.m., and to fix them some breakfast as she had called the Cawein home and the children were up but not Mrs. Cawein. She (Betty Strother) states that when she picked the children up, she checked in the bedroom for Mrs. Cawein and found her dead in the bedroom chair. She states that she wanted to be sure no one else told the Cawein child and that is the reason she was waiting for all the children. AND THAT IS THE REASON SHE BROUGHT THE CAWEIN CHILD AS THE CAWEIN CHILD DID NOT SWIM FOR THE TEAM BUT SHE BROUGHT HER SO NO ONE ELSE WOULD TALK TO HER ABOUT HER MOTHER'S DEATH."

From the tone of Fryman memo and the amount of capital letters he used, it was obvious that the detective was frustrated over the difference in the two different versions of events. He wrote his entire report of Betty Strother's first version, which she had given Carter of how she found Marrs Cawein, in capital letters.

Fryman interviewed judge Johnson who told him that he saw Betty Strother talking to his wife. Later the judge watched the swimming practice and left the club at 11:15 a.m., just behind Betty Strother.

The part of Betty Strother's interview, which bothered Fryman the most pertained to the day after Marrs Cawein' death. "On the morning of 7-6-65-8:30 a.m., Mrs. Strother called her (Priscilla Johnson) and told her what she told her yesterday was a mistake; that she had found Mrs.

Cawein in bed and she had her night clothes on and that this was better for Mr. Swinebroad."

Three days later, on August 19, Fryman re-interviewed Priscilla Johnson at her home on Fairway Drive. Again, she recounted the same sequence of events. The detective wrote at the bottom of his report, "This does not check out with the statement from Mrs. Strother."

Mrs. John Merrit, at whose lake cabin Skip Cawein spent the night that his mother died, told detective Fryman that she was told (she did not say by whom) that Betty Strother was called by her daughter, Elizabeth, who told her that they (the three girls) had found Marrs and thought she was sick and she went over to the Cawein home to pick them up and found her dead.

Sarah Knuckles, who had chatted with Marrs the night before at the Idle Hour Country Club, heard about her death on the golf course around 3:30 p.m., on July 5. She left the country club and went to the Cawein home to pay her respects. She told Fryman that a maid was moving through the house and that Madison Cawein said the maid was cleaning.

Returning to the Cawein home about 6:00 p.m., with her husband, Sarah Knuckles told Fryman the family was talking about how Marrs Cawein was found in bed wearing her nightclothes. She also told him that her husband went out to buy liquor for the family and guests, as there was only a three-quarters full bottle of Heaven Hill in the kitchen cabinet.

Quoting Sarah Knuckles, Fryman wrote, "Also at this time Dr. Cawein had called for the autopsy report of his wife's death and was told that no natural cause was found and he began to explain to the group that (the) death had been natural and that they must have overlooked something and went into medical terms explaining these terms about the heart and brain."

The Knuckles left and returned to the Cawein home again around 9:00 p.m. Around midnight, the telephone rang and Alfred Knuckles answered. "A slow drawl eerie type voice stated Mrs. Madison Cawein III is dead and the voice was going to say something else but Mr. Knuckles hung up," Fryman wrote.

"He (Knuckles) turned to Madison and told him the nature of the call and Madison showed no shock and stated that he had heard of these type of people and he been expecting such a call. Seconds later the phone rang again and Mr. Knuckles answered. The same voice gave a low eerie laugh and started to say something else but again Mr. Knuckles hung up."

Mrs. John Merrit told Detective Fryman she also went to the Cawein home to pay her respects. She described Madison Cawein as being reserve and calm. When she offer her assistance to the family, Cawein refused saying, "I don't need any help; I can handle it alone." During the course of the evening, she told the detective, Cawein kept stressing the point that his wife had died a natural death.

Walter and Frances Hillenmeyer told Fryman in one of their conversations with the Strothers, either Betty or Sam, quoted Madison Cawein as saying, "If he wanted to kill his wife he could have used seven different types of poison that couldn't be traced."

Frances Hillenmeyer told detective Fryman that Betty Strother came to her house around 11:00 a.m., looking for her daughter. She returned with the child, left her with the Hillenmeyers to go to the country club to pick up her older child and the Caweins' daughter.

The statement of Frances Hillenmeyer, as to the time frame, matched that of the Johnsons.

There were other alterations Betty Strother made to her original statements in her interview with detective Carter. "Another thing," she said, "that we soft pedaled was that I said to people that Madison had slept on the sofa at our house because it seemed to me there was something a little bit less attractive about him being drunk and sleeping on the sofa than Sam undressing him and putting him to bed. I don't know why but Marrs was dead and those were things that didn't make any difference."

Why Was She Dead?

There was no crime scene for detectives to investigate at the Cawein home after they learned her death was not natural. The Strothers, Madison Cawein, George Swinebroad and their friends decided items that could have been valuable clues were to be destroyed. The house was cleaned and vital evidence cast aside or thrown out.

Marrs Cawein's family and friends were, for the most part, the gang that could not shoot a straight story about their accounts of the evening of July 4 and the next day.

Fayette County coroner Chester Hager's initial willingness to accept Dr. William Winternitz's assessment that Marrs Cawein's death was probably the result of a heart attack and his failure to go to the death scene was indicative of the political clout wielded by Swinebroad and his friends, such as newspaper publisher Fred Wachs.

Wachs' publications, the *Lexington Herald* and *Lexington Leader*, printed a three and a half-inch page one article on July 6, saying Marrs Cawein had died, listed her survivors, visitation at Milward Mortuary on Broadway, services at Christ the King and burial in the Lancaster Cemetery in Garrard County. Later that month, an even smaller news item stated coroner Chester Hager was investigating her death.

There was a six-week blackout of news about Marrs Cawein's death in Lexington newspapers, which had rehashed articles, whether there was anything new or not, for weeks about the 1961 murder of Betty Gail Brown. Some of the details the newspaper printed about the Brown investigation were little more than rumors. When Hager, on August 13, finally officially announced Marrs Cawein's death was a homicide, the Lexington newspapers began their coverage. The publications did not suddenly discover the newsworthiness of the mysterious and puzzling murder in their own town weeks after the autopsy report revealed an unnatural death had occurred. The newspaper publisher, allegedly due to his friendship with George Swinebroad, refused to write about the death of his daughter, which was national news.

Sports Illustrated wrote about Marrs Cawein's murder, calling it the case of the "Carbolic Acid Cocktail Murder," in their September 20, issue.

Since early August, the *Kentucky Post*, a Covington., Kentucky, newspaper, had been saturating its news columns with details of the socialite's death. *Post* reporters developed a timeline of events in the case, conducted their own investigation, interviewed those who could become witnesses and, in general, made coroner Chester Hager's life miserable.

There was such a clamor for news of Marrs Cawein's murder, the *Post* printed extra press runs and shipped them to Lexington.

Lack of local media coverage helped hide Hager's bungling of the investigation. The failures of the Strothers, Cawein and Swinebroad to coordinate their statements with others such as Winternitz, the Milward Mortuary attendants and close friends occupied much of detectives' time.

The Strothers and Madison Cawein told one version of their story to detectives. Then, Betty Strother was apparently dispatched to call Priscilla Johnson and Frances Hillenmeyer on July 6, and tell them a different story from the one she repeated to them on July 5.

Sam Strother, in his July 9, interview with detectives Carter and Freeman, provided the same details as his wife up to the point he and Cawein rushed to the Cawein home. Like his wife, Strother provided little in the way of a time frame and the reason soon became apparent.

He told detectives when he and Madison Cawein went into the house, the doctor went into the bedroom and he stood in the doorway and looked inside the room. "I knew what to expect," he said, "since Betty told me she was dead."

"I was in the hall," he continued, "and he came out and handed me the glass, which had about one-half of a drink left in it and the beer can. I don't know what he said—I think at this time we all thought it was a heart attack—we didn't realize then that we were covering up anything. I took them, (the half-empty glass and beer can) to the kitchen and poured the drink out and threw the beer can away."

Strother, in an earlier interview with coroner Chester Hager, said Cawein told him, to "get rid" of the contents of the glass and the beer can.

"There was a whiskey bottle on the counter," he continued, "and I put that back in the cabinet. People drank out of this bottle as they came in throughout the day."

Detective Freeman asked Strother twice who drank from that particular bottle of whiskey and he could only remember the Knuckles and provided no other names.

"I went back into the living room from the kitchen," Strother said, "and Madison came in and said, 'Marrs is dead.' I said, my God, or something like that. I said to Madison, I have said this before, why don't you put her in the bed? He said, 'I don't think we can.'"

They could not put her into the bed because her body, still clad in the cocktail dress, was in full rigor from sitting in the blue chair for hours.

"He tried to call Thornton Scott, the doctor who is a close friend of his and couldn't get him," Strother continued. "He called Dr. (William) Winternitz and he came over and went in there (the bedroom). He came back out and said, 'Well, you want an autopsy?' Madison said, 'yes.'"

Strother said he and Winternitz signed the request Cawein authorized for an autopsy as witnesses.

The timeline Winternitz gave detectives Carter and Freeman supported the original story Betty Strother gave Priscilla Johnson at Idle Hour while their children were swimming and what she initially told Frances Hillenmeyer.

Carrick Shropshire's statement to detective Freeman also supported Winternitz's time line of events. Shropshire, another real estate agent, saw the advertisement Marrs

Cawein had placed in the local newspaper to sell their house. He called the Cawein home around 9:45 a.m., July 5, and a child answered the telephone. She said her mother was not up and to call back later.

Shropshire's call placed Betsy Cawein at her house at the same time Betty Strother claimed she was took the child to Idle Hour. Shropshire called the Cawein house again at 10:30 a.m. He said, "A cultured male voice answered and, after advising him why I had called, stated the house was not for sale and asked me to hang up."

Winternitz, who was on duty at the Medical Center, said he took Madison Cawein's call around 10:00 a.m., but had to check out of the hospital and arrived at the Cawein house around 10:30 a.m., which was the time Betty Strother was already at Idle Hour talking to Pricilla Johnson about finding Marrs dead in her blue bedroom chair. When he arrived, Winternitz said Madison Cawein showed him into the bedroom where he found Marrs Cawein sitting in the blue chair with her head tilted to the left; her eyes were open and dry.

"Dr. Winternitz pronounced Mrs. Cawein dead at 10:45 a.m.," detectives Carter and Freeman's report stated. Winternitz's statement and the time line he provided contradicted Cawein's and Betty and Sam Strother's statements to detectives about who found the body and at what time.

"Dr. Winternitz stated that he searched the room but did not recall searching the closet and found nothing that would have caused her death. The room was not disarranged and the bed was tightly made. He did note a book open on the lamp table and the name of the book was *Venetian Affair*." The spy thriller was written by Helen MacInnes in 1963.

"Dr. Winternitz stated that Dr. Cawein indicated that the death was due to natural causes," the report continued. "However, they did search the bathroom medicine cabinet with negative results. Dr. Winternitz then asked Dr. Cawein if he wanted an autopsy and Dr. Cawein said yes. At this time, Dr. Winternitz stated he took a piece of paper and wrote out in long hand permission to do the autopsy." Winternitz confirmed that he and Sam Strother signed the permission slip as witnesses.

Winternitz said that Marrs Cawein's body was in full rigor when he pronounced her dead. Two hours later, the ambulance attendants had great difficulty getting her body to stay on the gurney as they had to leave her legs as they were, which was in a sitting position.

Coroner Hager confirmed, in an August 5 statement, that Winternitz called him on the morning of July 5, no time given, to inform him of the death of Marrs Cawein. "He stated that he (Winternitz) was Mrs. Cawein's doctor," Hager's statement said, "and he was on the scene; that he did not think there was anything mysterious or wrong with the death that he could see. I asked him would he sign the death certificate and he said yes, that nothing looked unusual but that they were going to have an autopsy performed at the University of Kentucky Medical Center. I told Dr. Winternitz that was the proper thing to do and if they found anything unusual about this death that I would like to know about it."

Strother said Winternitz asked him if he would take his wife to the Medical Center for her cancer treatment while he waited for the mortuary attendants to arrive. He did after calling and asking Betty Strother to come back to the Caweins.

Winternitz pronounced Marrs Cawein dead at 10:45 a.m., on July 5. However the funeral home attendants did not arrive for nearly two hours. Winternitz said he made a perfunctory search of the bedroom, bathroom medicine cabinet and other areas of the house finding nothing suspicious. He found her black patent leather shoes in the bathroom.

What was Cawein doing during this time? Of course, there were relatives to notify but it was doubtful that took two hours while Marrs Cawein's body remained in the blue chair. The Swinebroads were not called until after Betty Strother returned to the Cawein home.

Carlton Case, a Milward Mortuary employee, told detectives they were called between 12:00-12:30 p.m., to go to the Cawein home and pick up a body. Case and Douglas Wallace, another funeral home employee, arrived at 12:40 p.m. They were met by Winternitz, who told them the coroner had already been notified and they were to take the body to the third floor of the UK Medical Center for an autopsy.

If Winternitz did not accompany the hearse, he was not far behind. He was at the Medical Center when Dr. Wilmier M. Talbert, Jr., began the autopsy at 1:45 p.m. Assisting Talbert in a portion of the dissection was Dr. John Koepke. Also in attendance for the major portions of the autopsy were Drs. W. B. Stewart, Edmon Pellegrino and Winternitz.

When Talbert began his procedure, he described Marrs Cawein's clothing: a yellow and black print dress, full white slip, white bra and a wide black cloth belt.

There was a bloodstain on the right side of the dress, near the hem, and smaller blood stains on her slip. Talbert found the bloodstains came from a fresh puncture wound on the right thigh. There was a similar injection site on the left thigh. The skin around the right thigh puncture was removed for toxicological analysis and the bloodstains on the dress were cut out and saved for analysis. The back of her dress was stained by dried urine and dried saliva was found on the left shoulder of the garment.

In Marrs Cawein's stomach, Talbert found phenol, more commonly known as carbolic acid. The pharynx and esophagus, the pathologist found, had intact white mucosa free of autolytic change. "Beginning at the cardio-esophageal junction and involving one-half the lesser and two-thirds to the greater curvatures there are 2 to 3 cm wide strips of black leathery mucosa with flecks of yellowish material attached," he wrote.

According to the *Oxford English Dictionary*, carbolic acid is referred to as phenol or phenol alcohol. Its powerful antiseptic qualities made it an ideal disinfectant, if properly diluted, as well as an equally poisonous substance if taken internally. A tiny drop of carbolic acid on the skin immediately provides a burning sensation. If ingested by mouth, phenol can literally burn tissue as it is swallowed causing the victim excessive pain, creating violent thrashing movements and screams of agony.

Although a deadly poison, carbolic acid had its medical uses. Joseph Lister first used carbolic acid to sterilize contaminated wounds and keep them sterile in Glasgow, Scotland, in March 1864, according to the *Canadian Medical Association Journal* of November 14, 1964.

Marrs Cawein had no open wounds to be treated and there were no wounds to indicate she swallowed the poison. Talbert's autopsy revealed no burns or stains were found on her lips, gums, tongue and tonsilar region or the upper portion of the esophagus. Yet, in her stomach, Talbert found the carbolic acid. Upon reaching the stomach, carbolic acid would have begun its deadly corrosive work resulting in accelerated breathing, rapid heart rate, yellow skin, convulsions and coma. People have been killed by 1.5 grams of carbolic acid, just enough to moisten the bottom of a teaspoon.

If Marrs Cawein was conscious while the acid did its deadly damage inside her body, why was her clothing not in disarray? Why were the lamp, book, glass and beer can not knocked off the table by her thrashing? Why was everything in the room in such perfect order? Or, had the room been in disarray and everything put back in order?

Did the agony from the carbolic acid cause her to scream? If so, did the three young girls, sleeping upstairs, hear her cries? No one questioned them about any noise they might have heard during the night. Or, was she gagged to keep the sounds of her pain quiet?

Even Case, the mortuary attendant, commented about how everything in the bedroom was so neat when he helped place Marrs Cawein's body on the gurney.

Betty Strother described Marrs Cawein as looking yellow. Did Madison Cawein or William Winternitz, both physicians, notice the color of her skin? If they did, there was no mention in their case file interviews.

Talbert's autopsy report found Marrs Cawein's bladder to be empty, a rather unusual finding considering how much liquid she had consumed that evening but he did locate some congestion in her kidneys. His autopsy report did not address the size of the urine stains on her dress.

Management of Poisoning: A Handbook for Health Care Workers, a 2006 World Health Organization publication, described phenol as being so lethal that poisoning can occur when it is absorbed through the skin. The publication said kidneys are one of phenol's main targets in the body. Acute renal failure, according to the publication, can result from systematic absorption of phenol and coma and seizures usually occur within minutes.

There was evidence Marrs Cawein also suffered from acute alcohol intoxication. Talbert found 395 mgs of ethyl alcohol in her blood, 395 mgs in her liver and 320 mgs in her kidneys.

Even more mysterious and puzzling were those puncture wounds, in the back of one thigh and front of the other, in the body of a woman who was so scared of syringes and needles she was unable to bring herself to donate blood for a friend. Did blood from those puncture wounds find it way to the arm of the blue chair?

Talbert's seven-page autopsy report was notable for what was missing. There was no toxicology information about the substance that was injected into her thighs. Supposedly, there is still a specimen from the Cawein autopsy in the toxicology laboratory at the Medical Center. The pathologist also failed to mention if the material from her dress and slip had been tested or if the blood on her clothing belonged to Marrs Cawein.

Nor did Talbert address how the carbolic acid reached her stomach without burning her mouth and throat?

Marrs Cawein had not had sexual relations recently, according to the autopsy report. That ruled out a brief interlude with Sam Strother on the night of her death.

With the information available in Talbert's 1965 autopsy report, sixteenth district state medical examiner Dr. Gregory J. Davis said, in a 2007 interview, if he had an autopsy similar to that of Marrs Cawein, he would have ruled the manner of death as undeterminable. Davis used as reference Talbert's six-page autopsy report from the coroner's file and detectives' case file.

Bits and pieces of research turned up the idea there might have been two different autopsy reports on Marrs Cawein, one for the coroner and another to be kept private. Items missing in the autopsy report Talbert gave the coroner such as the time of death, the substance injected into her thighs and whether or not the blood stains on her dress were from the victim also raised questions.

When the autopsy was finished on July 5, Talbert said he notified coroner Hager that he might want to investigate the circumstances of Marrs Cawein's death. The next day, July 6, Talbert called the coroner twice: once at 11:00 a.m., to give him a preliminary review of his findings and again at 2:00 p.m., to tell him that the poison in Marrs Cawein's body had been identified.

Had the coroner taken action on that date, July 6, when he learned that Marrs Cawein died an unnatural death, detectives might have been able to conduct a more complete investigation and actually determine who killed the woman. At the very least, they could have preserved some of the crime scene. Instead, Hager waited until Marrs Cawein was buried to begin his coroner's investigation.

In an August 5, statement Hager made at the Detective Bureau, he neglected to mention Talbert's first call to him was on July 5. Hager did mention the pathologist's second call on the morning of July 6, but said Talbert's third call was on July 7.

Hager said on July 8, after Marrs Cawein had been buried, he went to the Lexington Police Department and informed Captain Gilbert Cravens about what he knew of Marrs Cawein's death, the information he was given by Talbert and requested Cravens' assistance.

On the same day Hager and Cravens, not detectives, went to the Keeneland Race Course to talk to George Swinebroad.

Hager, as coroner, was keeping control of the death investigation instead of turning it over to Police Department detectives, who were better trained to conduct such inquiries.

Normally, the spouse of the deceased is considered the next of kin and the first person interviewed by authorities. But in this case, the coroner chose to talk first with the father probably because he had the most political clout. That political clout was important with an election only a few months away.

Hager's account of the meeting sounded almost like he was asking Swinebroad's permission to look into his daughter's death. During the meeting, Swinebroad lied through his teeth about the existing relationship between his daughter and son-in-law.

The purpose of the meeting with Swinebroad Hager wrote, "Was to inform him that the death of his daughter was an official coroner's case at this time and that the death was not a result of natural causes. Mr. Swinebroad was informed as to the causes of death of his daughter as well as the unusual circumstances surrounding the death."

On July 8, Hager, his own words, acknowledged that Marrs Cawein did not die a natural death. Yet, he waited until August 13, to rule that her death was a homicide.

In responding to Hager's questions about the medical and personal background of his daughter, Swinebroad told them, according to the report, "That his daughter was in especially fine health and spirits. She was most happy with the recent forming of the partnership of Swinebroad, Denton and Cawein Real Estate Offices, that he had talked to her recently and that, as far as he knew, the Caweins were most happy at this time."

Swinebroad may have spoken recently with his daughter but it is doubtful if the conversation was about her health and marriage. Swinebroad was preparing for his busiest time of the year, Keeneland's July Selected Yearling Sale, which attracted Thoroughbred buyers from all over the world. As Keeneland sales director, it was his responsibility to see everything went smoothly before, during and after the sales. The Keeneland sales were noted for operating like a well-oiled machine.

Hager persisted in asking about Marrs Cawein's marriage. "Mr. Swinebroad was questioned as to the marital status of Dr. and Mrs. Cawein; if they were on the best of terms at this time. Mr. Swinebroad stated that he thought that they were the happiest that they have ever been since their marriage," Hager wrote.

"Mr. Swinebroad did inform us that over the past year or two Dr. Cawein was involved in an affair with a Dr. Lappat, who was also employed at the University of Kentucky Medical Center. This information was taken from Mr. Swinebroad by Captain Cravens and myself as we proceeded to leave at this time," Hager wrote.

Hager and Cravens left Keeneland and drove to the Cawein residence to question the deceased's husband. It was another softball interview. Hager said, "Dr. Cawein was informed for the first time of the actual cause of the death of Mrs. Cawein by myself." That may have been the first official notification of the cause of Marrs Cawein's death but her husband knew the final results of the autopsy before Hager did.

The coroner continued his statement, "When Dr. Cawein was informed as to the true cause of death of Mrs. Cawein and was told about the phenol and the large quantity of alcohol found in the body, Dr. Cawein questioned the ability of the pathologist at the University of Kentucky Medical Center who performed this autopsy. He stated this could not be possible, that his wife would not have committed suicide, that he did not believe phenol to be the cause of death. He stated there was some mistake."

Cawein asked Hager if Dr. Randolph Meulling, the pathologist in charge of the UK Department of Legal Medicine and Toxicology had performed the autopsy? Cawein knew exactly who performed the autopsy. If he had not spoken with Talbert, he certainly talked with Winternitz, in front of witnesses, on the night of July 5. Cawein requested that Meulling be asked to review the case.

Hager replied that four Medical Center doctors had witnessed the autopsy and all four told him phenol was discovered in Mrs. Cawein's body and they felt the poison was the true cause of death. Hager had no problem with Meulling reviewing the autopsy procedure and report.

"We asked Dr. Cawein," Hager continued, "to search the residence for anything that might have phenol present in his household." The coroner, who was charged with making the legal determination of Marrs Cawein's death, *asked* her husband to search his own house in the officials' presence three days after his wife died!

Hager confirmed that Cawein made a search of his home while they were there and, of course, no phenol was found. "Captain Carvens and myself briefly checked the room and the chair that Mrs. Cawein's body was discovered in," the coroner said. "We found one recent blood spot on the right arm of the bedroom chair on the upper surface. Dr. Cawein stated he did not know what this was; that one of the children may have gotten blood on the chair."

A month later, in an August 9 memo to Cravens, detective Frank Fryman confirmed he had picked up the chair that day from the upholsters on National Avenue, along with the old blood-stained, blue upholstery, and turned it over to Talbert at the Medical Center. Cawein said he asked Betty Strother, at an earlier date, to see that the chair was reupholstered.

Another piece of evidence lost.

"We asked Dr. Cawein for any type of evidence that might have been found in the room when he arrived at the residence" Hager's report continued. "He stated there was nothing." At Hager and Craven's request, Cawein demonstrated the position of his wife's body, in the blue chair beside a lamp table, when he arrived at their home on the morning of July 5.

There was nothing in the report to indicate if Hager and Cravens asked Cawein if his wife's skin was yellowish or about the set of her mouth.

"We asked Dr. Cawein was there anything liquid or otherwise sitting on this table. Dr. Cawein stated there was nothing found." In fact, Cawein had asked Sam Strother to get rid of a half-filled glass sitting on the table and a beer can.

Cawein also told them that his wife was healthy and did not take any type of medicine or drugs with the exception of aspirin and Alka Seltzer. The prescription medication in the bathroom, Cawein said, belonged to him. There was nothing in Hager's report that detailed what the prescription medication contained.

According to the case file, that was Cawein's last interview with authorities for more than a month. He took his children on a vacation in the interim.

On August 7, detective Fryman interviewed Cawein at his home. Fryman said he informed Cawein he did not have to talk with him but he agreed to the interview.

Cawein told Fryman there were no needles around his wife's body or any evidence that those he kept in the bathroom had been used when he arrived at his home on the morning of July 5. Actually, there were needles and medical equipment through out the Caweins' bedroom.

The doctor also told Fryman there was nothing in his house that contained any preservative. Apparently, Cawein was referring to the methyl paraben found around the injection sites on his wife's thighs.

The detective quoted Cawein as saying, "His wife was in a very (high) spirit and was as happy as he had ever seen her. He states that he had been having an affair with Dr. Lappat but that it was over and had been since last fall. He further states that he had met Barbara Leapman about two weeks ago and thought he had fallen in love with her. He had been treating her and had cured her and during this time began to have lunch with her. He states that Mrs. Cawein found out about this and that they had an argument about this and he stated that he asked for a divorce but that he was drinking and the next morning the matter was dropped and was not brought up again."

The interview ended with the detective writing, "He topped the talk off with that his wife was scared to death of needles and would not have shot herself with any needle. He said that she would not have killed herself and that she seemed to be very happy as they were buying a new house that she wanted and making plans for the future."

Obviously, Fryman did not buy Cawein's happy-ever-after theory. If he and Marrs Cawein were so happy, why did she tell her mother, a few days before she was killed, that she was upset that Madison Cawein might lose his medical license because he was treating Barbara Leapman at the same time he was having an affair with her? Why did Marrs Cawein tell her stepbrother that her husband hated her and their marriage was at an end?

Meanwhile, the coroner was doing some strange surveillance.

On July 8, three days after Marrs Cawein's death, Hager placed the Cawein residence at 326 Chinoe Road, the Strothers' home at 409 Bristol Road and Lappat's house at 1506 Beacon Hill Drive under surveillance from 8:00 p.m., until 3:00 a.m. There was no explanation in the case file for surveillance of the three houses, the strange time frame, perhaps it coincided with police shifts or any indication how long it lasted.

Something else unusual occurred on July 8. George Swinebroad recanted a portion of his previous statement to Hager and Cravens. Swinebroad got in touch with Capt. Cravens and confessed he had not been exactly candid with them. Hager said, "He had not told us everything involving his daughter's personal life when we talked with him the previous day. Mr. Swinebroad's information was that his daughter and Dr. Cawein had had martial troubles for several years and that Dr. Cawein had been dating Dr. Lappat and that recently Dr. Cawein had asked for a divorce."

When Hager and Cravens made an appointment for a conference with Talbert on July 10, they took county attorney Armand Angelucci with them to the Medical Center. The pathologist, according to Hager, placed the time of Marrs Cawein's death between 2:00 a.m., and 6:00 a.m., July 5.

By his own admission, Sam Strother said he left the Cawein home about 2:30 a.m., on July 5.

There was no time of death mentioned in Talbert's autopsy report. Hager, in his coroner's report, stated that death probably occurred from thirty to forty minutes after Marrs Cawein ingested the small quality of phenol.

The amount of phenol found in her stomach was not measured or even estimated possibly because her vital organs had absorbed much of the poison. Talbert found congestion in her lungs, spleen and left kidney.

While they were at the Medical Center, Angelucci called Dr. Emma Lappat and asked her if they could also speak with her. Lappat told him it was impossible. When Angelucci suggested the next day, which was Sunday, she said she was having company. The county attorney pressed for an interview with her the next week but Lappat said she would have to let him know.

Since no ruling by the coroner that an unnatural death had occurred, authorities were unable to force her to speak with them.

Having no luck with Lappat, Hager, Cravens and Angelucci headed for the Idle Hour Country Club to interview employees about the evening of July 4. There was nothing new except for the bartender, Avery Martin, who saw Strother make a pass at Marrs Cawein by patting her on the buttocks. He said Strother said, "I would like to have some of this."

From the Idle Hour, they visited Madison Cawein to go over the case with him. Hager made no notations of that conversation.

Hager, Cravens and Angelucci left the Cawein home and drove to the Swinebroad home on Tahoma Drive to report to Marrs Cawein' father what they knew. There was no more telling indication of just who had control of the investigation.

Hager said Swinebroad told them he wanted a complete investigation and began spouting a fount of information. Swinebroad told them about Lappat coming to the Cawein residence uninvited the previous Christmas, bringing presents for the Cawein children. Swinebroad said that was the first time he had met Lappat. "He also stated," Hager recorded, "that he had heard Dr. Cawein was involved with some doctor's wife. He thought this lady was a nurse and he had heard this doctor (her husband) had attempted to shoot Dr. Cawein after he found out about the relationship."

Cawein, in the face of the mounting evidence that his wife's death was a homicide, was still trying to build a case that she had died from a heart attack. While Hager, Cravens and Angelucci were talking to Swinebroad, Cawein called Elizabeth Swinebroad and told her he had just returned from the Medical Center where he reviewed the cause of Marrs Cawein's death with the pathologist. Hager's report did not name the pathologist Cawein allegedly spoke with about the autopsy. "He stated that the pathologist said that Mrs. Cawein had probably just taken too many alka seltzers; that gas built up in the system and had apparently caused a heart attack; which he had previously told the Swinebroads was the cause of death."

One had to wonder if, at any time, Cawein ever considered that his actions, particularly his affair with Lappat, might have contributed to his wife's death.

They Were Sticking to Their Story

While Hager, Cravens and Angelucci were talking with Swinebroad and Cawein and trying to pin Lappat down for an a time to interview her, detectives Frank Fryman, Morris Carter, Nolen Freeman and Robert Cisco were questioning the Strothers at Don Sturgill's law offices on July 9.

Sturgill was acting as the Strothers' temporary attorney since Gene Oliver, their regular attorney from Strother's father's firm, was out of town.

Detective Nolen Freeman was unsuccessful in attempting to get more information out of Sam Strother about what transpired after he brought Marrs Cawein home. Strother said he did not remember. At the beginning of the interview, Freeman told Strother that he did not have to make a statement in the investigation of Marrs Cawein's death; that if her death turned out to be a homicide and he became a suspect, such a statement could be used against him in court.

Strother told Freeman that Marrs Cawein had on the same dress, when he left her bedroom early that morning, that she had worn to the party.

"There have been rumors flying about in this case, Sam, no use in us trying to fool around with you," Freeman said. "One, do you have any idea of the location of any of her underclothing?"

"No," Strother replied.

"Did you find any of her underclothing the next day when you found her?" Freeman continued in the same line of questioning. Again, Strother gave a negative reply and added, "They asked me that. Marrs and Madison hung all their pajamas on the back of that bathroom door and Capt.

Cravens had said that she didn't have any pants on when they found her."

Strother hardly needed a captain of detectives to tell him Marrs Cawein was wearing no underwear the evening of July 4. He knew about that first hand, so to speak. However, he artfully evaded the question.

"When I went into that bathroom that morning," he replied, "after we had gotten over there and all this stuff was happening and they could have been on there (the back of the bathroom door), I don't know."

Strother told Freeman that he suggested to his wife that, with all the people who would be using the bathroom that day, all the pajamas and things should be taken off the back of the door. He said when she checked there was nothing hanging on the door.

"Did you happen to notice a syringe or anything like that around on the floor or one of the tables?" Freeman asked.

"No, he never had anything out like that," Strother said. He indicated Cawein had been especially careful with medicines and medical supplies since two of three years earlier, when a little girl who lived behind them had gotten some pills out of his car. "As far as I know," he continued," he didn't carry his bag with him anymore."

"Did she administer herself a shot from a syringe while you were there?" Freeman asked.

"No," Strothers replied.

"You did not either?" the detective asked.

"No," Strother said, "Marrs was scared to death of shots."

When Freeman asked how he knew, Strother said a few years earlier he and Marrs Cawein went to the Medical Center to donate blood for a friend who had leukemia. "We got out there and Mary Marrs was scared of the needle and wouldn't give any," he said.

Freeman continued quizzing Strother if he knew of anyone in Marrs Cawein's family or among their friends who were diabetics and used syringes for injections of insulin.

Strother said he did not but then remembered that her half-brother was a diabetic.

Freeman, nevertheless, pursued that line of questioning. "Do you know of any way or any one," he asked, "who might have administered her anything with a needle?"

"No," Strother said. "What you are asking me now is speculation on my part." He turned to Sturgill and asked, "Should I go ahead and answer?"

The lawyer said, "Sam, as I told you when we started you tell them what you know and you can't speculate. If you know something, you answer; if you don't just say I don't know. If you have an opinion, you answer it."

Strother asked Freeman, "Should I give you an opinion?"

"Sure," the detective replied.

Sturgill interrupted again saying, "Not unless it is based on fact, don't just guess."

Strother was on a roll and wanted to get something off his chest. "I would say the only one who had anything against Mary Marrs was this Dr. Lappat."

"We would like for you to qualify that; why do you think that?" Freeman asked.

Strother's reasons for suspecting Lappat were entirely circumstantial. They included his wife finding her lurking behind the Cawein house after the trip to Shakertown; Marrs Cawein finding stools placed outside their windows; Madison Cawein not getting a divorce but leaving home on Friday nights and not returning until Sunday afternoons. "She is the only one who could have had any reason to do anything like that," he stated.

Investigators were thinking the same thing that Lappat might be their best suspect.

Did She Do It?

Detectives apparently had a difficult time finding Dr. Emma Lappat to question her about her relationship with Madison and Marrs Cawein.

She gave the county attorney the run around when he tried to pin her down on an interview time in July. Then, she invited herself on an August vacation trip with friends from the Medical Center. The only interview with Lappat found in the case file was one conducted by detective Frank Fryman and dated January 1, 1966.

The Police Department's seven-page witness list, of people interviewed in their investigation of Marrs Cawein's murder indicated that Fryman's January 1, 1966, interview was the only one conducted with Lappat. What Lappat told Fryman about her activities on July 4 and July 5, certainly did not match what others said.

Lappat had an alibi for the early portion of the July 4 evening. However, she and her escort differed on where they had dinner.

She told Fryman she had dinner the evening of July 4 with Ed Long, who picked her up between 6:00 and 7:00 p.m. at her home. They went to his home for drinks and had dinner at the Holiday Inn. Long brought her home around 10:00 p.m., and she retired for the night.

Long told Fryman, in a December 7, interview, he picked Lappat up at her home and they stopped at his home on South Hanover for before dinner drinks. Lappat made a telephone call from Long's house while he was in the kitchen mixing drinks and he did know who she called. Long said they had dinner at the Campbell House. If, indeed they ate at the Campbell House, the route they traveled that evening was interesting. Lappat lived in a development, off

Lane Allen Road and behind the Campbell House; Long lived across town in the east end near the Caweins.

After dinner at the Campbell House, Long said he took Lappat home between 10:30 and 11:00 p.m. That was Long's second date with Lappat. He told the detective he did not know her well and had not dated her since. Long told Fryman he had never had contact with nor was he friendly with the Cawein crowd.

There was another conflict in Lappat's story about the evening of July 4.

Borys and Frida Surawicz, he was a cardiologist and she was a psychiatrist at the Medical Center, asked Lappat to have dinner with them on July 4, and go to the Lansdowne Club to watch the fireworks display. The Surawiczes told Fryman Lappat was unable to accept their invitation because she had some visitors and could not get them out of her house.

Long said nothing, in his interview with Fryman, about Lappat having visitors when he was at her home to pick her up.

Lappat told Fryman she got up around 7:00 a.m. on July 5. She dug up some honeysuckle for her friend, Saeed Salehi, who was teaching at Transylvania College while working at the Medical Center, and went over to the Surawiczes' home to meet Salehi. The four of them went blackberry picking in rural Jessamine County, which is adjacent to Lexington and Fayette County.

They returned to Lexington around noon, Lappat continued. She dressed for work at the Surawiczes' home, on Overbrook Drive, and went to Medical Center Around 4:00 p.m., she saw Winternitz and he told her Marrs Cawein was dead.

"She at first denied making any telephone calls to anyone that afternoon after learning of the death of Mrs. Cawein but later admitted that she had called the Cawein home and had talked to Betty Strother and had called the Surawiczs and Mr. Salehi," Fryman wrote.

"She states that she thought the death to be a suicide but thought the suicide to be a threat and not meant to be successful and thought the injections to be someone trying to save her (Marrs Cawein)."

Betty Strother did not mention, in any of her interviews with authorities, Emma Lappat calling the Cawein home on July 5, and speaking with her.

Lappat told Frida Surawicz that Madison Cawein called her at 2:00 a.m., on either Thursday or Friday, before the holiday, and asked her to take his duty rotation at the Medical Center that weekend.

The Surawiczes provided detectives with interesting information about Lappat's actions on July 5. Borys Surawicz told Fryman that Lappat called him around 12:00 p.m., shortly after she got to work, and said she had just learned about Marrs Cawein's death. That was almost a four-hour difference from her account to Fryman about learning of Marrs Cawein's death from Winternitz around 4:00 p.m.

Borys Surawicz told the detective, after Lappat called him, she came over to their house to talk about Marrs Cawein's death. Frida Surawicz had taken their children to the country club to swim. He said there was nothing unusual in his conversation with Lappat.

There was something quite unusual in a conversation Emma Lappat had had with Frida Surawicz more than a year earlier about what sounded like an intervention for Marrs Cawein. The psychiatrist related to detectives that Lappat told her Marrs Cawein was disturbed and needed medical help and asked she and her husband to treat her. Frida Surawicz refused saying someone outside the Medical Center should treat her.

Wonder how Lappat planned to convince Marrs Cawein that she needed psychiatric help?

When Lappat learned the Surawiczes were leaving on August 31 for a vacation in the east, she invited herself along. The Surawiczes said they would be glad to have her if she could get off work. The day before they left, Lappat called and said she was able to get off work.

After Frida Surawicz told her about an August 30, newspaper report that Marrs Cawein's death could possibly be murder, Lappat rushed over to the psychiatrist's office to read the newspaper, according to the case file. Surawicz said when she read the aarticle, Emma Lappat burst into tears and said it was all a frame up caused by George Swinebroad because he would not believe his daughter committed suicide.

The Kentucky Post, on August 30, carried an article inferring that Marrs Cawein died from carbolic acid poisoning. It was interesting that Lappat was so upset by the article on carbolic acid, when the coroner had already announced on August 13, that he was ruling Marrs Cawein's death a homicide.

Lappat also called Saeed Salehi and discussed her suicide theory. He thought it was the night of July 4, but was not sure, that Lappat told him Marrs Cawein had been found dead. Since her death, Salehi said Lappat told him Marrs Cawein had suicidal tendencies and she (Lappat) could not understand why everyone was trying to make something else out of it.

The relationship between Salehi and Lappat, was somewhat reminiscent of her association with Dr. and Mrs. Ralph Kniesley, in Oak Ridge, Tennessee, four years earlier. Salehi went to great pain to tell Fryman that his relationship with Lappat was on a friendship, not romantic, basis.

He told Fryman that he first met Lappat when she and Cawein were treating his wife for leukemia in 1962. Both physicians were with his wife when she died in July 1963. Salehi said Lappat had been very supportive of him after his wife died in helping with his children and his wife's funeral arrangements. At one time he had borrowed $500.00 from Lappat but said he paid it back. Again, he emphasized they were not romantically involved. Lappat's actions while on vacation with the Surawiczes called that assertion into question.

Frida Surawicz said when her family and Lappat arrived in Williston, Vermont, for their vacation, Lappat made several telephone calls. Surawicz did not know the nature of those calls. Lappat announced that she was going to take the bus to Carlisle, Pennsylvania, and asked the Surawiczs if they would pick her up there on their way back to Lexington. While in Pennsylvania, she said Lappat stayed at the home of Julian Ripley and was joined there by Saeed Salehi.

Salehi told Fryman he did not expect to meet Lappat in Pennsylvania at his friends, the Ripleys. He said his trip had been planned for some time. During their time in Pennsylvania, Salehi said Lappat did not mention Marrs Cawein.

Lappat and the Surawcizes returned to Lexington on September 9, and Emma Lappat must have discovered detectives had been probing into every aspect of her life.

Sgt. James Perkins sent Cravens a memorandum about Lappat having keys to unauthorized supplies at the Medical Center. A former Medical Center employee, who requested anonymity, said Lappat certainly had access to such materials. Not only did the physicians in the anatomy, pathology, and surgery departments and the morgue have access to the carbolic acid kept under lock and key at the Medical Center but so did their assistants. Since carbolic acid was used as a disinfectant, it would have been easily obtainable in any of those departments.

Perkins searched the garbage cans at Lappat's home on Beacon Hill Drive and found a bottle, which he took to the Medical Center to have the contents tested. Through the door of Lappat's house, Perkins could see a note she had left for Harrison Fields, asking him to take care of her house and get her mail while she was on vacation.

On August 5, detective Fryman spoke with Fields, who lived with his wife in the Suburban Trailer Park, about his relationship with Lappat. Harrison said he worked for her and she asked him to take care of her house and mail while she was on vacation. Fields and his wife Gail had been to three parties with Emma Lappat. Two were at Lappat's house and the third was at the home of another Medical Center employee, Tom Roach, on Chestnut Street. Fields said he did not see anything wrong at the parties; just that some of the people were a little far out.

Fryman also interviewed another Medical Center employee, Gus Hauche, the same day. He told the detective he and his wife were friends with Cawein and Lappat and went to parties with them. "He states," the report read, "that there is a lot of hearsay in reference to an affair with Dr. Cawein and Dr. Lappat; and he states that both of these people were fine people but that he didn't care for Mrs. Cawein as she was stupid and he didn't blame Dr. Cawein if he was having an affair."

Hauche told Fryman the last party he attended with them was at Tom Roach's house on July 2. Hauche said the party started about 8:00 p.m. and ended sometime in the early morning. "He states," Fryman wrote, "that Mrs. Cawein got drunk and made an ass of herself."

It was 11:30 p.m. that night by the time Fryman got to Roach's home to talk to him about his party three days before Marrs Cawein died. Roach told Fryman that he did not know of anything unusual that occurred at the party. The detective recognized Roach as one of the men arrested in April in an investigation of homosexuals at the "Gilded Cage" nightclub. He wrote that Roach gave his name as Jackson at that time but he recognized him.

Not only were Lexington detectives digging into Lappat's current and past life, *The Kentucky Post* made their own contributions. In their August 11 issue, reporter Arlo Wagner had a long article on carbolic acid and the fact there was no antidote. In the same issue, the newspaper mentioned the cars that were seen at the Cawein home at 3:00 a.m., on July 5

On August 13, the same day coroner Chester Hager, finally ruled that Marrs Cawein's death was a homicide, the newspaper printed an extensive page one story, with headlines in a type size that was larger than their masthead type, about the home invasion Marrs Cawein had a year earlier with an unknown woman. The day after the article appeared, acting police chief Wallace McMurray announced that authorities had found a witness to the fight.

The Out-of-Town Newspaper and The Coroner

By the first of August 1965, the small town of Lexington was quite curious about the mysterious death of socialite Marrs Cawein. Detectives, despite spending long hours, were making little headway in their preliminary investigation.

Until the coroner ruled an unnatural death had occurred, they had done about all they could. Some of the Caweins' upper crust friends were not only, not talking, they were lawyering up. Cawein's death swelled the coffers of several local law firms.

All who thought they might be involved rushed out to get lawyers. George Swinebroad, for some unexplained reason, had two attorneys representing him. One Lexington lawyer, from a prominent family, was slow to seek representation and found that he had to go all the way to Prestonsburg, in eastern Kentucky, to find an attorney for himself.

Long time friends began to wonder if their own social relationships were out of kilter. A courthouse secretary was quoted in *The Kentucky Post* as saying, "If I were in that social group, I'd want to help an investigation or I'd be afraid of my friends after something like this."

Coroner Chester Hager, with his mostly softball investigation, had the case in such a mess that many wondered if it could ever be straightened out or if the truth about Marrs Cawein's painful demise would ever emerge.

City officials, including police brass, mayor Fred Fugazzi and city manager John Cook, held a closed-door meeting on July 28, to discuss the Cawein case. County attorney Armand Angelucci began to take a management role in the investigation and said all future information would come directly from police headquarters instead of the coroner leaking out bits and pieces of information.

But, there was no keeping coroner Hager out of the loop because everything hinged on what he ruled was the official cause and manner of Marrs Cawein's death. On August 3, Hager was quoted in the *Post* as saying the investigation was being hampered because many of the principals in the case refused to be questioned.

No indication was found in the case file of anyone who refused to speak with detectives. Some requested that their attorneys be present during their interviews. It was difficult to ascertain to whom Hager was referring. Even Lappat eventually had an interview with detective Fryman.

Hager, irritated with *The Kentucky Post* coverage of his death investigation, toyed with their reporters by speculating, sometimes wildly, about the source of the carbolic acid that was found in her stomach. Occasionally, he came upon the truth.

The August 12, issue of the newspaper quoted Hager as saying, "Mrs. Cawein was fed carbolic acid which probably caused her death early July 5 as she sat in a chair in her bedroom at 326 Chinoe Road." Was it possible that someone inserted a tube down Marrs Cawein's throat and poured the carbolic acid into her stomach? The autopsy report said there were no burns in her mouth, throat or upper esophagus.

As for evidence in the case, much of it evaporated because there was no crime scene. The blue chair could have told its own story if Hager had removed it for evidence before Madison Cawein had Betty Strother send it to be re-upholstered.

Despite all the incompetence, bits and pieces of evidence came to light. Detective Howard Rupard had an interesting interview with Howard Orme, who embalmed Marrs Cawein's body at Milwards Mortuary. Orme said he did not notice any bruises on her arms and legs and, if they had been there, he probably would not have seen them. Orme paid particular attention to Marrs Cawein's mouth being in such an awkward position. He said her tongue was slightly between her teeth indicating that she was in much pain when she died. Orme said when a person died a normal death, the mouth was usually in a normal position.

Could Marrs Cawein have been gagged to keep her quiet and avoid waking the three children sleeping upstairs? Authorities would never know as she had been buried just two days after she died. There was nothing in the case file that mentioned exhumation. One can only imagine the hue and cry George Swinebroad and Madison Cawein would have raised in putting a stop to such action.

If Hager's statement to the newspaper was correct and she was fed carbolic acid, then what was injected into the woman's thighs?

Talbert found an antiseptic, methylparaben, outside the injection sites on Marrs Cawein's thighs. The substance was commonly used to cleanse the skin before a syringe injection was given. The injection site on the left thigh was more pronounced as the pathologist called it a "puncture wound," while referring to the right thigh as having an "injection site."

Did Marrs Cawein, given her fear of needles, put up such a fight that whoever gave her the injection tore her skin with the needle? More importantly, what was in the injections?

If Hager truly had a problem with witnesses refusing to be questioned all he had to do was call a coroner's inquest and put them under oath. One of the *Post* reporters made such a request and Hager and Angelucci lost their cool.

On August 6, at Good Samaritan Hospital, *Post* reporter John Zeh handed Hager a notarized letter asking him to hold a coroner's inquest into the death of Marrs Cawein. Zeh referred to Kentucky Revised Statute 72.030, which allowed a responsible citizen to ask for a coroner's inquest.

"He merely placed it in his pocket and said is that all," Zeh wrote.

"Asked if he would honor my request, he replied, 'I don't know. I'll have to turn it over to the county attorney. He'll decide if we can have it (inquest) and when.'"

"I then asked if there was any reason why not? 'He replied, 'no.'"

Zeh contacted county attorney Angelucci at home and informed him of the letter he had given Hager. "You are not entitled to it," he quoted Angelucci as saying. Angelucci previously had exhibited a friendly relationship with *Post* reporters but Zeh said his voice took on a note of defiance.

When Angelucci asked Zeh what interest he had in the case, the reporter replied, "After conferences in *The Kentucky Post* editorial offices in Covington, I felt an inquest was necessary to move the investigation forward."

Angelucci, Zeh wrote, disagreed. He quoted the attorney as saying, "A continued investigation will reveal more than an inquest. An inquest, he said, could shut the door to new clues."

Investigators were already shut out, partly due to Hager's dragging his feet in making a legal determination as to whether an unnatural death had occurred. By using the *Post*'s news columns, police were practically begging the public to come forth with any information they might have regarding Marrs Cawein's death.

On August 13, nearly six weeks after Marrs Cawein died and a week after Zeh's request for a coroner's inquest, Hager called a news conference. He read a list of names of newspapers, television and radio stations and wire services entitle to receive the prepared statement on his ruling on Marrs Cawein's death. *The Kentucky Post* was not on Hager's list.

"I have reached the conclusion," Hager's statement read, "in the death of Mrs. Mary Marrs Cawein and I hereby enter an official coroner's verdict that it was homicide. Acting in my official capacity as coroner and in full accord with others investigating the case, I have signed a death certificate to the effect Mrs. Cawein died of unnatural causes and not by her own hand."

Hager, according to the next day's *Post*, said he reached his conclusion after a thorough and extensive investigation conducted in cooperation with all law enforcement agencies.

At last with Hager's official ruling, the *Lexington Herald* was forced to acknowledge that such a brutal crime had actually occurred in their town and began to give Marrs Cawein's death some coverage. The local newspaper quoted Hager as saying he would keep in mind conducting a coroner's inquest at a later date when it would be meaningful and in the public interest.

The coroner claimed he had viable witnesses who refused to be questioned and he was avoiding putting them under oath in a coroner's inquest to get answers. It appeared he had problems seeing beyond his prejudice toward the out-of-town newspaper and his concerns about being re-elected.

Hager pandered to the local newspapers, which, with the exception of two small items, had provided no previous coverage of the socialite's death investigation. "We compliment those who have refrained from enlarging on the rumors that have circulated and the distorted stories (published) by the northern Kentucky newspaper," he said. Hager added that it was fortunate so few people in Lexington read *The Kentucky Post* so a future jury pool would not be tainted.

Once again the coroner was mistaken. The northern Kentucky newspaper was the fastest selling print commodity in town.

Hager blamed the *Post* for making extra work for investigators by printing irresponsible rumors. The biggest handicap investigators had to overcome was apparently Hager's refusal to rule on the cause and manner of Marrs Cawein's death while evidence evaporated and potential witnesses lawyered up.

The coroner's statement did not address that portion of the investigation.

Hager had not finished lambasting the out-of-tow newspaper. "Pressures have been applied against me by a northern Kentucky newspaper to add to their shameless keyhole version of the circumstances surrounding the mysterious and unfortunate death of Mrs. Cawein," he said. "I have refused to lend credence to their trashy, sordid account of the tragedy. I would only become a party to too many distortions of fact and shabby sensationalism. Because gossip, in my opinion, has been greatly intensified by the lurid and, in many instances, erroneous reports printed in an out-of-town newspaper."

Hager's four-page statement bounced from one aspect of the case to another in which he gave himself credit for working day and night to solve the case. He did compliment the police for, what he called, their diligence. According to the case file, Hager might have spent a week, or less, on the investigation.

The coroner, of course, made no mention of the thousands of hours detectives spent on the case not only interviewing witnesses but doing house-to-house checks of the Cawein neighborhood, all deliveries made in the vicinity and the delivery personnel. The detectives developed time lines and grid charts, checked drug stores for sales of carbolic acid and looked at the Caweins' charge account at Begley Drug stores.

Hager lauded Lexington, where this dreadful murder occurred, and its people for its sense of fair play. "The fact that all of the irresponsible accounts about the death and all the outcry for officials to join in muckraking have come from the outside," he said, "shows we live in an area where people are imbued with fair play and are prone to base their opinions on established facts."

Many of those "imbued" people Hager talked about, were quaking in their boots at the thought of becoming involved in the investigation of Marrs Cawein's death. Those individuals were not courthouse secretaries, plumbers or retail clerks. They were some of the town's most prominent citizens who feared their livelihoods as well as their reputations, socially, politically or otherwise, could be irreparably damaged.

Buried in the middle of Hager's statement was a paragraph, which explained the coroner's actions in the Marrs Cawein case, his own re-election.

"The circumstances surrounding this tragedy are such that indiscriminate disclosures of all persons who might be remotely linked with some facet of the case or any of the central figures in the case would amount to character assassination of innocent people on a wholesale basis," he explained. "I have no desire to become a party to such malicious mischief. In my opinion, it is descent and honest to preserve the rights of those who although subject to questioning or even considerable investigation can prove they are innocent of any involvement or wrong doing."

There it was!

Hager's reason for refusing to rule on the cause and manner of Marrs Cawein's death for six weeks was, at last, clear. He intended to protect his friends and insure his re-election.

Hager said if a coroner's inquest, would be helpful in the future, he would call one and make it open to the public and the press. "I have no further comment at this time," he said, "except to say I will continue to work with police and officials of our courts."

Except, Hager was not actually working closely with investigators to solve Marrs Cawein's murder. Detective Frank Fryman had been begging for weeks for a coroner's inquest to force witnesses to get their stories straight. Finally, he asked Capt. Carvens to request a coroner's inquest in order to find the truth. "Every time a discrepancy is found the witness will state that he didn't say it or that he doesn't remember or that he will try to think about it," he told Cravens. "In any attempt to make an appointment with witnessed referenced (in) this case, it takes sometimes weeks to catch them in a free moment.

"I feel a coroner's inquest would at least give us one set statement of what happened and as close to the truth as we can get. We must have this in order to be able to check information that may come in on this case in years to come," Fryman said.

It was patently obvious that neither Fryman nor Zeh would get their coroner's inquest. However, the *Post* editor had an answer for Hager's actions.

Post editor Vance Trimble had no intention of accepting Hager's self-serving excuses and his attempts to turn his newspaper into a tabloid. The crusty editor was accustomed to chewing up and spitting out politicians, like Hager, from his days as the head of the Washington bureau for Scripps Howard newspaper. In 1960, Trimble won a Pulitzer Prize for a series of articles exposing nepotism in Congress.

Trimble, in an editorial entitled, "And Now They Decide It Was Murder," agreed with Hager that Marrs Cawein's death was a terrible tragedy, but disagreed with him about everything else in his news conference tirade.

"From the very onset," Trimble wrote, "there was more mystery and odd circumstances in this case than you'd find in a Perry Mason mystery story. And certainly not the least baffling was the lethargic approach Fayette County officialdom took toward the investigation. Just why there was such an effort to 'play down,' almost to the point of forgetting, this questionable death of a prominent citizen puzzled and frightened us."

Trimble lauded his reporters, Arlo Wagner and John Zeh, for their efforts to interview every person known to have been involved with Marrs Cawein on the last day of her life and the next day, when her body was found.

Post reporters, however, were not very successful in interviewing the men in Marrs Cawein's life. Her husband refused interviews, always referring them to his attorney, John Y. Brown, Sr., a Lexington insider and one-term U.S. Representative. Brown told Wagner, "I don't care to discuss this case with the newspapers; if they (the police) have anything to present, let them present it."

Don Sturgill ran interference for Sam Strother telling the *Post* on August 13, "It would not be to his advantage to talk to the press at this time." Sturgill, the article continued, "said Strother had willingly answered all questions of authorities." No record of an media interview with George Swinebroad could be found. There were those who insisted that he dotted on his only child regardless of his public persona of non-involvement in the search for her killer.

Among the many mysteries of Marrs Cawein's murder were statements by her father. George Swinebroad first lied to authorities in regard to the Caweins' marriage and then recanted. He was an influential man in Lexington and his friends sat in positions of power. One would think such a person would use every resource available to him to find what happened to his only child.

Swinebroad did have the backing of friends in the Thoroughbred industry during the investigation of his daughter's murder. The Thoroughbred Club of American raised more than $5,000 as a reward for information that would help solve the crime. There was never an occasion, according to the case file and media reports, to use the money and, presumably, it was returned to the donors.

Discrepancies

If detective Frank Fryman had been successful in his efforts to have Chester Hager call a coroner's inquest, he just might have solved the murder of Marrs Cawein. From the evidence in the case file, nobody worked harder than Fryman in an effort to solve the case. He conducted twenty-nine interviews, the most of any detective.

The detective found numerous discrepancies in statements from Sam and Betty Strother, Madison Cawein and Emma J. Lappat. In the statement of two of the people involved in the investigation of Marrs Cawein's death, Herschell and Barbara Leapman, Fryman found no discrepancies.

Resolving the discrepancies in just the statements of Betty and Sam Strother, Madison Cawein and Emma Lappat would have possibly taken the case farther toward a solution if the witnesses had been under oath.

That was not going to happen because Chester Hager refused to impanel a coroner's inquest.

Fryman was curious about why the Strothers' stories about the discovery of Marrs Cawein's body went in so many different directions. In a coroner's inquest, the Strothers might have been compelled to tell whichever of their versions was true.

Another of Fryman's concerns was why the Strothers' stories differed so much from Cawein's about where the doctor left his clothes at their house on the evening of July 4. Another concern was why the physician stayed so long at the Strother home that morning instead of going to his home.

In particular, Fryman pointed to Carrick Shropshire's two telephone calls to the Cawein residence. Shropshire's first call placed Betsy Cawein at her home when Betty

Strother said she was eating breakfast at her house. His second call placed Cawein at the death scene at 10:30 a.m., earlier than the Strothers' version.

The detective suspected Sam Strother was at the Cawein home later the evening of July 4, than he admitted. He pointed out that one of the automobiles seen at the Cawein home that morning, around 3:30 a.m., fit the description of one of the Strothers' automobiles, the Chevrolet convertible.

Most importantly, the detective wanted to know why Cawein destroyed the glass and beer can that were sitting on the lamp table beside his wife's body. Later, the physician denied there was any drink or beer can sitting on the lamp table.

Cawein first told detectives, there were no syringes in his house. When Hager finally rendered a legal opinion that Marrs Cawein's death was a homicide, detectives were able to search the house. They found a drawer full of syringes and other medical equipment in an antique washstand in the Caweins' bedroom. In addition, they found a syringe in the lamp table drawer, with a solution in it, and the needle intact with Madison Cawein's fingerprints on it. Cawein maintained the apparatus had been planted by someone who wanted to frame him. There was no information in the case file about the content of the solution in the syringe.

Fryman was confused about the Caweins' on and off divorce. Cawein told detectives he had asked for a divorce when he was drunk but they were not getting a divorce. Marrs Cawein thought they were. She told her mother and stepbrother that her marriage was over and her husband hated her. Nobody seemed to know if she had agreed to the divorce.

Fryman had a theory that Marrs Cawein and Emma Lappat might have been working together in checking on the whereabouts of Madison Cawein and Barbara Leapman. If his theory was correct, it would have been an unusual collaboration of two former adversaries joining together in opposition to what they perceived to be a common enemy,

Barbara Leapman. Fryman had evidence to back up his theory.

In his interview with Fryman, Dr. Herschell Leapman said, when he went to the Medical Center to see Lappat on June 30, he had to wait in her office. On her desk he saw a telephone message to call Marrs Cawein. Leapman thought Lappat was the woman who called him at midnight the last week in June to tell him his wife was seeing Cawein. On June 28, Leapman received a letter at his work, the U.S. Public Health Hospital on Leestown Road, with the same message.

On July 4, while he was on duty at the hospital, the operator called Leapman at approximately 3:00 a.m., and said a woman, who identified herself as his wife, called and said he was needed at home. He knew that Cawein had been seeing his wife at the Leapmans' home and told detective Fryman that he suspected a set-up.

On his way across town to their apartment on Jennifer Drive, Leapman decided to stop at Fayette County Police headquarters and seek some advice. He was told, by the officer on duty, to check the license numbers of cars in his apartment complex to see if any belonged to Cawein.

Leapman drove to Jennifer Drive and returned a short time later to police headquarters with the license plate numbers. None of the numbers matched Cawein's license plate. Detective Fryman said Leapman, agitated over the entire situation, had a fender-bender when he was leaving police headquarters, which required a dated and signed accident report. Afterwards, he checked his apartment and found his wife in bed asleep, alone, and returned to work around 6:00 a.m. on July 5.

Whoever attempted to set Leapman up to take the fall for Marrs Cawein's murder, certainly did not expect him to go to police headquarters and then have an automobile accident in front of the building. Fryman questioned whether Lappat ever knew about Leapman's activities after he left the hospital the night of July 4, in response to what was probably her telephone call. She had called Hager and Angelucci and told them that Leapman could solve the murder of Marrs Cawein.

Leapman would be transferred to another hospital in three months and it was no wonder he said he never planned to be in Kentucky again.

Perhaps the most puzzling of Fryman's questions had to do with Cawein and his daughter. The detective made out his list of discrepancies in March 1966, eight months after Marrs Cawein was murdered. As of that date, Fryman said, Cawein had not discussed what happened at their house on July 5 with his daughter. Marrs Cawein's mother, who the nine-year-old visited a few week after her mother's death, said Betsy never mentioned her mother.

Emma Lappat presented a long list of questions for Fryman. He never was able to figure out why she threw the acid-like substance into Martha Kieckhefer's face. Nor, did he understand the reasons for all the violence apparently perpetuated by Lappat toward Marrs Cawein, why she peeped in their windows, hid in shrubbery and sat on stools beside their house.

He was interested in any contact Lappat had with Marrs Cawein the last of June and the first four days of July. If they were working together, it brought up the possibility that Cawein might have been using his relationship with Barbara Leapman to get away from both women.

There were no answers to why Lappat denied going to Long's home before their dinner date on July 4, and of making any telephone calls from his house. If Lappat had visitors on July 4, as she told friends, where were they while she was out with Long?

Had Hager called a coroner's inquest, many of Fryman's questions might have been answered. All the principals were still around, except Marrs Cawein.

One Last Chance

In September, the Fayette County grand jury took on an impossible task, investigating a homicide that defied a solution. Unlike a coroner's inquest, which did not occur, results of grand jury proceedings were secret. From all indications, the grand jury made their own decision to investigate Marrs Cawein's murder.

After all, the coroner and the county attorney declined to further involve themselves in finding the answer by refusing to call a coroner's inquest. Detectives were at a dead end, so to speak.

Apparently the commonwealth attorney's office felt the same way. George Barker, an assistant commonwealth attorney, was surprised the grand jury wanted to spend any time on the Cawein murder. Barker, later a circuit court judge, was quoted in the September 22 *Post* as saying the jury was, "A scrambling one which asks for more information rather than being content to study only those cases and information presented to it."

What a unique idea!

Someone, other than detectives, was interested in a murder case that seemed to be an embarrassment to Marrs Cawein's family and friends.

However, there could be a problem with the grand jurors. The foreman was Ronald Collins, a vice-president of First Security Bank and Trust Company, one of the entities making up the Lexington establishment. Of course, Collins being on the jury could simply have resulted from a spin of the jury wheel.

Others on the grand jury were John Boyce, an International Business Machines (IBM) data processor; Robert T. Jackson, a GMAC janitor; Charles Blankenship, a National Cash Register repairman; Woodrow Hamm, Lexington sales manager for the Louisville *Courier-Journal* (Kentucky's largest newspaper); Janice Broughman, a stenographer; Gladys Inski, a housewife whose husband George Inski was president of the Fayette Tobacco Warehouse Company; James Blackburn, an insurance agent; Harvey Case, a department manager at Sears Robuck; Rev. R. C. Porter and Dorthy Birch whose husband Abner Birch was an IBM technician.

Before the grand jury met, Cawein took a polygraph test administered by the Kentucky State Police and passed. His attorney, John Y. Brown, Sr., told the August 2 *Post*, "He was very firm that he knew nothing about the cause of death and that he had nothing to do with it."

All Cawein tried to do was convince everybody his wife died of a heart attack, destroyed evidence, cleaned up what should have been a crime scene and lied about wanting a divorce.

Betty and Sam Strother were accompanied to the grand jury proceedings by his father, attorney Sam Strother, Sr., and another lawyer in the firm, Gene Oliver.

Betty Strother complained to the August 2, *Post*, that the murder had disrupted her family life. She said she and her husband were "Near a nervous breakdown because of being in the middle of all this mess. It could have been anybody else who had dinner with them that evening we just happened to be the ones."

The evening was certainly no picnic for Marrs Cawein.

Betty Strother still had problems getting everything straight. It was not what happened at dinner at the Idle Hour Country Club that involved them. It was what they did afterwards.

Marrs Cawein's father, George Swinebroad showed up for the grand jury with two attorneys, Nathan Elliott, Jr., a relative of his wife, and high profile Lexington lawyer Harry B. Miller. They were all seen reading *The Kentucky Post*'s coverage of the murder while waiting to testify. Why would a father want to read about the brutal murder of his only child?

Lexington Herald editor Herndon J. Evans attempted to explain the newspaper's recent coverage of Marrs Cawein's murder after a drought of nearly six weeks. Evans made his excuses in a September 30, editorial. He said the newspaper's lack of coverage of the murder was due to the police and coroner giving out a minimum of statements.

His newspaper received the same statements as did *The Kentucky Post*. The real difference was that Evans did not assign investigative reporters to cover the case. In all likelihood, Fred Wachs, publisher of the *Herald* and the *Leader*, told him the newspapers would not cover the murder.

Evans used the Betty Gail Brown murder coverage as a reason for not pursuing and printing articles about the Cawein murder. "It is generally understood that too many newspaper stories were carried in the case of the murdered Betty Gail Brown on the Transylvania campus and that many persons' names were brought into this case doing irreparable damage to their reputations and standings in the community," he wrote.

What a novel idea, protecting potential witnesses instead of pursuing justice for the victim.

Herald-Leader reporters obviously did not agree with their publisher and editors. When the news staffs voted on the top Kentucky news story of 1965, they selected the murder of Marrs Cawein, a story initially they were not allowed to cover.

After hearing from four of the principal figures in the case, the Strothers, Swinebroad and Talbert, the pathologist, the jury wanted to hear more witnesses and asked for a three-day extension, which was granted. Jurors questioned Betty Strother for an hour and her husband for forty-five minutes. Swinebroad was in the jury room for an hour and a half. Jurors kept Talbert in the room for an hour and forty minutes.

Earlier testimony was heard from police chief E.C. Hale, coroner Chester Hager and detectives Morris Carter and Nolen Freeman. No indication was found that detective Frank Fryman testified before the grand jury but he could have. His pages of witnesses' discrepancies alone would have provided jurors with fertile information.

Two other grand jury witnesses, Madison Cawein and Emma J. Lappat, caught the attention of *Post* reporters who thought it was curious that the two longtime research associates and alleged lovers never made eye contact nor spoke to each other while waiting to testify.

Cawein was in the grand jury room for an hour and ran from the courthouse to avoid photographers.

Lappat spent three hours in the grand jury room. Leaving the courthouse, she darted into a shoe store to avoid photographers and reporters. When she returned to the sidewalk, she got into a scuffle with *Post* reporter John Zeh, a UK journalism student who also covered the Cawein story for the student newspaper, *The Kernel*. As Zeh attempted to take a picture of Lappat, she grabbed for his camera, which was fastened to a leather strap round his neck As they wrestled for possession of the camera, other photographers had a field day.

Some of the photographs of Lappat and Zeh's camera tug-of-war appeared in *The Kernel*. Lappat wrote a letter to Medical Center officials asking them to do something about Zeh because of the pictures and his articles about her.

Others appearing before the grand jury included: Winternitz, newspaper carrier George Ferrell; a Cawein neighbor Rosa Beard; baby sitter Phoebe Edwards; Idle Hour Country Club manager Robert Lewis; Mrs. John Merrit, who owned the camp where Skip Cawein spent the night of July 4; Herschell Leapman, whose wife Barbara was also subpoenaed to testify but did not appear; W. F. Owsley, another employee of the U.S. Public Health Hospital, and Dr. Frank Cleveland, a Cincinnati pathologist.

Apparently, Cleveland appeared on behalf of his friend, Chester Hager, to convinced the grand jury that the coroner had handled the case properly.

After they heard from witnesses in the Cawein case, three options were open to the grand jury: they could issue indictments, make a written report or leave the investigation for a future grand jury.

Jurors spent six days of their nine-day session on the Cawein murder case. They issued a seven-page report, which contained only thirteen lines on their findings about Marrs Cawein's death. The jury did, however, return forty-five indictments for various other crimes and made reports of their investigations of the jail and city dump.

The grand jury report, however, lauded the police and coroner for their investigation while criticizing *The Kentucky Post* for its over-zealous reporting. Foreman Ronald Collins refused to talk with reporters about the jury's report. Another juror, who asked *Post* reporter Arlo Wagner not to use his name, said, "I disagreed about the reference to the news reporting but the majority of the jury thought we ought to have it in the report. Actually, they got that from the police and coroner Hager."

It is now 2008, forty-two years since Marrs Cawein met her tortured death and her murder remains unsolved.

Many of those connected to the investigations have died.

George Swinebroad died in May 1975, at age seventy-three, in Houston, Texas, as he was being rushed into emergency cardiac surgery. "For some 50 years Swinebroad's gravely voice ruled over major horse auctions, both Thoroughbred and Standardbred, in the United States," *Herald* sports editor Tom Easterling wrote on May 11, "It is estimated that more than $1 billion worth of horse flesh passed under his gavel."

Swinebroad's obituary listed his grandchildren, Madison Cawein IV, as living in Versailles, and Elizabeth Webb Cawein was in Cincinnati.

The Strothers did not buy the house on Richmond Road that Marrs Cawein planned to show them. Instead they moved to Fairway Drive, near the Idle Hour County Club. In 1978, Sam Strother, Jr., died at his home on Riva Ridge Drive. His obituary in the February 25, 1978, *Lexington Herald*, listed among his survivors two daughters from Dallas, Texas. The obituary identified him as a former Idle Hour Country Club member. There was no mention of Betty Strother in his obituary.

Since Marrs Cawein died without a will, Madison Cawein was appointed administrator of her $43,000.00 estate on May 19, 1966. Her stock portfolio, according to the estate inventory in the Fayette County clerk's office had dwindled down to $4,200.00. In June 1966, Cawein sold their home on Chinoe Road to Louise R. and P. Porter Douglas III, for $25,400.00. The Caweins paid $23,000.00 for the house in 1959.

Cawein left Lexington and apparently spent some time in New York. He married the former Joan B. Roper and they lived in Cincinnati where he worked for the Merrell Dow Pharmaceutical Company. Roper collaborated in producing *A Picturography of Madison Cawein*, her husband's grandfather.

Cawein died in 1985 at Deaconess Hospital in Cincinnati, from cancer at fifty-nine. His survivors included his father, who lived in Danville, New Jersey, his son who lived in Louisville and his daughter who lived in Denver.

Madison Cawein IV, attended Harvard from 1968 to 1971, and graduated from the California Institute of The Arts in 1973. As adapt with a paint brush as his great-grandfather was with words, Madison Cawein IV is an outstanding artist. Many of his still life flowers are almost photographically perfect in details He also works in vanitas, a genre of still life that flourished in the Netherlands in the early seventeenth century. A painting, entitled, "Vanitas II," is of a skull, whose jawbone sits on a thick book, perhaps a medical book, while the back of the skull rests on two similar volumes.

Vanitas paintings, according to the *Encyclopedia Britannica*, are symbolic of the inevitability of death; the transience and vanity of earthly achievements and pleasures and exhort the viewer to consider mortality and to repent.

Cawein has held one-man shows across the country and prices for his some of his paintings are in the five figures. His works are exhibited in art museums in Massachusetts, Kentucky and California.

Elizabeth Webb Cawein was the most elusive member of Marrs Cawein's family. Except for her name being mentioned in the obituaries of her father and maternal grandfather, little was known about her.

Emma J. Lappat remained at the Medical Center until 1968, when her contract was not renewed, also became an elusive figure. She was ostracized by many of Cawein's former associates. She sought refuge behind her closed office door as Cawein's friends would bang on the door and call her unspeakable names.

Lappat went from UK to the M. D. Anderson Cancer Center, in Houston, Texas. She was there a year before being let go due to a budget crunch. Her trail grew cold until she surfaced after the turn of the century as an internist at a Los Angeles Comprehensive Care Clinic, where she retired in 2005.

Madison Cawein's other associates at the Medical Center scattered. Medical School dean William Willard led an exodus from the Medical Center to the University of Alabama, where they established the College of Community Health Sciences. Winternitz was part of that group known as the "Kentucky Mafia."

Pathologist Wilmier Talbert also left the university. Borys Surawicz went to Indiana University, where he retired.

Most of the detectives who worked the Marrs Cawein murder case are retired or deceased. Nolen Freeman, who was later chief of police in Lexington, and Morris Carter, who became an assistant chief, are both dead. None worked more diligently to solve the crime than Frank Fryman, who is also deceased.

Chester Hager retired as coroner in 1989, and sold his Whitehall Funeral Chapel, which was located in an elegant mansion, once owned by chief justice Thomas A. Marshall. The building now houses a catering firm.

Kentucky Post reporters, Arlo Wagner and John Zeh, moved to Washington, D.C. In 2007, Wagner was still working for the *Washington Times*. Zeh worked for *Rolling Stone, The Village Voice* and reported for "All Things Considered," a program on National Public Radio. He returned to Cincinnati, after losing a leg when a Washington transit bus ran over him, but continued his advocacy work for the homeless and gays before his death in 2006.

After more than four decades, there is little chance Marrs Cawein's murder will ever be solved. Her death could be considered the perfect crime giving credence to the axiom, that justice delayed is truly justice denied.

Carlton

Elliott

Ray

Four Bullets to the Head

Dr. Carlton Elliott Ray, 27, finished his rounds at St. Joseph Hospital, in Lexington, on Friday, April, 1, 1977, went out into the damp spring evening and got into his Ford Torino. For weeks, he had told family, friends and patients that his life was being constantly threatened. He may have check the glove compartment of the car to make sure the .32 Smith and Wesson pistol he recently purchased was still there.

He drove south on Tates Creek Pike to Merrick Place, a posh development where he had recently moved to be near his twice-divorced girl friend, Sheila Day. Ray's apartment, at 3301 Commodore Drive was off Humphrey Lane, where Day lived, in Merrick Place. His apartment was sparsely furnished with only a sofa. He may have intended to spruce it up a bit since he had, among other items, two pairs of green drapes in his car.

Ray parked his car in front of Day's apartment.

The couple apparently planned to get married as soon as his divorce was final.

In recent conversations with friends and patients, Ray indicated he felt the continual threats on his life were behind him. Those conversations appeared to have coincided with his filing for a divorce from Nancy Bowles Ray the middle of February.

The threats on his life, however, were real.

Someone had decided the young doctor was going to die that evening and they were waiting in the Merrick Place parking lot for him.

Ray was well turned out that evening in a blue shirt underneath a three-piece Palm Beach-brand blue suit, the trousers were in a matching check, and his blue tie had a white design. Perhaps he thought it was unnecessary to take his gun out of the glove compartment to walk the short distance from the parking lot to the entrance of Day's apartment building. It was doubtful he would have had time to use the weapon as his assassin held the element of surprise.

As Ray got out of his car a fusillade of bullets burst forth, fired at point blank range, into his head. He fell to the pavement, between his car and another vehicle in the parking lot. Three .45 caliber bullets tore through his skull and another bounced off a bone causing an enormous amount of damage inside his brain, according to the autopsy report.

The assassin, whom detectives later described as being about 5'9", in his early twenties with sunken cheeks and thick hair, not only left the weapon at the scene but three handkerchiefs, a pair of rubber gloves and three crumpled empty Camel cigarette packages as well.

The hour was late and many Merrick Place residents were out for Friday evening and/or the weekend, were entertaining, had gone to bed or were watching television.

John F. Summersett, of Lexington, was visiting his girl friend Polly McNair, who lived with her roommate, Susan Moberly, in a second floor apartment across the hall from Sheila Day. Both apartments were on the end of the building that overlooked the parking lot where Ray was shot. Summersett and McNair were watching television when they heard the volley of shots, then silence.

Summersett, in an 2007 interview, said he looked out the window on the parking lot but was unable to see anything due to the darkness and trees. He ran downstairs, out into the parking lot and saw a person, he determined to be the shooter, crawl into the back seat of a two-door vehicle, parked at the edge of the lot. The vehicle immediately drove away. Apparently the two men were more interested in leaving the scene quickly than they were in taking a shot at a potential witness.

Summersett said the interior light of the getaway car was on but he was not able to get a good look at the assassin, the driver or the vehicle. He added that the driver appeared to be familiar with the complicated layout of the development since there was no hesitation as he made the correct turns and drove away. It was possible to exit Merrick Place from the front entrance on Tates Creek Road or by the side street, Dove Run Road.

Blood, with its metallic odor fouling the fresh spring air, was pouring on the pavement from Ray's head when Summersett found him. When McNair came downstairs and started out toward the parking lot, Summersett asked her to go back inside and call police.

Summersett placed the time of the shooting at around 10:00 p.m. "The shooting occurred just as the Division of Police was changing shifts," he said. "That was the reason they didn't arrive for about a half an hour."

He said he was the only person at the shooting scene and he remained there until the police and coroner arrived around 10:30 p.m. Ray's car door was open, the keys were in the ignition and the .32 pistol he purchased for protection was still in the glove compartment. Inside the car was a sheet of yellow paper with the names and telephone numbers of people for authorities to call in the event the doctor was murdered.

Sheila Day, Summersett said, was absolutely scared to death for her safety and that of her sons, who were in her apartment at the time of the shooting, before the detectives arrived. Unfortunately, Day's witness statement, along with thirteen others, including Summersett's, was missing from the case file. Apparently, detectives were concerned enough about her safety to post a police guard outside the door to her apartment for the remainder of the night.

Summersett recalled that Day's two sons, then around seven and eleven years old, told detectives they thought the car, they saw from their second floor living room window leaving the parking lot, was a Cadillac. He questioned the accuracy of their description since the darkness and trees also obscured the view of the parking lot from their windows.

Polly McNair Summersett, in a 2007 interview, said Day told her a few days before the shooting that Ray said he had a "real creepy feeling," and suggested if anything happened to him Day should check and see where his father-in-law Charles G. Bowles was.

At detectives' request and in hope of refreshing his memory in describing the assassin and the get-away car, Summersett said he later underwent hypnosis administered by the famous psychiatrist Dr. Cornelia Wilbur. Wilbur was the psychiatrist who treated and wrote about Shirley A. Mason, better known as Sybil, the woman deemed to have multi-personalities, whose life story became a movie.

Summersett said the hypnosis, performed in Wilbur's office in downtown Lexington, was of little value as he remembered a only few details, such as the tail fins on the get-away car. He remembered nothing more about the description of the assassin or the driver.

The empty cigarette packages the assassin left behind indicated he was either a chain smoker or he had been waiting some time for the doctor's arrival. Today, the items the shooter left at the scene of the shooting would have provided invaluable DNA information and possibly could have led to the convictions of Ray's murderer and those who might have been accessories before and after the fact.

But, the year was 1977. "Forensic DNA analysis was first used in the United Kingdom in 1985 to solve two related sexual homicides," according to the June 30, 2006 issue of the *New England Journal of Medicine*.

Aside from Summersett, there was another witness at the scene.

Gerald W. Helton, of Lexington, was referred to in the case file as an eye witnesses to the shooting. Helton's witness statement was also missing from the case file. Summersett said he wondered where Helton was since he did not see him at the scene. Summersett said he remained there until authorities arrived and, when the parking lot was no longer a crime scene, called the fire department to come out and wash the blood off the pavement. The media was on the scene soon after the police and the coroner's office arrived.

Mary Cox, whose apartment also overlooked the crime scene, told the *Herald-Leader*, she heard several shots. "I was on the phone at the time and thought it was firecrackers-or hoped it was," she was quoted as saying in the April 3 edition. Another neighbor, who asked the newspaper not to print her name, said she heard the shots and also thoughts they were firecrackers. She called out her window, "What's going on out there?" She said a male voice yelled back from the parking lot and told her to stay inside or she might be caught in the line of fire "When someone tells you something like that, you listen," she told reporter Marti Martin.

Deputy coroner William P. McCarney set the time of death at 10:30 p.m., which was when he arrived on the scene, and that was normal procedure. McCarney removed the body to Whitehall Funeral Home, which was also the office of Fayette County coroner Chester Hager.

With information provided by Sheila Day, in her interview at 11:20 p.m., about alleged threats from Ray's father-in-law and the list in Ray's car of people to be notified in case of his death, detectives were able to rapidly accumulate statements which appeared to implicate Charles G. Bowles, of Russellville, and the father of Nancy Carolyn Ray, in his son-in-law's murder.

At 2:10 a.m., Sgt. Drexel Neal interviewed the physician's sister, Roberta M. Ray, who lived in Kettering, Ohio. Two hours later she gave the Kettering Police Department a statement outlining the numerous times Bowles had threatened to kill her brother, or have him killed, from the time he and Nancy Bowles were married in 1968, until a few days before his death. Her information about Bowles' supposedly actions came from conversations with her brother.

She mentioned that her brother had obtained a restraining order against Bowles the first of February and had hired a bodyguard. In her witness statement, in the case file, the sentence concerning the restraining order was underlined. No other mention of a restraining order, nor the document itself, was found in the case file.

Forty minutes after Roberta Ray's interview with detective Neal, investigators began efforts to pick up Bowles, who was apparently at his home in Russellville, Kentucky. Nancy Ray, a registered nurse, had voluntarily committed herself to the psychiatric ward at Good Samaritan Hospital, in Lexington, a week earlier. The victim's wife, according to the case file, had attempted suicide on three previous occasions.

Detectives went to Nancy Ray's apartment on Shaker Drive off Harrodsburg Road, where she had lived with Ray before he filed for divorce, looking for Bowles. Only Carolyn Bowles, her mother, was there. She had been staying there while her daughter was in the hospital. Detectives telephoned Charles Bowles in Russellville at 1:15 a.m., he answered the call and was informed of Ray's death He agreed to drive to Lexington immediately.

At 6:30 a.m., investigators began interviewing Merrick Place residents as they left the complex. Detectives checked gas stations to see if attendants could identify anyone matching the description of the shooter. Shortly thereafter, detectives contacted the Russellville Police Department concerning Bowles' reputation. Later, investigators checked the time and mileage for a trip from Russellville to Lexington and back to Russellville.

Bowles appeared to be investigators' primary and only suspect.

Five hours later, detectives went Nashville, Tennessee, where the Rays lived while he did his internship at Vanderbilt University Hospital. At 7:00 p.m., detectives re-interviewed Day and Summersett. Elliott Ray's divorce lawyer, Walter Tackett, was also interviewed. None of these statements were in the case file. According to the case file, there was some discussion about asking Day to take a polygraph test but nothing was found to indicate that she did.

Before the day was over, detectives had re-interviewed the Merrick Place neighborhood, personnel at St. Joseph Hospital who had contact with the physician the previous evening and Ray's friend, Dr. Judson E. Chalkley.

The two detectives, who went to Nashville, interviewed those who knew the doctor and his wife when they lived there. A person of interest there was Charles P. Hand, a real estate executive with the firm of Dobson and Johnson, Inc. Another was Ed Smith, a former Davidson County deputy sheriff, who had been suspended fifteen years earlier for informing another officer he was the subject of an internal investigation. Smith's numerous applications for reinstatement had been denied. Neither Hand nor Smith's statements were in the case file.

Former Lexington detective Philip Vogel said Ray and Smith began friends when the doctor was in Nashville and that Smith apparently did some investigative work for the physician. Vogel added that he suspected Smith was blackmailing Ray.

Commonwealth attorney Larry Roberts was quoted in the Lexington newspaper as saying, "Hand had been questioned because he was engaged in an extra marital affair with Mrs. Ray during her residency in Nashville." Tennessee authorities said Hand has some knowledge as to the ill feelings of the wife toward her late husband. Lexington detective John W. Bizzack, was quoted in the Lexington and Nashville newspapers as saying, "We have determined a motive in the crime but we are not releasing the identity or number of people we have identified as suspects."

The next morning, April 3, at 8:00 a.m., detectives contacted Randy Thornton, at General Telephone Company's security office, in Lexington, about a conversation Ray with him about the doctor's telephone line being tapped. Detectives also collected long distance telephone records for Ray and Day's telephones.

In a 2007 interview, Thornton said he could not determine if there was a tap on Ray's telephone line. He added that, in his opinion, the physician's death was a professional hit. Thornton's witness statement was also missing from the case file.

Detectives John Bizzack and William Read interviewed Charles and Carolyn Bowles the first thing Saturday morning. Bowles' witness statement was in the case file, but Carolyn Bowles' was not. After lunch, they went to Day's apartment to check for Ray's personal items, records and other data.

Later that evening, according to the case file, Bizzack and Read contacted the Kentucky State Police (KSP) for intelligence on Bowles' operations. That reference may have concerned his bookmaking on basketball games and other people who were involved. It would not be a large leap to consider some of the unsavory characters engaged in bookmaking operations might have had information concerning murder-for-hire.

The next day, detectives met at Ray's office with his staff, indexed Ray, Bowles and Day's telephone records and interviewed Jane S. Farmer, of Lexington, the first wife of F. P. Farmer, Day's second husband.

By April 3, eight detectives were conducting interviews in Kentucky, Tennessee and Ohio. Also involved in the investigation were the Federal Bureau of Investigation (FBI) and the Treasury Department's Bureau of Alcohol, Tobacco and Firearms (ATF). John F. McCauley, a FBI senior resident agent, told the Lexington newspaper his organization and detectives were sharing information.

There was no indication in the case file as to what that information was.

Ray's murder stirred up a boiling cauldron of acrimonious emotions. His family had deeply held convictions that Charles Bowles had either murdered their son and brother or had hired a hit man to kill him. The Bowles family felt that Ray, after receiving their financial assistance to complete medical school, had behaved rather shabbily toward their daughter who worked to put him through medical school and his internship.

As for Sheila Day, since her witness statements were among those missing from the case file, there was no documentation of her reactions.

Day, one of the pivotal figures in the case, had two former husbands who gave detectives two distinctly different descriptions of the woman who had been their wife. There was little doubt, had he lived, Day intended to marry Ray.

One of the Other Women

When a murder involves a triangular relationship, the victim, Elliott Ray, his wife Nancy from whom he had filed for divorce and one of the other women he dated while still married, Sheila Day, detectives would normally look first at the surviving spouse.

In this case, Nancy Ray had the perfect alibi. She was in the psychiatric ward of a Lexington hospital the night of the murder. Sheila Day also had an alibi. She was at home, according to numerous witnesses, with her two sons when the physician was shot in front of her apartment building.

Detectives delved deeply into Day's background by interviewing her former husbands. Apparently, they came across something that caused them to go down this trail.

Sheila Day, an attractive, petite, dark-haired woman, had lived a fast paced life in her thirty-four years with two former husbands, two sons, a career and was planning a third marriage to a doctor seven years her junior.

In between marriages she earned a bachelor degree from the University of Kentucky and worked in a department store in Cumberland, Kentucky, for Columbia Gas in Lexington and for a personnel firm, Dunhill of Lexington.

The marriages and divorces of Sheila and Tony Day, from Bean Station, Tennessee, and of F. P. and Jane E. Farmer, from London, Kentucky, followed a parallel track. The Days were married in 1961, had two sons and divorced in 1971. He remarried a year later. The Farmers were married in 1962, had a son and daughter and were divorced in 1972. Sheila Day and Farmer were married in 1974, and she filed divorce less than a year later.

Although she collected child support from Tony Day, it was not clear whether Sheila Day received any assistance from Farmer, the London lawyer, after they split. She filed for the divorce from Farmer in Harlan Circuit Court, civil action # 2894. Since Farmer lived and practiced law in Laurel County, perhaps Day was more comfortable filing for divorce in her home county. The divorce document stated, "There are no property rights, child support or separate maintenance to be determined in this action. The petitioner (Day) and the joint petitioner (Farmer) have executed a Separate Agreement to that effect."

The impressions Sheila Day's former husbands had of her could not have been more different. Their remarks were taken directly from their interview statements with detectives.

Detectives Philip Vogel and Al Borne went to Bean Station, Tennessee, on April 3, to interview Tony Day. He told them he had never met Ray and had never traveled to Lexington to see his ex-wife.

"When was the last time you saw Shelia?" detective Borne inquired.

"About, I don't really remember the date," Day replied, "but it was about five or six weeks ago; they were down here one weekend. My son told me she brought this very tall doctor with them. In fact, I didn't see her that time, I didn't see her at all."

Where did Sheila Day and the doctor stayed on that visit, Borne asked?

"They have a summer home right over here on the lake," Day said. "It's about 800 yards from here." Day was referring to Douglas Lake, formed from the French Broad, Nolichucky and Pigeon rivers in the foothills of the Great Smokey Mountains, where his former father-in-law had a home.

Day had nothing nice to say about his former father-in-law. In answering Borne's question of what type of person he was, Day answered, "I don't think he is a very honest man. He's devious. He'll do anything to get his inch."

Detective Vogel asked Day if his ex-wife was having any financial difficulties?

"I think she is," he replied. "At least she says she is. This is one of the things I always get from her every time I talk to her, hear from her--money." Day said he was paying her child support. "She's had me in court twice in the last year trying to get this (child support) increased even though I'm caring for one of the children myself and it is my personal feeling that she should care for one and I would completely care for the other. That's not the way the judges see it," Day added.

"Let me ask you also, are you at this time or Shelia at this time trying to gain custody of both children?" Vogel inquired.

"Yes, I am," Day said. "She has repeatedly run off and left them in the custody of her parents ever since we've been divorced. She's only been with them about nine months since 1971, had them in her possession, under her guardianship and she did it again in October of this year, ran off to Lexington and I just felt like it was time for me to make a move on it."

"Has she ever spoken with you about her relationship with Dr. Ray?" Vogel asked.

"No," Day answered. "I hate to say this but she was, she goes out quite a bit and dates a whole lot of fellas from what I understand is a swinger and that sort of thing, so it doesn't surprise me if she changes dates once a week."

"Do you know her second husband F.P. Farmer?" Vogel probed.

"No," Day said. "I never met him. She wanted to introduce me a couple of times and I just sort of walked off, I didn't respect him very much. He had mistreated my children, at least that's what they told me, so I didn't want to be around him because I didn't trust myself in a situation like that."

"Do you know if Mr. Farmer had any animosity toward her or say anybody she would date?" Borne asked. Day's answer was missing from the typed version of his tape- recorded witness statement.

Vogel picked up on the same subject asking, "In discussing her marriage and relationship with F. P. Farmer it lasted about a year, do you think she has had contact with Mr. Farmer a couple of time since they were divorced?"

Day replied, "Yes, I know of one time, I know of at least two times they were separated and I don't know if they were divorced at that time, anyway he came to the lake down here and she was down here one weekend and she said he was there, down on the boat or something like that. I was over picking up my kids and I didn't meet him or see him or anything. And then I heard that she and he had been out about shortly before Christmas or shortly after Christmas she had been running and gone somewhere with him."

The detectives spent about as much time questioning Day about Farmer as they did asking about his ex-wife. Vogel asked if the London lawyer had another ex-wife? Day's reply was in the affirmative and indicated that he had spoken with Jane Farmer.

"Does she know Sheila?" Vogel asked.

"Yes," Day replied.

"Are they friends?" Vogel continued.

"No, they are not friends," Day answered. "As a matter of fact, again I hope this is confidential because I don't want to get her (Jane Farmer) in trouble, she's really concerned about F.P., Jane is. They had a custody fight not too long ago and I talked with Jane afterwards. She said she (he) had gone into court and told things about her, terrible things about her and lied about her and lied about her relationship with the children so F.P. could have custody of the daughter, which Jane had had since their divorce."

In the same reply, Day described his ex-wife, "Sheila is completely unprincipled. She'll lie for one minute if it suits her ends and she'll turn around and lie exactly the other way if it suits her ends the other way."

Day said his ex-wife had made threats toward him after their divorce. Vogel asked him to explain.

"This was in September when I had a discussion with her about child support and I wasn't able to work. She said if

I took Bradley away I would be dead in a week. I told her something like what do you mean or what are you talking about and she said she would have me killed. That was the jest (gist) of the conversation."

In prefacing his next question, Vogel said of Ray's murder, "It appears to be a set-up. The doctor himself was worried that someone was watching him, that he was being set-up; he was carrying on a relationship with Sheila, one and everybody saw it. Could there be any suspicion in your mind that Sheila would be capable of playing two ends against the middle and setting him up for something as serious as murder?"

Day replied, "I just wouldn't know. I used to think I knew her but she's surprised me some in the last few years with the things she's done. To me she is completely without principle. That's about it. I don't know what she's capable of doing."

Day repeated, "I don't know what she's capable of doing. I know she threatened me and so forth but I've never been afraid of her or her family either one, as far as my own personal safety, you know I'm not worried but as I say to me she is completely without principle and I don't know what in the hell she would do."

Borne asked, "Do you know of any reason she might have done something like this?"

"I have no way of knowing," Day replied, "I do understand she has a problem with alcohol, I don't know if that's true or not, I just hear this from common friends."

Vogel followed up with another question. "You wouldn't know if she had any friends or acquaintances that were part of a rough crowd that might be capable of following or engaging in any kind of conduct which would lead to something like what happened to Dr. Ray?"

"Not of my own knowledge, no," Day replied. "However, as I said, I've heard some things about her since our divorce, you know marijuana and (word left blank) and things like that. I don't know where she gets it or what she does but I have heard those things but I can't say of my own knowledge either one of them. But, you know those kinds of people generally follow that special kind of crowd."

Detective Borne had some more questions for Day to answer about Farmer. "What had you heard about him, besides him being involved?" Borne asked.

"Well, my kids didn't like him, which is enough for me," Day replied. "When children don't like somebody there's something wrong with 'em. Most everybody gets along with kids, they didn't like him. As I say, with his (former) wife, I talked with his wife on about three occasions since December and she's told me some things he has done and said and I understand that he beat her up, beat Sheila up several times while they were married which tells me his ex-wife Jane says his is violent, has a horrible temper, during the hearings for custody he would get so violent and horribly upset that he would just walk out of the courtroom, the judge would reprimand him because he can't control it."

Day further described what he knew of his former wife's second marriage, "Well they got married in December of '74. She took the kids out of the Lexington public schools and entered them in the London schools. They were there 27 days and she sent them back to Cumberland to live with her parents. She tried to keep this from me because I would call or Bradley would call up there and they wouldn't say if the kids were there, wouldn't let the kids talk to Bradley. When I questioned her about it later she said it wasn't safe for them there--what that means, whether it was F.P. or what."

Vogel asked, "I wonder if he was jealous and wanted her to reconcile and come back or would Jane know this?

Day replied, "She may. I know that he did want to patch things up. That was shortly before they separated but I don't know what their problems were but it was something to do with the kids, apparently he didn't want her kids, you know. It finally dawned on her that here's a guy she married to that doesn't want her children so she's not going to stay married to him and he apparently didn't want to change his mind so…"

"Who filed for the divorce?" Vogel asked. "Did Sheila?"

Day failed to answer the question directly. "I went, when I left here Friday, I went to London. This thing all sort of fell in, it spooked me, I thought man, maybe I can get tied up in this thing. I went to London and talked to the clerk at the court (house) there and asked surprised me that it was held in Harlan. So, apparently she had left F.P. and gone back to Cumberland and then filed for divorce and it was heard in Harlan so as I went through Harlan I just called my lawyer who is handling my custody case and told him to get those pleadings from the court."

Detectives Vogel and Borne also interviewed F. P. Farmer in London, the same day they questioned Tony Day. Vogel asked Farmer to tell them about his relationship with Sheila Day and how often he saw her after their divorce.

"I've been divorced from her since November of '75 and in the last six months I've had not too much contact with her," Farmer replied. "I've probably seen her two times, maybe three. I talk to her on the phone occasionally. As far as what kind of a person she is, she is a very fine person. I think she's a very kind person, nothing malicious about her. She wouldn't hurt anybody. She's a good person. We had a friendly divorce--we're still friends."

"What prompted the divorce or the split between you two?" Vogel asked.

"Well, see we were just married for less than a year," Farmer said. "She had children from a previous marriage. I had children from a previous marriage. We got married without a permanent home for the children. We both tried it and it just didn't work out. I can't put my finger on any one particular thing."

It was odd that Farmer stated there was no permanent home for both his and Day's children. When he asked for and was granted a divorce in 1972, from Jane E. Farmer, Laurel Circuit Court civil action # 910, the court awarded him the family's residence at 1308 Shady Lane, then valued at $65,000, in an upscale London development.

"When was the last time you had contact with her?" Vogel asked.

"I was in Lexington probably about I would say around three weeks ago or a month ago," Farmer replied. "I stopped in the office of one of my clients, it was insurance claim for a man here in Lexington and she is working in the same building, although I didn't know it at the time. But, when I left his office I had a note to stop by her office so I stopped by her office, it was three or four weeks ago."

Vogel's next question was more specific, "When was the last time you talked with her on the phone or had any conversation with her?"

"Well, she called me Friday night," Farmer said, "she called me Friday night."

"About what time?" the detective inquired.

"I would say about 11:00," the lawyer replied.

If Farmer's recollection was correct, Sheila Day called him within an hour after Ray was murdered.

"Can you tell me what extent your conversation was then?" Vogel asked.

"Yes," Farmer said. "She told me that well she was extremely upset. She told me that someone had just been shot out in front of her apartment and she told me she tried to reach her parents and couldn't contact them and that's really about all, that's basically was what she was telling me."

"Did she tell you who was shot?" Vogel asked.

The lawyer replied, "I don't know if she mentioned a name or if she just said a friend of hers, I'm not sure. She may have mentioned a name or she may have just said a friend of hers, I'm not completely positive about that."

Vogel asked Farmer if he had never met Elliott Ray. "No, I've never heard of him," the attorney replied, "I never heard his name mentioned, I don't remember whether she mentioned his name Friday nigh. I called her again Saturday morning just to see how she was and I'm sure she mentioned his name Saturday morning and she may have Friday night, I'm not sure but that's the first time I had ever heard the name."

Farmer told Vogel there was no chance of his reconciling with Day.

Under questioning by Borne, Farmer said he was at his mother's home in Hyden when Sheila Day called him after Ray was shot. "I understand," Farmer said, "she did try to call my home and my office and my sister in Corbin and she finally located me over there."

"Has Sheila ever talked to you or expressed any concern that someone might be following her or Dr. Ray or that there had been anonymous phone calls to her?" Vogel asked.

"As I told you before, I never, I had never heard the name Ray mentioned, Dr. Ray mentioned until Friday night or Saturday morning, whichever one it was she told me," Farmer said. "I didn't know who she was dating. We just didn't talk about that; we discussed other things so I had never heard the name mentioned. She had not mentioned anything about phone calls or threats or anything like that."

Why did Sheila Day call you Saturday morning, Borne asked Farmer?

"She didn't," he replied. "I called her Saturday morning. She was, when she called me on Friday she was extremely, she was very upset. As a matter of fact we got cut off. I was over in Hyden and that's a pretty bad telephone system and after we talked a few minutes we got cut off. She was extremely upset so I just called her back Saturday morning about 11:00 or so just to see how she was. As a matter of fact, her father was there at the time and he answered the phone."

Vogel asked Farmer for his telephone number, home address and his itinerary for Friday, April 1st, the day Ray was murdered.

"I was here in my office until about say about 4:00," Farmer explained. "At that time I went home, took my son to Corbin, Kentucky, to my sister's home to spend the weekend there and drove from there with my daughter to Hyden, Kentucky, and got there about 7:30 and was at Hyden until

Saturday about 5:00 or 6:00 in the afternoon and I left to come back to London."

"When you were in Hyden," Vogel asked, "did you go any place or with any friends?"

"I was in the presence of several people all the time," Farmer replied. "I stayed at my mother's apartment; she was having, she was opening a new store and the grand opening was Saturday and I was over there for that purpose. She was there and my sister was there and my daughter and myself. We went out to dinner at a motel there in Hyden and we saw a couple in the dining room of the motel."

The detectives asked Farmer when he would next be in Lexington. The attorney said he had depositions scheduled there for Monday, Tuesday and Wednesday of the next week. Vogel asked him if he could stop by the police department, then located on Forbes Road, on Monday when he finished his depositions.

Farmer said he would. Then, he asked, "Why would you like for me to come out there?"

"In case we would like to ask you more questions on interview," Vogel replied.

"Maybe get a statement down in writing," Borne added. "We are trying to get as many people eliminated as we can as soon as possible so we can narrow our investigation."

"He said I was some kind of suspect," Farmer protested.

"We don't want you to appear as a suspect," Vogel explained, "but I think you have to understand this is a crime we can't put the finger on any one person as yet and through process of elimination it is almost methodical sometimes."

"You being at your mother's would eliminate you there," Borne said.

After arrangements were made for the meeting at police headquarters, Farmer asked to make another statement about Sheila Day. "I want to emphasize this point," he said, "that in my opinion she is a very kind person. In my opinion she would not do anything to hurt anybody under any circumstances, there is nothing malicious about the girl. She wouldn't do anything to hurt anybody, friend or enemy."

While Vogel and Borne were in Tennessee and London, other detectives were conducting interviews in Nashville among the Rays' friends and acquaintances there.

Meanwhile, the medical examiner began the autopsy.

No Surprises

Twelve hours after Ray died in the Merrick Place parking lot, Dr. James T. McClellan, the 13th district state medical examiner, began the autopsy on the doctor's body at St. Joseph Hospital, in Lexington, where the body was taken from Whitehall Funeral Home, owned by coroner Chester Hager and his family.

Hager, similar to his actions in the Betty Gail Brown murder case, had already embalmed Ray's body before McClellan began the post-mortem examination. McClellan noted when he first saw Ray's body it was already embalmed and the external blood cleaned up.

Often funeral homes embalmed bodies, which were destined for other establishments, for the extra income. If a body was going to be shipped out of state, as Ray's was, then embalming was required but not necessarily before the autopsy was performed.

When asked about embalming practices in 1977 murder cases, the current 13th district state medical examiner, Dr. Gregory J. Davis, said, "Back in the '60s it (embalming bodies before autopsies) was a lot more common. It's a decision sometimes made if refrigeration was not available or if the body is going to be transported long distances." Davis added that embalming a body before an autopsy was not customarily done in 2007.

The autopsy was requested by Hager's deputy coroner, William P. McCarney. Present for the procedure were McCarney and detectives John W. Bizzack, William Read and Luther Cole.

There were no surprises about the cause and manner of Ray's death, four bullet wounds to the head fired at close range. However, there was a great deal of mystery about the

.45 caliber weapon the unknown assassin used to fire the shots.

"There are 7 wounds to the head," McClellan wrote in his autopsy report. "Four are determined to be wounds of entrance and three are determined to be wounds of exit. The Police present produced an automatic Colt pistol, Model 1911, Caliber .45 Government, which was found on the scene. They also found four cartridge cases and two spent bullets." As one bullet was still in Ray's skull, then one spent bullet was still missing.

The medical examiner found damage to Ray's brain so extensive that he was unable to determine the order in which the bullets were fired. "However," he said, "an attempt is made to trace the bullets through the head. For this purpose the bullets' tracts are numbered by myself and the police officers and are plotted and designated 1, 2, 3 and 4."

According to the autopsy drawings, bullet 1 entered Ray's left chin and exited the top of his head. The medical examiner said, "The bullet tract took a course through the bones of the face producing extensive fractures and entered the cranial cavity through the medial petrous portion of the left temporal bone." Bullet 2 entered Ray's right chin and exited above his left ear. This bullet, McClellan pointed out, took an upward course, straight toward the top of the head, passing through the brain.

Bullet 3, McClellan said, "Entered the head just anterior to the right ear, passed across the base of the skull where it passed somewhat diagonally through the bones of the base of the skull producing a considerable amount of bone to go through. This bullet then struck the side of the cranial cavity on the left and bounced back into the brain and was found lodged in the left occipital lobe of the brain. This bullet produced a tremendous amount of brain damage in the left occipital lobe."

McClellan was unable to find a clear tract for bullet 4, nor could he find a straight line between the entrance and exit wounds. "This bullet appears to have veered off after striking bone in the skull and exited from the right occipital region of the skull. It appears to have been deflected by bone of the calvarium or off the base of the brain."

The bullet the medical examiner removed from Ray's skull, designated as number 3, was considerably deformed, he said, but some barrel markings were present The bullet had an "M" marked on it and was turned over to detectives Bizzack and Read. McClellan said he found no deposit of powder residue in the wounds of entrance or along the bullet tracts within the skin.

McClellan dissected the chest and neck organs. "There was no bullet tract extending down into the neck," he found. "There is no blood in the neck region or around the thyroid gland." Of course, there was no blood, the coroner had already embalmed the body.

"After the neck was demonstrated to be free of bullet tracts or of blood," he continued, "there was no further entry into the chest cavity."

Ray's body was released to Tobias Funeral Home, in Dayton, for his family to make arrangements. Roberta Ray said Sheila Day did not attend the physician's funeral because Nancy Ray was there. She described her brother's widow, who apparently left the hospital for the services, as "Being sort of groggy" at the funeral.

The medical examiner ruled that Ray's death was caused by four bullets to the head. The weapon that fired those bullets, however, was not so easily identified. An attempt to file off the gun's serial numbers made identification even more difficult.

McClellan, in his autopsy notes, referred to the gun as a Colt .45 M, government issue. The Department of Treasury's Alcohol, Tobacco and Firearms (ATF) laboratory, where the weapon was sent for identification by detectives, described the gun as a .45 caliber automatic Ithaca M 1911 A1.

The pistol could easily have been a Colt, an Ithaca or a combination of both. The M 1911 A1 weapon was a modernized version of the side arm used extensively in World War I, according to *Hallock's .45 Auto Handbook.*

Before the start of World War II, the US Army, recognizing the need for an additional supply of the sidearm, decided to experiment by having the M 1911 produced by a company with no prior firearms experience. The Singer Sewing Machine Company, in Worchester, Massachusetts, produced only 500 of the side arms before the government moved production to the Ithaca Gun Company, in Ithaca, New York. The demand for the .45 caliber gun during the World War II was so great that Colt and Remington-Rand also produced the M 1911 A1. With three major arms companies producing the same model, many parts were interchangeable.

In order to trace the weapon, investigators needed the entire serial number. The ATF laboratory was able to determine only the last two digits, -----36.

Without disclosing her source, Roberta Ray related some interesting information about the weapon found at the site of her brother's shooting. She said the gun was reported stolen in Las Vegas, Nevada, a couple of months earlier, and that Charles Bowles was in Las Vegas at the time the gun was reported stolen.

Young Love Gone Bad

Tall and handsome with sandy hair, an insatiable intellect and an engaging personality, Elliott Ray grew up in the middle class Dayton, Ohio, suburb of Kettering, one of five children. Ray's father was a welder at Wright-Patterson Air Force Base, in Dayton.

A band scholarship brought the young man to Lexington to attend the University of Kentucky. "He was the first freshman honorsman in the UK marching band," Roberta Ray, his sister, said in an interview with the author. Also in the band was a vivacious, young brunette studying to be a nurse, Nancy Carolyn Bowles, of Russellville.

Teri Ray Bittner, the doctor's niece, remembered meeting Nancy Ray after she and her uncle were married. "She was the most beautiful woman I had ever seen at that time since I was only a child," Bittner recalled. In an interview with the author, Bittner said she was only nine when her uncle was killed and his death was a terrible blow. "I thought he was the greatest thing since sliced bread," she recalled.

Roberta Ray, from her interviews, made it plain that she absolutely adored her younger brother and made no mention of what turned out to be his darker side.

Elliott Ray and Nancy Bowles fell in love and eloped in April 1968. As events in their lives played out, the idea of having a wife working as a registered nurse to support him through medical school might have occurred to Ray.

When the couple told their families about their marriage, they experienced different reactions. Teri Bittner had fond memories of family holidays when her uncle and aunt came to Dayton. She lived in Milwaukee with her parents, he was Lawson Ray the doctor's brother, and her older sister Chris.

Roberta Ray indicated her family liked Nancy Bowles but said the bride's father threatened to shoot Elliott Ray upon hearing the news of their nuptials. Roberta Ray said, "At this point (being told about the marriage), Bowles took a weapon and threatened Elliott. Elliott took the weapon away. Bowles pulled another, which Elliott also took away. Soon after Bowles went to Elliott's apartment and threatened to kill Elliott. He stated he would do it or get someone else to do it for him. Indicating that he had the power and resources to get it done." This information, she told investigators, came from her brother.

Had Bowles been serious about shooting his new son-in-law, he would have had his choice of weapons from his own arsenal. He owned two .12 gauge, a .16 gauge, a single barrel and double barrel shotguns; .30-30 and .22 rifles and a snub-nosed .38 Italian pistol, according to the case file.

After his freshman year, Ray changed his major from music to pre-med and UK allowed him to keep his academic scholarship. Roberta Ray talked about her family's health problems, which could have influenced his decision to switch majors.

One of the five Ray siblings died of pneumonia at fifteen months and another succumbed to cancer just before her high school graduation. Roberta Ray was stricken with polio when she was seven but went on to become one of the first handicapped physical education teachers in Ohio. Their mother suffered from cancer.

Bowles, 63, according to the case file and media reports, was financially comfortable, if not wealthy. A native of Beattyville and a World War II veteran, he moved to Russellville where he owned movie theatres, a golf and country club and other property. He was a heavy-set man, accustomed to physical labor.

Bowles had another interesting vocation. He made book on basketball games. Bowles apparently made little effort to hide his bookmaking activity as several of his acquaintances knew about it.

Bowles' disapproval of their marriage was never clear. Was it Ray he objected to or any man who married his daughter? From all indications, he put his initial feelings aside and gave the couple with considerable financial assistance while both were in college.

Bowles told detective Bizzack he provided the couple with food, furniture and $160 per month while they were in school. He also told the detective that he used his influence to have Ray made a resident of the commonwealth. By doing that, Ray was eligible for the much lower in-state tuition rates at UK. "Happy Chandler (former governor A. B. Chandler) got the resident status done for us," he told Bizzack. "We bought him (Ray) some clothes and books. I didn't want anything back and nothing was said between us to pay me back."

Both the Rays worked while they were in college to supplement Bowles' stipend and assistance. One of the places they worked was the Barn Dinner Theatre, near Winchester. Elliott Ray worked there in the summer of 1972. Nancy Ray worked there for about a year as a hostess. After Nancy Ray graduated from the UK College of Nursing, she worked while her husband completed medical school.

On occasions, both families visited the couple in Lexington to attend football games and had dinner with them. For a while, everything appeared to be amicable.

Ray reportedly completed medical school with a 4.0 grade point average. In his last two years, he was president of the UK student chapter of the American Medical Association. "He did a lot to give leadership to his class and I really enjoyed working with him," Dr. Roy Jarecke, assistant dean for academics at the medical school, told the April 3, 1977, *Herald-Leader*.

A medical school graduate with Ray's academic credentials probably had his choice of prestigious institutions for his internship. Ray selected Vanderbilt University Medical School, in Nashville, Tennessee. "Vanderbilt did not have a general practice internship program at that time,"

Robert Ray said, "so they allowed Elliott to set up his own course of study."

In Nashville, while Elliott Ray worked the long arduous hours his internship required, Nancy Ray was employed as a registered nurse. Their marriage began experiencing problems and both of them engaged in extra-marital affairs, according to the case file.

Despite his rigorous schedule, which sometimes required him to be on duty for seventy-two-hour stretches, Ray apparently found time for the ladies. Detective Vogel, who investigated some of the Nashville leads in the murder case, said, "Ray lived a loose and fancy free life." Also while in Nashville, Ray became associated with a former Davidson County sheriff's deputy, Ed Smith, who had been dismissed from his job.

Nancy Ray was hardly languishing away while her husband was interning and pursuing other interests. According to media accounts, she was reported to be having an affair with Charles P. Hand, a Nashville real estate executive.

Paula Harrison, in her witness statement, told detective Robert S. Giles that she worked with Nancy Ray in Dr. Chase Allen's Lexington office for nearly three years while Ray was in medical school. "Nancy brought Charles Hand to the office to meet me around October 1976," Harrison said. "This is the only time I ever saw him. Mr. Hand would call me from time to time to ask about Nancy--usually where she was or where he could get in touch with her."

After finishing his internship at Vanderbilt in the summer of 1976, the Rays returned to Lexington. Since Harrison told detectives Nancy Ray introduced her to Charles Hand in October 1976, obviously her relationship with the real estate executive continued after the Rays left Nashville.

In October, Ray borrowed $36,600 from First Security Bank and Trust Company, in Lexington, to pay for leasing office space in Physicians' Mall at 1725 Harrodsburg Road. Physicians' Mall, according to the case file, was built by a partnership of some of Lexington most prominent physicians and businessmen: Drs. James B. Holloway, R. Herman Playforth, Raleigh R. Archer, Edwin J. Nighbert and Richard M. French and George B. Carey and Robert T. Mays.

A July 19, 1976, cancelled check, written for $3,000 in cash, indicated that Ray was practicing at the same address three months before he signed the lease.

Documents in the case file indicated his income for August and September 1976, was $1,405. However, his income rapidly improved.

Roberta Ray, in her witness statement, recalled a conversation with her brother at an October open house event, probably the formal opening of his office. She said her brother told her Charles Bowles was back in his old form threatening to kill him. "Elliott also indicated that his phone was tapped and he was being followed," she recalled. "His reasoning for that assumption came from his wife and his father-in-law knowing in detail his movements and his phone calls."

Normally, a wife would know about her husband's schedule but the Rays' marriage, by this time, was now far removed from normality.

Teri Bittner, said she came to Lexington with her family for a visit shortly before her uncle was killed but did not see Nancy Ray.

The Rays moved into an apartment in Harrodsburg Square, which was just behind his new offices. From that point, their married life appeared to go from bad to worse. Nancy Ray, according to the case file, had taken an overdose of drugs on three occasions in the few months they lived there.

Not only was their relationship strained but it was tempestuous and violent. Ray told one of his patients that his wife had shot at him. When detectives searched their apartment, after his murder, they found a bullet hole in the kitchen ceiling.

Either Lexington at that time had a shortage of general practitioners, Ray was exceptional at attracting patients or he received numerous referrals from other physicians. In the first full month, November, in his new practice, Ray generated an income of $10,482, according to the case file. By the middle of December, his office bank account had a balance of $59,000.

At the time of his death, having been in practice only five months, Ray had over 1,000 patients, according to First Security loan officer Ben. J. Elkins' business report in the case file. Ray's projected income statement, also in the case file, had his annual income reaching $75,000 by June 1977, and a conservative $125,000 two years later. The statement projected his office expenses, without insurance, would only increase from $50,950 to $61,150 during that period.

In addition to his other insurance, Ray had a life insurance policy with Minnesota Mutual Life. "Elliott had a large life insurance police and his wife was the beneficiary," Roberta Ray said. He had been advised to change the beneficiary after filing for divorce, she added, but had not done so at the time of his death.

In her statement to detectives, Roberta Ray recalled, "Approximately 1-1-77 to approximately 2-1-77, Elliott was having problems concerning a restraining order against Charles Bowles. Bowles was again threatening to kill Elliott or to have one of his friends do it for him. It was during this period of time that a soldier of fortune type friend of Elliott's was being used by Elliott in the fashion of a bodyguard. He (her brother) had also begun to drive an auto owned by his girl friend Sheila due to his auto having become known."

There was no mention of a restraining order in either Ray's murder case file or in court case file when Bowles was indicted and charged with the doctor's murder. Nor was there any mention of a bodyguard.

On January 26, 1977, Nancy C. Ray signed, as an individual guarantee, for a six- month loan for Ray from First Security National Bank and Trust Company for $89,000. Four days later, Nancy Ray was again in the hospital for an overdose and her parents came to Lexington. Bowles, in his witness statement, said his wife and Ray had an argument at the hospital over the pills Nancy Ray took. "My wife was raising cain about the pills," he said, "and Ray told her to back out of his life." Bowles said he returned to Russellville on January 31.

The source of the pills Bowles referred to raised a number of questions. Who prescribed the pills for Nancy Ray? Was it Ray or another physician? Did she have a physical or mental problem requiring such medication? Did Ray's accumulation of more than 1,000 patients in less than five months in practice have anything thing to do with the manner in which he dispensed prescriptions?

Former detective Philip Vogel discounted the prescription drug angle. "I never really thought he'd trade his Vanderbilt medical degree for a tag of a dope dealer," he said. "After all, he had everything going his way."

Out of further concern for their daughter, the Bowles returned to Lexington on February 3. Carolyn Bowles returned to Russellville on February 11. "On the 12th we learned about the divorce papers," Charles Bowles said, "and Nancy and I went back to Russellville."

Ray, represented by Walter Tackett who was later a Fayette Circuit judge, filed for dissolution of his marriage to Nancy Carolyn Ray on February 11, 1977, less than two weeks after she signed documents for the $89,000 loan for the doctor.

After signing the divorce documents, Ray and Sheila Day left Lexington and spent the weekend in Dayton with his family, his sister said. "At that time Mr. Bowles was still issuing death threats to Elliott," Roberta Ray recalled.

From all indications, Nancy Ray was distraught over the divorce. Although her father was in Lexington with her, she called Robert F. Potts, with whom she and Ray had worked at the Barn Dinner Theatre, to come over to her apartment because she needed somebody to talk with about her husband.

"I hadn't seen Nancy for close to two years and I really didn't know what was going on with her and Elliott," Potts said in his witness statement. "She related to me that Elliott was leaving her and that she was so upset she didn't know what to do. She felt heart broke over the thought of losing him and was upset and crying very much. She tried to relate some events of her past year. She talked of her attempted suicide(s) and her father was also upset, due, I believe to the fact that Nancy was upset."

"They were also hurt by the fact, they stated, that Nancy had worked so hard to get Elliott through school and now that he was a doctor he didn't want her any more," Potts continued. "Nancy's father gave me the impression of a protective father of his daughter and was also upset at the prospect of Elliott kicking her out." Potts added that he got the impression that Bowles would do whatever he could to protect his daughter from any unnecessary hurt.

Nancy Ray and her father returned to Russellville on March 12. Potts said Nancy Ray called him three times from Russellville to see if he had heard anything about the divorce. He added that she was "Sobbing, etc., feeling down about herself and the divorce, like she was a loser and had lost her husband."

On March 22, Ray's office filed a report that his wallet and credit card had been lost. The document stated he had no idea of where he lost his wallet. An entry on the report read, "Wife is making numerous purchases." Another entry said the loss was discovered "Week of 12th of Feb." That date coincided with his filing for divorce from his wife.

Whether Nancy Ray was charging items on her husband's credit card was questionable since she had been in and out of the hospital since the end of January and had gone to Russellville with her parents on February 12. Neither was it clear when she returned to Lexington.

Bowles stated, "I wasn't back in Lexington again until the 24th of March. The 26th Nancy was put in the hospital. On the 25th we were in court (apparently referring to the divorce hearing). On the 26th of March, I went back to Russellville. My wife has been here ever since."

The case file indicated that Sheila Day was not the only woman the physician was seeing while he was married to Nancy Ray. In the case file index to witness statements, Jeanne Howard was listed as, "Dr. Ray's employee (close)." The same document stated that Margaret Faye Holtzclaw, one of Ray's patients, dated the doctor.

In her April 2, witness statement, Holtzclaw said, "I remember on several occasions Elliott told me that I just could not believe what was involved with the situation with his wife. Then around the first or second Wednesday in February, the 7th or 14th, he told me that his wife had made several threats to kill him. Then he went on to say that I wouldn't believe this, but there were people out there carrying gun(s)."

Holtzclaw added, "He went on to say that it was really too involved to explain and told me that he did not want to get me involved in it for my own safety. He also said that she was really crazy, meaning his wife."

Elliott Ray also discussed his personal problems with another patient, Randy Burke, a former Lexington police motorcycle officer. Burke, in his witness statement, said, Ray's lawyer, Walter Tackett, called him when the doctor was in his law office to draw up the divorce papers. "He said he (Ray) and his wife were separating and that he (Ray) was very afraid of his father-in-law," Burke recalled. "He (Tackett) said he was going to give Dr. Ray all 3 of my telephone numbers. The reason was that he felt I could easily contact the police for him."

Burke, who had left the police force had a nightclub and later a tool business, said, "Around the middle of November or the 1st of December, I went to see Dr. Ray for an appointment. He said, 'I guess Walter told you most all about my problems.' He wanted to know the law on buying a gun and the procedure on carrying a gun. I told him to call the police and he said it wouldn't do any good because no one had done anything yet. I think it was this visit that he said his father-in-law was crazy and didn't care. He said he wanted the gun for protection. He never made a real threat but I knew in my mind why he wanted it. He told me he would talk to me later."

Burke said Ray came to see him at his club around Christmas but they did not have time to talk.

"I next saw him for an appointment on January 18, 1977," the former policeman said. "We talked for a minute and he said nothing had changed with his personal problems but that he still wanted to get with me and talk." Burke was unable to reach Ray until more than two weeks later. "At this time," he recalled, "he said he though he had it worked out and everything was ok. That was the last conversation I had with him."

Burke's last conversation with Ray occurred near the time the physician filed for divorce from his wife. During the second week in February, Ray also made a mysterious trip back to Nashville.

Geraldine Trinler, of Lexington, was identified in the case file as a friend of both Ray and Sheila Day's. She told detectives how upset Day was at that time. "She told me that Elliott had gone to Nashville to find out if there was a contract on him by his father-in-law," Trinler told detectives. "If there was (he was going) to try and get one against his father-in-law to stop him. Elliott called while I was there (in Day's apartment), from Bowling Green, and said he was coming home. Sheila told him we were going to Nellie Kelley's and for him to meet us (there) when he got home."

Trinler said Ray met them three hours later at the popular restaurant, which was located across the street from Merrick Place. According to her statement, Trinler told Ray she felt like someone had been watching them earlier. "I felt like I know what he looked like, due to the mental picture I developed of him," she said.

"Elliott then asked, 'did he have a baseball cap on?'"

"I said no," Trinler recalled.

Charles Bowles often wore a baseball-type cap.

Ray's trip to Nashville raised a number of questions. If he was truly being followed and in fear for his life, why did he make such a trip alone? How did Ray know there was a contract put out on his life by Bowles? Who did he really see in Nashville? Did Ray visit Ed Smith, the former deputy sheriff, while he was in Nashville?

On February 8, Ray withdrew $4,000 from his First Security office bank account. A copy of the cancelled check was in the case file. The check memo read, "Transfer." A copy of a July 19, 1976, check withdrawing $3,000 from his office account was also in the file and the accompanying check memo also read, "Transfer." Copies of those checks indicated that detectives had an interest in where that cash went especially since his income for the entire month of February 1977, was only $8,576.

The physician's brother, Lawson O. Ray, told investigators his most recent telephone conversation with his sibling was in January to see how things were going, "He said things were going fine if he could wear a bullet proof vest."

"I said, 'is it that rough?'"

"He said, 'yeah, Charlie's gotten mad.'"

"I asked how he knew Charlie was that mad and he said, 'I've been shot at twice.'"

Lawson Ray asked his brother how he was protecting himself? "He was driving friends' cars, never staying at the same place more than twice and not letting anyone know where he was going," Lawson Ray said his brother told him. "Then he said his phone was tapped and he said a private detective was working on seeing who it was."

Elliott Ray was a very intelligent young physician who appeared to have trouble keeping his mouth closed about his personal life. He seemed to be headed toward a professionally satisfying and financially secure future, which he apparently had no intentions of sharing with his wife. Divorce would free him to marry again but he had another more pressing problem.

Somebody was supposedly threatening to kill him. The most likely suspect appeared to be his father-in-law.

The Father-in-law and His Alibi

Charles G. Bowles' biggest problem in this case was shooting off his mouth to various people about killing Ray. However, those statements did not prove he shot Elliott Ray.

Bowles' inability to decide, in his various witness statements, whether or not he had ever threatened Ray's life immediately made him a most attractive suspect.

However, it also appeared that he was at his home in Russellville at the time Ray was shot in Merrick Place.

In detective John Bizzack's interview with Bowles on Sunday, April 3, Ray's father-in-law recounted his activities on the day Ray was shot, Friday, April 1. Those statements appeared to place him at his home, 378 West 7th Street in Russellville, Kentucky, at the time of the shooting.

Bowles came to Lexington after being called at his home in Russellville by a detective around 1:15 a.m., April 2, with the news of Ray's death and after also speaking with his wife Carolyn Bowles, who was staying at their daughter's apartment on Harrodsburg Road while Nancy Ray was in the hospital.

Russellville was in the Central Standard Time (CST) zone; while Lexington, being in the Eastern Standard Time (EST) zone, was an hour faster. The time difference was critical in determining if Charles Bowles was involved in his son-in-law's murder as was the 200-mile distance between Russellville and Lexington.

Bowles related his movements and the people he interacted with on Friday, April 1, in his witness statement. Presumably, detectives interviewed these witnesses but their statements were not in the case file.

Bowles said, that after running some errands, he mowed the grass at his golf course until 3:00 p.m. (CST). He then went to Ralph Morgan's restaurant where he ate some cold chicken and left there around 4:00 or 5:00 p.m. While at the restaurant, Bowles got a call from a man who had upholstered the front seat of his car and arranged to meet him at his home to pay him for his work.

"I met Bill at my house and paid him $45.00," Bowled recalled. "I watched the news, fixed a fire, it was cool and my wife called about then. I told her if it rained Saturday, I'd come on to Lexington. I watched To Tell The Truth and Redd Foxx. In the program there was a woman dressed up like a man. You know how Redd Foxx is. I was home the rest of the night. No one came by to see me and I didn't receive any telephone calls. About 1:15 or 1:30 a.m., Russellville time, I got a call from my wife and a detective about Elliott."

"What did you do after the call?" Bizzack asked.

"I talked to one of the detectives who was with my wife," Bowles replied. "He asked me to come up there and I told him I'd come as fast as I could. It's about a four-hour drive. It's two hundred miles."

Remember, Summersett said a half hour lapsed between the time he found Ray's body, called authorities and when they arrived at the scene because of the shift change.

Consequently, Ray was most likely shot at 10:00 p.m., EST or 9:00 p.m., CST. If Carolyn Bowles' April 1 telephone call to her husband was between 6:00-7:00 p.m., CST, and Ray was shot at 9:00 p.m., CST, it was unlikely that Bowles drove the 200 miles to Lexington, negotiated his way through an unfamiliar development, and shot his son-in-law and returned to Russellville in time to answer the detective's early morning telephone call.

That is not to say that he did not hire someone else to shoot the doctor.

Bowles appeared to be authorities' prime, perhaps only, suspect.

"Did you ever threaten Ray's life?" Bizzack asked him in his initial witness statement.

Bowles replied, "Sir, I sure never did. I never had an argument with him, no way shape or fashion. My wife argued with him over them pills, but I made her hush. He never threatened me either. Me and Elliott never had a word no way."

Bowles' waffling over whether or not he threatened to shoot his son-in-law was best explained in a memo from his attorney, Mike Moloney, to commonwealth attorney Larry Roberts. "Mr. Bowles initially stated after being advised that he was a suspect in the murder of Elliott Ray," Moloney wrote, "that he had in fact made threats toward Ray in the past. He then changed that statement to the effect that he had never made any threats toward Ray and then changed the statement again to the effect that he had made threats toward Ray. He then stated that he had not shot anyone, but that a man does get mad at some things that go on concerning his child."

Lawson Ray, the doctor's brother, also had some revealing information about Charles Bowles. In his April 3 statement to detectives in Kettering, Ohio, Lawson Ray talked about Bowles and his brother getting into a fight several years earlier. "I don't know what it was over," he told detectives.

"There was also the time," he continued, "that Charlie's wife left him and Elliott said he would protect her and Nancy. He told him if he got caught, Elliott would shoot him. I offered to have Elliott send them to our house in Wisconsin."

"Do you know why Charlie's wife left him?" Lawson Ray was asked by detectives.

"No, I don't," he replied. "Elliott told me that it had been a knock down, drag out fight and that Charlie had beat her."

Detectives had little trouble finding people, outside the family, who heard Bowles threaten his son-in-law. John Allen Martin, of Russellville, told detective Bizzack that he and Ike Duncan, also of Russellville, ran into Bowles in the middle of March at the state basketball tournament, where he was making book on the games.

Martin said Bowles asked him, "Did you know that son of a bitch left my daughter?"

"I replied no," Martin said, "that the last time I saw them was at a U.K. football game back in the fall and I though they were doing all right."

According to Martin, Bowles replied, "Elliott has been screwing my daughter for eight years and he screwed me out of paying for his medical education and now that he's hung out his shingle, he's left my daughter for another woman who's a divorcee with two children. I'm going to kill the son-of-a-bitch and you can bet that within a year he will be looking up at daisies instead of looking down at them."

Martin said he just laughed and said, "Charlie you ain't going to do anything. He replied back 'if I don't kill him, I've enough connections to have his head blown off for five hundred dollars.'" Martin said he had known Bowles practically all his life and that, while he had a reputation of drunk and erratic behavior, he had stopped drinking three years earlier.

The case file contained a similar statement from Woodrow P. Sosh, no address listed, about Bowles' earlier threats toward Ray but was more specific about the marriage break-up. Sosh said that in February Bowles told him about his daughter taking an overdose of drugs in an attempt to take her own life. "He (Bowles) stated that Ray had come in one day and told Nancy that he didn't love her any more and to get out," Sosh said. "He stated, that upon learning all of this, that he and his wife attempted to talk to Ray but that all Ray would tell them was that he didn't love Nancy any more.

During this conversation, Bowles told Sosh that he had warned Ray, "If anything happens to Nancy, I will get you." Bowles then told Sosh, "I'll kill him."

After his April 3 interview with detective Bizzack, Bowles was interrogated again on April 16, but was not arrested for fourteen weeks.

Ray's murder case hit two snags. First, investigators had the father-in-law's motive but placing Bowles in

Merrick Place on April 1 or proving he hired someone to kill Ray was increasingly difficult. Second, another case detective Bizzack was working at the same time began to intersect with Ray's murder investigation.

Cases Intersect

Detective Bizzack, at the time of Ray's murder, was also working a missing person's case, the investigation of which eventually connected some former officers from the Division of Police's narcotics unit to a nation-wide drug and weapons smuggling racket. The missing person case became such a high-profile case that it might have diverted investigators' attention from the Ray murder.

Initially, detectives appeared to be spending an enormous amount of time and effort on solving Ray's murder.

On May 9, Sgt. David Childre was quoted in the Lexington newspaper as describing the Ray case, "I think we're making progress. We wouldn't be expending that much time and that many resources if we weren't." As many as twenty-five detectives were reported to be working on the Ray murder case. At the same time, detectives asked the public to call them if they had noticed a car loitering near or speeding away from Merrick Place the night Ray was shot.

Detective Bizzack, on June 29, told the Lexington newspaper that investigators had suspects and were certain more than one person was involved. "The more time that has gone by the more information that has become available," he was quoted as saying. "We are not going to limit our opportunities to be thorough by making an arrest just to clear the investigation."

Yet, in the end that was exactly what happened.

The Melanie Flynn missing person case begun to dominate the headlines and the names of prominent local people cropped up in connection with the case. It appeared Bizzack and his superiors stumbled all over themselves to close the Flynn case as soon as possible. Officers, now retired, said it was common department practice at that time to clear murder and homicide investigations quickly to improve their statistics on closed cases.

If that was the case, the Ray murder proved to be the exception.

Ray's murder occurred two months after Kentucky High School Athletics Association secretary, Melanie Flynn, the beautiful 24-year-old daughter of former state legislator Robert Flynn and sister of Major League Baseball player Doug Flynn, disappeared under mysterious circumstances.

The scandal Flynn's disappearance created involved prominent businessmen, former lawmen and sports and political figures in Kentucky and across the nation. The saga was chronicled in Sally Denton's 1990 book, *The Bluegrass Conspiracy, An Inside Story of Power, Greed, Drugs and Murder.*

Flynn, something of a gadfly who tried a wide range of careers from being a jockey to singing to working as a secretary, was closely involved with two Lexington narcotic detectives who had ties to the drug trade: William T. Canan, a Mt. Sterling native known to use forceful intimidation in his work and Andrew Thornton, from a prominent Bourbon County Thoroughbred family, who saw himself as an exceptional survivalist. Their persona of dashing men about town appealed to Flynn, Denton wrote.

Neither of the men lasted long on the police force after Flynn disappeared. Thornton resigned from the Division of Police a few months after Flynn was reported missing and Canan was fired by the Lexington Fayette Urban County Government Council in 1979, for insubordination. He attempted, in vain, through the courts to get his job back for several years.

Denton described the two men's lifestyle, in which Melanie Flynn apparently participated before her disappearance. "Canan and Thornton had gained a reputation for this fast-paced life that included the best parties and nightclubs, flashy rolls of hundred-dollar bills, guns discretely tucked into their ankle and shoulder holsters and flashy cars with high-tech audio equipment--all, ostensibly, in the name of the war on drugs," she wrote.

Flynn left her office at 5:00 p.m., on the evening of January 26, 1977, to keep an appointment with her psychiatrist and have dinner with her parents. The petite, 5'1", woman, with light brown hair and brown eyes, failed to keep either appointment and was never seen again.

Two days later, her boss called Robert Flynn to find out why his daughter had not been at work for past two days. Flynn called Canan, a married detective who had been seeing his daughter, and asked for assistance.

From all indications, Canan made little effort to locate the missing woman. *Kentucky Post* reporter Tom Scheffey described Flynn and Canan as a "Striking pair. He with his tree trunk physique and bushy red top; she an aggressive, vivacious little thing who knew just how to use her sexy good looks to get into a fellow's mind." Flynn told friends they were engaged; Canan said she was just his snitch.

Bizzack, Denton said, assured the Flynn family everything that could be done, would be done to find their daughter. "The investigation was in the most competent hands with the Lexington police and they would pursue every lead Bizzack assured the Flynns," she wrote.

On February 6, Flynn's car was found parked behind an apartment building in an area of north Lexington known for drug dealing. Her red leather coat and unpacked suitcase, from a trip to Louisville the previous weekend, were still in the car, according to the Lexington newspaper. However, her keys and purse were missing.

Other than the proximity of time, the Ray and Flynn investigations normally would have had little in common. One was a homicide and the other a missing person case. However, the two cases became inexorably intertwined though Bizzack, who appeared to be the lead detective on both.

Speculation that Bizzack attempted to cut short the Flynn investigation appeared to be valid. There was always an inference that there were those within the Division of Police who attempted to cover up information linking Flynn's disappearance to the Canan-Thornton crowd, which had connections to a nation-wide stolen weapons and illegal drug ring called, The Company.

One of those inferences came from her brother. The Lexington newspaper quoted her brother Doug Flynn as saying, "It looks like somebody was trying to cover up something down at the police department; somebody down there got caught."

Former KSP Sgt. Ralph Ross, the primary source in Denton's book, had another theory. He told the Lexington newspaper that Lexington police officers did not pursue Flynn's disappearance because they were afraid of Canan and Thornton. ""He said Lexington police used to call him to work cases that targeted Canan and Thornton because of that fear," he was quoted as saying. Ross said Canan and Thornton emerged as the two chief suspects (in Flynn's disappearance) in reports that he had seen. Ross was arrested on a wire-tapping charge and had to resign from the KSP. He was later indicted but served no prison time.

Two weeks before Ray was shot and two and a half months after Flynn disappeared, a Danville teacher was in Florida with students on spring break and they met a woman who introduced herself as Melanie Flynn. John Thompson, the teacher, asked her if she knew his aunt and uncle, Mildred and John Carr, in Lexington? She said she did.

Thompson called his aunt, who then called Ella Flynn. Mrs. Flynn quickly relayed the message to Bizzack. *Kentucky* Post reporter Tom Scheffey wrote, "Bizzack immediately flew down to Florida. In two days of investigation Bizzack saw enough people who believed they'd seen Melanie to close the case. But, he didn't see Melanie."

Bizzack returned to Lexington and, according to Scheffey and other media accounts, announced that Melanie Flynn was alive and well in Florida. He was quoted as saying, "The possibility of foul play as being a part of her disappearance has been eliminated and due to that elimination the investigation has ceased."

Case closed.

Without having seen Melanie Flynn, Scheffey wrote, Bizzack insisted that the missing person case was closed.

Ross, then the head of the KSP's Organized Crime and Intelligence Section, decided to double check on Bizzack's efforts in locating Melanie Flynn since he had some problems working with him on other cases, according to Denton. Ross, Denton wrote, contacted a Federal Bureau of Investigation agent he knew in Florida and provided him with pertinent information about Flynn and Bizzack's statements concerning the case. According to Denton, the FBI agent told Ross, after conducting his own investigation, the woman in question was not Melanie Flynn.

In the middle of April, while still investigating the Ray murder, Bizzack made another trip to Florida concerning the Melanie Flynn case. This time he was accompanied by detective Al Borne, who was also working on the Ray homicide.

According to media accounts, they interviewed several people who said they saw someone who looked like photographs of Flynn, distributed flyers and contacted other police departments.

Apparently, Bizzack was not questioned by the media about why he was yet again in Florida, looking for the Flynn, when he had already announced the her missing person case was closed.

Meanwhile, the Ray murder also investigation continued with gaps here and there where the Flynn case appeared to take over. Detective Bizzack appeared to have his hands full with both investigations.

Bizzack came from wealth and political power. His family owned and operated Bizzack Brothers Construction Company, in Frankfort, which for decades was the highway contractor of choice for state road contracts. But, he chose to go into police work.

On May 9, according to the Lexington newspaper, Nashvillians Charles P. Hand and Ed Smith testified before a Fayette County grand jury in connection with Ray's murder. The article said neither man was a suspect in the homicide. Sgt. Drexel Neal was quoted as saying authorities were using the grand jury as an investigative tool at that time and they were not seeking indictments. "Their appearance before the grand jury was to verify their previous statements," Neal said.

Neither Hand's nor Smith's statements were in Ray's case file nor Bowles' court case file.

Bizzack was in Russellville on May 11, according to the case file, purchasing brown cotton gloves, and yellow and orange Playtex gloves from Higgins Grocery Store presumably attempting to match the gloves left at the murder scene in an effort to obtain evidence against Bowles.

By June 29, the *Lexington Leader* reported that more than one suspect was involved in Ray's murder but the investigation appeared to be at a standstill. Bizzack was quoted as saying that time was in the police department's favor; the more time passed, the more information authorities had been able to gather.

Through the summer of 1977, the Ray and Flynn families complained about the investigators' progress in both cases.

Roberta Ray, in an October 2006, said she thought her brother not being a Lexington native was a factor in investigators' failure to apprehend his killer. "It was like he wasn't from Lexington and therefore they (investigators) didn't consider it important. Our conversations with the police department indicated they just didn't care; told us not to come to Lexington." Roberta Ray did not recall the names of those in the department her family talked to about the case.

Unlike Ray's family, Ella Richey Flynn had the political connections to call attention to the case of her missing daughter. He husband was a former legislator with ties to governors and was a Lexington Fayette Urban County

Government council member. Those connections provided her some political clout but it was evidently not enough to push authorities to delve any deeper into her daughter's disappearance.

In August there was action in both cases. A Fayette County grand jury on August 2, after hearing witness testimony from Bizzack, Charles Hand, Ed Smith, Carolyn Bowles and Charles Bowles, indicted Bowles. The True Bill stated that Bowles, "And other persons whose identity is unknown to the Grand Jury murdered Dr. Elliott Ray by shooting him."

There was no problem impaneling a Fayette County grand jury to investigate and indict Bowles for Ray's murder, despite the fact detectives were unable to place him in Lexington at the time of the homicide. There were, apparently, a great many problems with impaneling a grand jury to investigate the case of the missing Melanie Flynn, who was last seen on Cooper Drive in Lexington the previous January.

As soon as the bench warrant for Bowles had been signed by Fayette Circuit Court judge N. Mitchell Meade, according to the arrest history, detectives Bizzack and Read traveled to Russellville and met KSP detective Wendall Jackson who served the warrant on Bowles. "After he was processed at the Russellville Police Department," the document continued, "we transported him back to Lexington where he was booked in the Fayette County jail under a $100,000 bond. The bond was reduced on 8-3-77 to $50,000 and Bowles was released until trial date."

Bowles' attorney was Mike Moloney, whose law firm was also representing his daughter in the divorce proceedings instituted by Ray, according to the August 3 *Lexington Leader*. The newspaper quoted Moloney as saying Bowles' bail would be posted that day. He pleaded not guilty at his arraignment the same day.

There was no problem finding bail money. Bowles' sister and brother-in-law, Millard and Myrtle Hacker, of Manchester, put up a house, lots, warehouse, a car wash and stocks, which Clay County property evaluation administrator, James A. Sizemore, attested to be worth $308,440 in court documents. It was strange that Bowles turned to his family to raise bail money when he owned considerable property in Russellville.

While Lexington detectives were in Russellville, the KSP executed a warrant and searched Bowles' home at 387 West 7th Street. They collected hairs from six dogs and confiscated two screwdrivers belonging to Bowles as well as clothing, records and books.

Bowles was given a Harrison-Gilroy gunpowder residue test to determine if he had recently fired a weapon but no date was found in the case file indicating when the test was conducted. However, according to a Division of Police's request to the KSP crime laboratory, the date evidence was submitted for the Harrison-Gilroy test was May 19, more than six weeks after Ray's murder.

Commonwealth attorney Larry Roberts told *Herald* reporter Scott Smith that the real question was whether or not Bowles fired the gun that killed Ray. Smith wrote that scientific tests performed on Bowles' clothing were inconclusive as to whether of not he fired the shots that killed Ray. Bowles, according to the case file, was accustomed to carry loose bullets in his pockets.

Smith quoted Roberts as saying, "We found a positive reaction during a Harrison-Gilroy test which was taken to determine if he had fired a weapon. However, the test only showed there were deposits of lead found on his clothing. There was no barium."

Meanwhile, bombshells were exploding in the Flynn case.

On August 3, the *Kentucky Post* began a series of four in-depth articles on Melanie Flynn's disappearance. Reporter Tom Scheffey's page one story was headlined, "Curious case of the missing playgirl, Kentucky's greatest dead-or-alive mystery grows more baffling." Scheffey interviewed Canan, Bizzack, and a vast number of friends, associates and acquaintances of Flynn's in a less than complimentary account of the detectives' investigation of the missing woman.

On August 12, a purse, similar to one owned by Melanie Flynn, was found in the Kentucky River, near Camp Nelson in Jessamine County, south of Lexington. Canan, Thornton and former policeman Danny Murphy reportedly owned land along the bank of the river where the purse was found.

Inside the purse was a tube of lipstick, a perfume atomizer and two containers for prescription medicine. Ella Flynn identified one of the medication containers as being her daughter's prescription antihistamine. The KSP crime laboratory confirmed Mrs. Flynn's identification of the medication.

Denton told an interesting story in her book about the Jessamine County farm reportedly owned by Canan, Thornton and Murphy and their connections to detective Bizzack. Denton wrote that the Division of Police refused KSP Sgt. Ross and his team access to certain Fayette County drug cases, particularly those relating to former detectives Thornton and Canan. The farm the trio apparently owned in Jessamine County was fair game to the State Police since it was outside Lexington police's jurisdiction.

Sgt. Ross, according to Denton, knew about paramilitary maneuvers and other strange events taking place on the farm and sent a KSP plane to fly aerial surveillance over the property. Denton wrote, "Bizzack told Ralph he was conveying a message from the owners of the property, Drew Thornton, Bill Canan and Danny Murphy, if the State Police plane (again) flew over the Triad (the farm's name) the plane would be shot down."

Rumors persisted that Melanie Flynn might have been buried on that farm or her body had been tossed in the river.

In late August, according to the Lexington newspaper, Bizzack and detective Al Borne, who was also working on the Ray murder, made yet another trip to Florida seeking information on the missing Flynn, a case Bizzack had proclaimed closed months earlier.

Detective Bizzack's numerous declarations that Melanie Flynn was alive and well in Florida and his continual assertions that the missing person case was closed, were denied by his superior.

Lexington police chief Nolen Freeman, in August, issued a statement to the Lexington media stressing that the investigation into Melanie Flynn's disappearance was not closed.

Both the Ray murder and the Flynn missing person cases were in turmoil. Charles Bowles, who apparently was not in Lexington at the time of the shooting, had been indicted and arrested for Ray's murder. Flynn's alleged abductors, or murders, appeared to be invisible as well as beyond the law.

A Not So Surprisingly Ending

Although detectives had witness statements from a number of people that Charles G. Bowles had publicly threatened to kill his son-in-law, Elliott Ray, they were unable to place him in Lexington at the time the doctor was shot.

In preparation for Bowles' murder trial, the commonwealth attorney, on August 23, began asking for money to fly a prosecution witness to Lexington from Rhodesia for the trial. Commonwealth attorney Larry Roberts was a state official preparing to try a state case, yet he sent one of his detectives, Jim Horine, to ask the Urban County Council for $1,700 for airfare for the witness, according to the Lexington newspaper. Horine was quoted as saying, "We simply have to have him to try the case."

Horine told the Council the man was an engineer and he was living in Lexington at the time of the murder. Was this the mysterious Gerald Helton? The council approved the expenditure with the hopes of getting a refund from the state at some future date.

Whether the witness flew back to Lexington was not known, as Bowles was never tried for the murder of his son-in-law.

On September 15, according to court documents, commonwealth attorney Roberts filed a motion in Fayette Circuit Court asking that the indictment against Charles G. Bowles be dismissed for lack of evidence.

It might be construed that Bowles' arrest and indictment had served their intended purpose, drawing the public and media's attention toward the Ray case and away from the events occurring in Melanie Flynn case.

In his Motion to Dismiss, Roberts listed these reasons: scientific tests were inconclusive; based on those results, there was a high probability a jury trial would result in a deadlock or a not guilty verdict; by dismissing the charges before the trial, the commonwealth could at a later day, if more evidence was found, secure another indictment; the case would last two weeks, and the expenses for bringing witnesses from out of state and out of the country would be considerable.

"This case is not over," Roberts was quoted as saying. "I have been assured that the police will continue their efforts to follow up every angle."

A separate court order directed that all items given to or seized by the Division of Police be returned to Charles Bowles. The document required Bowles' signature on an attested copy of the court order that his property had been returned.

Bowles' attorney, Mike Moloney, commended Roberts on his decision to dismiss the charges against his client. *Herald* reporter Scott Smith quoted Moloney as saying, "They had no case whatsoever. Russellville city police knew Bowles was in Russellville the day of the shooting. They told metro police just that. Apparently they (detectives) never got around to following it up."

His failure to solve the Ray murder and Melanie Flynn missing person cases apparently did not hurt Bizzack's career. According to Lexington newspaper articles, he rose from detective in 1980 to captain by 1989. He retired after twenty-five years with the Division of Police and, after making sizable contributions to the campaigns of two governors, Democrat Paul Patton and Republican Ernie Fletcher, was appointed commissioner of the Department of Criminal Justice Training in the Kentucky Justice Cabinet at Eastern Kentucky University, in Richmond.

Bizzack wrote four books. They included *Criminal Investigations: Managing the Results*, *No Nonsense Leadership*, *Police Management for the 1990s*, and *Professionalism & Law Enforcement*. He edited another book, *Issues in Policing: New Perspectives*.

Bizzack also had a country music band called "Pistol River" and owned an extensive cattle farm just outside Lexington. In 1993, he obtained a Ph.D. from Walton University, in Minneapolis.

Walden, according to its 2007 Web site, opened their correspondence school in Naples, Florida in 1971. The next year, Walden awarded forty-six Ph.D.s and twenty-four Ed.D.s. Ten years later the school moved to Minnesota, and is now controlled by Sylvan Learning Systems.

Neither the Ray nor Flynn families were afforded closure in the loss of the loved ones.

In 1980, Russell Ray, by then a widower, was nearly blind and living alone in Kettering Ohio. He told a *Herald* reporter, "I'm living with it but I don't like it. I haven't forgotten it and will not forget. There are no answers-no answers." He died never knowing who killed his son.

Roberta Ray told the reporter, "I miss him terribly. I really do and I'd do anything to have him here. It's such a waste all the good this man could have done and someone has to stop it with four lousy bullets to the head. I think if they could kill my little brother, they could kill someone else...I'd hate to see another family get a telephone call saying the person they care for is dead."

Teri Bittner recalled the terrible night her family was notified of her uncle's death. "I heard the telephone ring and my dad wailing and my sister crying. My mother told me Elliott had been killed. She put me in bed with my sister and we held each other. My mother told me that our grandfather was coming over to stay with us and she and my dad were going to Dayton." Bittner said her father, so devastated by his brother's death, cried the entire eight-hour trip from Wisconsin to Dayton.

Afterwards, Bittner recalled, her father wanted to kill Charles Bowles and kept a gun in his bureau. "My mother finally took it away," she said.

In 1993, Ella Flynn, equally devastated about the disappearance of her only daughter, decided to speak out about her daughter's disappearance. "We think information was suppressed," she told the Lexington newspaper. "We don't know why. We tried to work within the system all these years and we were told that if we spoke out we would hurt the investigation. And I just felt like it was time we told our side of it."

Ella Flynn speculated that some lawmen might have played a role in her daughter disappearance. "I think they were involved in her disappearance and probably her murder," she added. The article continued, "She was especially critical of Capt. John Bizzack, one of the first detectives assigned to the case. Bizzack said last night that there is nothing he can say publicly about the case."

The January 26, 1987 *Herald-Leader*, in doing a ten-year anniversary story on the Melanie Flynn case, said, "Several years ago then Commonwealth Attorney Larry Roberts told a Herald-Leader reporter that Miss Flynn had been murdered and that he knew who was responsible. But he said there was insufficient evidence to obtain a conviction. Roberts declined last week to discus the case."

The newspaper also quoted Bizzack as saying that his investigation had not been so conclusive. "I don't think anyone can say that,"

Melanie Flynn's friends Canan and Thornton eventually paid a price for some of their nefarious and illegal activities.

In the early morning hours of September 11, 1985, Andrew Thornton was found splattered on a driveway in Knoxville, Tennessee, with duffle bags, filled with $74 million in cocaine, weapons, money and survival rations, strapped to his body. He wore a bullet-proof vest over his combat-style fatigues, carried identification papers in two different names, had infrared night-vision goggles and his feet were clad in Gucci loafers. Thornton's main parachute failed to open and he died from a ruptured aorta. His plane, supposedly being chased by US customs agents, crashed in the North Carolina mountains.

In an April 1993, federal drug case against Canan, former police officer George Umstead, then serving a 36-

month sentence on federal drug violations, testified to the following conversation with Canan, according to the Lexington newspaper:

"I said, 'who killed Melanie Flynn?'"

"He (Canan) just smiled. I asked him if he killed Melanie. He just...nodded his head as if saying, 'yes.'"

"Umstead also testified," the article continued, "that a mutual friend, drug smuggler Andrew Thornton once told Umstead that Canan killed Flynn 'because he loved her.'"

Also testifying was FBI agent Jim Huggins, who headed the Lexington office. "The agent," the article continued, "testified that Bonnie Kelly, convicted of killing a Florida prosecutor investigating her husband, had told him that she overheard Canan discussing Flynn's disappearance with drug smuggler Andrew Thornton, who has since died. They were not worried Higgins said she told him because Melanie Flynn would never be found."

That was also the opinion of former KSP Sgt. Ralph Ross. In an April 17, 1993, WLEX-TV interview show, Ross said that Canan and Thornton were, in his opinion, the chief suspects in Melanie Flynn's disappearance.

When federal agents raided Canan's home, in connection to the drug case, they found, along with directions for converting a shotgun into a grenade launcher and other weapons' manuals, a hand-drawn poster, labeled "Canan's Alley." One of the pictures on the poster, according to the newspaper, was a photograph of Bizzack in the cross hairs of a rifle. Others on the poster, which included commonwealth attorney Larry Roberts, had bullet holes drawn between the eyes.

The fourteen missing witness statements from the Ray murder case file paled in comparison to the entire Melanie Flynn missing person case file being shrouded in mystery. During his trial, Canan's court appointed attorney Fred E. Peters asked the court to obtain the Division of Police's case file on Flynn and the judge denied his motion.

Ella Flynn in 1993, according to the Lexington newspaper, accused the Division of Police of losing or allowing her daughter's case file to be stolen. Then police chief Larry Walsh denied the case file was ever missing. However, he did not give a location for the file, which was apparently well traveled.

KSP Sgt. Ralph Ross related to the April 17, 1993, *Herald-Leader* that he "Asked the Lexington police whether he could see their file on the (Flynn) case but they told him he couldn't because it had been placed in a bank vault." A retired detective recalled being given the same explanation as Ross received, that the Flynn case file was kept in a bank vault.

Why was the Flynn case file so valuable that it was kept in a bank vault when the Ray murder file had so many missing witness statements? If the Flynn case file was that volatile, why not destroy it?

The author made an Open Records Act request to the Division of Police to examine the Melanie Flynn file in 2006 and was refused access. The reason, it seemed, was that the thirty-year-old Melanie Flynn missing person case was an active, ongoing investigation. There had been no sightings of Melanie Flynn for three decades.

Does a case file actually exist for the missing person Melanie Flynn?

Canan was found guilty and sentenced in January 1994, to seventeen years and eight months in prison. Ella Richey Flynn was there in the courtroom for the sentencing. She told a Lexington newspaper reporter, "It doesn't answer any questions for my family about our daughter..." She added, "I've always felt like Melanie was kidnapped and murdered and I think certain people in the metro police department had something to do with it."

Melanie Flynn, according to the August 4, 1993, *Herald-Leader* was declared legally dead in 1984 for insurance purposes.

"Somebody out there knows something," Ella Richey Flynn was quoted as saying. "Won't you please speak up."

To date nobody has spoken up.

Much like the Flynns, Roberta Ray's family suffered in silence knowing it was most likely the murder of their son and brother would never be solved. Thirty years later, Teri Bittner said the murder of her uncle still created sleepless nights for her.

For both the Ray and Flynn families, justice delayed was actually justice denied.

Rebecca Anne Moore

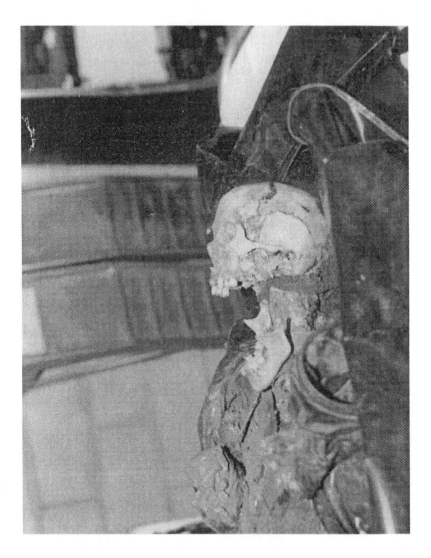

Rebecca Ann Moore's recovered body, shown above, at the coroner's officer before the autopsy. Note the black leather jacket's zipper and the material through the jaws.

She's Gone to Florida

The death of Rebecca Anne "Becky" Moore, of Cincinnati, who disappeared just before Christmas in 1980, remains officially classified as death from an undetermined cause. Her body was found in the Kentucky River nearly six months after she was reported missing.

Moore's disappearance followed that of Melanie Flynn, the Lexington woman who went missing after she left her office at the Kentucky High School Athletic Association three years earlier. Both Moore and Flynn had connections to the illegal drug culture, which encapsulated Lexington and Kentucky in the 1970s and 1980s.

Like some of the detectives who investigated the Flynn case, authorities charged with solving the Moore case proclaimed the same tired rhetoric, "She's gone to Florida,"

Moore, a beautiful, blond, gray-eyed college student left her Cincinnati apartment on Wednesday, December 17, drove to Lexington to attend a party given by Lexington man-about-town James Purdy Lambert, whom she was dating and who was her employer at the Trumps Disco in Cincinnati, or so she told her parents John and Barbara Moore. A 1983 Lexington newspaper article stated that Lambert, six or seven years earlier, had purchased a share of Trumps from his good friend, John Y. Brown, Jr., who was Kentucky's sitting governor when Moore disappeared.

Those with less than sterling reputations and law enforcement officials figured into prominently what little investigation there was into Moore's disappearance. They must have been startled when a friend of the Moore family started asking hard questions and made a real effort to find the missing woman.

Moore, a talented art student at Edgecliff College, which later became part of Xavier University, in Cincinnati, promised her mother she would be at their home in Lawrenceville, Indiana, the next day to help her with last minute preparations for the holidays.

After spending the night with Lambert at his well-appointed cabin on Upper Amster Grove Road, in Clark County, beside the Kentucky River, Becky was never seen alive again, with one exception.

From all indications, Moore got up that Thursday morning, dressed, put on Lambert's black leather jacket, with $1,100.00 in a pocket, over her jeans and sweaters, took either a sketch book or a note book and left the cabin. She was supposedly last seen by one of Lambert's neighbors who saw her walking along the river. It was doubtful if she even knew the money was in the jacket's pocket.

Lambert did not report either Moore or his money missing. By December 18, Moore's parents filed a missing person report with trooper Jasper White at the Kentucky State Police (KSP) Post in Richmond. The Richmond KSP Post covered both Fayette and Clark counties, areas where she was last seen.

The rapidity with which the Moores filed the missing person report indicated they harbored suspicions of both the crowd she was involved with and the horrible possibility of foul play.

Six months later their suspicions became fact when the Kentucky River, swelling from the accumulation of spring thaws, spewed Moore's decomposed body to the surface where it became entangled in tree limbs.

Kentucky medical examiner George R. Nichols, II, in his June 6, 1981, autopsy report, said the young woman's body was in such a state of total decomposition the cause of her death could not be anatomically determined. Moore was identified from her dental records.

Lexington police detectives and a deputy coroner appeared determined to push the theory that Moore's death was the result of an accidental drowning. There was some discussion about listing her death as natural causes.

Three days after Moore's body was discovered by four Madison County fishermen, near Clay's Ferry on June 3, 1981, detective John Bryant stated in his report that, "Deputy (coroner William) McCarney is ruling the death an accidental drowning based on information supplied to his office at this time." Nichols' autopsy was conducted on the morning of the same day.

After Nichols issued his finding of an undetermined cause of death, detectives' reports continued to insist that Moore died from either natural causes or accidental drowning. That action, plus the multitude of unanswered questions due to the scarcity of and missing case file material and some of the same people surfacing in both the Moore case and the Flynn missing person case created a parallel.

The coroner's office initially listed Moore's death as accidental drowning. After Nichols' autopsy report listed the cause of death as undetermined, the coroner changed his original ruling in Moore's death to match the opinion of the medical examiner.

At that time the coroner's office appeared to be clinging to an archaic operating style of hit and miss on death determinations. Associate state medical examiner William Hamilton in the December 22, 1980, *Lexington Herald-Leader*, blasted Kentucky's county coroners, Fayette County coroner Chester Hager's office in particular, for failure to conduct proper post-mortem examinations in questionable deaths.

"Fayette County is big enough," Hamilton wrote, "to need a forensic pathologist. It needs someone with formal training. I should point out that no one in the Fayette County coroner's office has taken the course (a four-day instructional workshop offered by the commonwealth) and it shows." Hamilton, who appeared disgusted with the entire process, later resigned his position saying the Kentucky coroner system was still in the middle of the nineteenth century.

Changes in the county coroner system, since Moore's death in 1980, have made the office more powerful.

Regardless of the opinions of forensic pathologists reached through careful post mortem examinations, county coroners may either accept their findings in questionable deaths or assign another apparently unrelated cause of death and those decisions are all legal. Now, coroners and deputy coroners are required to take extensive courses related to their work.

Since there was no media coverage of the Moore missing person case and little attention paid to the recover of her body, few questions were asked. To be fair, there were all sorts of breaking news during the middle of December 1980.

Col. Harlan Sanders, who created the Kentucky Fried Chicken (KFC) recipe in the 1930s in his Corbin, Kentucky, restaurant and who was one of the most recognized people in the world with his goatee and white suit, died on December 16. The colonel's death pushed many news items aside. A four-day mourning period was declared by Gov. John Y. Brown, Jr., in honor of Sanders.

In 1964, Sanders sold his chicken franchising business to Brown and Nashville businessman Jack Massey for $2 million. The year after Sanders' death, Heublein, Inc., paid Brown, Massey and their stockholders $275 million for KFC.

At the time of Moore's death, the Federal Bureau of Investigation (FBI) had launched an investigation into the alleged corrupt administrations of former governors Wendell Ford and Julian Carroll, who were Democrats. A federal grand jury, impaneled in Lexington under the friendly, watchful eye of Federal District Judge Bernard Monahan, also a Democrat, was investigating those allegations.

Also included in the FBI investigation were particular events connected to Lexington horseman Brownell Combs, who was chairman of the Kentucky Racing Commission, and a former commissioner, attorney Harold Kelly, from Ashland. Combs, whose father Leslie Combs was scion of Spendthrift Farm in Lexington, emerged unscathed and Kelly was tagged as an unindicted co-conspirator. Carroll escaped with little more than his reputation dented while his close friend, Howard "Sonny" Hunt, of Danville, took the fall and went to prison. Ford moved on to the US Senate.

Aside from all the breaking news in December 1980, there was an undercurrent of a jurisdictional turf war between the KSP's Organized Crime and Intelligence Unit, headed by Sgt. Ralph Ross, and some officers in Lexington's Division of Police, especially in its narcotics unit, over the shipments of illegal drugs that were inundating Lexington and the Commonwealth. Eventually the FBI became part of that investigation. It was rumored that Lexington narcotic officers were watching the KSP unit as they observed Lambert and others.

The FBI continued looking into the activities of Lambert and some of his friends several months after Moore's body was found.

Ross, whose unit had Lambert's home on Old Dobbin Road and other Lexington locations under surveillance for illegal drug activity, apparently knew nothing about Moore's disappearance until the following January. However, the missing person report was filed with the KSP by Moore's parents on December 18. Some Lexington detectives knew about Moore's disappearance but apparently shared nothing with the KSP.

One of the ironies of the Moore case was, much as Lexington detectives wanted to avoid the case, it ultimately ended up in their jurisdiction.

Precipitating the FBI and KSP's investigation and surveillances of Lambert and his friends were the illegal activities of perhaps the largest drug smuggling ring in the nation at that time, The Company, as it was known, included Kentuckians, both in law enforcement and in business, who were looking to make their fortunes in illegal drugs. A December 1980 article in the *Philadelphia Bulletin* stated that The Company had more than $26 million in assets including boats, airplanes and weapons. Guns, most of them alleged to be stolen, were traded to South American cartels for illegal drugs which were transported to Kentucky and other locations across the nation.

The prominent names connected to The Company's roster read like a Blue Book of Bluegrass society. The Company was organized by Bradley Bryant, whose sister was once married to the son of popular former governor, A. B. "Happy" Chandler. Andrew C. Thornton, II, from a Thoroughbred horse family in Bourbon County, apparently had a share of the business. The Company also included Henry S. Vance, Jr., once an aide to Gov. Julian Carroll, Wallace M. Kelly, an electronic genius and former narcotics officers William Canan, Jack Hillard, Steve Oliver, Rex Denver Hall and Danny Murphy. Dan Chandler, son of the former governor, appeared to be a facilitator to The Company.

Along with Lambert, Canan, Hillard, Thornton, Oliver, Hall and Bryant eventually received prison sentences related to the illegal drug trade. Murphy went to prison in connection with his wife's death and Vance for providing the gun used to assassinate a Florida prosecutor who was building an illegal drug trafficking case against Kelly.

Did Moore know more about her friends' activities than was healthy for her? Was she murdered and tossed in the river with the assumption that no one would be the wiser? A quarter of a century later those questions remain unanswered.

Moore's relationship with Lambert brought her in contact with wealthy and prominent people, including Kentucky's governor.

The close connection between Brown and Lambert had long raised high level of speculation in Lexington. In 1977, Brown, after divorcing his first wife Eleanor Durall Brown, sold Lambert his home on Old Dobbin Road for $130,000, according to an August 7, 1982, *Herald-Leader* article by reporter Ed Bean. Brown, according to Bean, lived with Lambert for some time after the sale. Brown was the only son of a volatile Lexington attorney who was a perennial candidate for public office and was elected only once to a term in the US House of Representatives.

Bean wrote that Brown and Lambert met while in college at the University of Kentucky (UK). Another close college friend of Lambert's was William C. Taylor, from Lexington. Both men became close business associates of Lambert's.

Lambert's wealth, Bean wrote, came from his Henderson, Kentucky, family who owned western Kentucky oil wells and a chain of grocery stores. Bean estimated Lambert's share of the oil wells amounted to approximately $2 million.

After the younger Brown and Massey purchased Kentucky Fried Chicken in 1964, from Col. Sanders, Lambert paid $50,000 for the KFC franchises in Norfolk, Virginia, Four years later, according to the newspaper, Lambert sold the franchises back to KFC for $1 million.

Lambert and Taylor, according to the Kentucky Secretary of State's office, were associates in a number of businesses, including The Library, a bar in a strip mall they developed on Woodland Avenue, near UK. The Library was alleged to be a well known hangout in the 1970s and 1980s for drug dealers, some narcotic unit officers, celebrities, local, state and national personalities as well as politicians.

The Lexington newspaper reported in 1974 that two local politicians were found drinking in The Library after the required closing time of 1:00 a.m., on a Sunday. The establishment only received a warning for remaining open after the required closing hour. Mayor Foster Pettit was quoted by the newspaper as saying no bar rules were broken.

Seems only the liquor had to locked up after closing time.

At one time or another, Lambert's name appeared on incorporation papers for Big Daddy Liquors, Kentucky Slot Car Racing, Heaven Private Discotheque, Campus Liquors, Danceland and Franchise Realty.

When Becky Moore met Lambert he seemed to be more of a man about town than a man with his fingers in a lot of businesses.

Phelps Lambert, who was chairman of the board of Farmers Bank and Trust Company, in Henderson, Kentucky, in 1982, told Bean that for the last ten years his brother has been busy devoting himself to doing nothing. The almost nightly gathering at his Old Dobbins Road home, friends and family members explained, were not the debauchery the media and rumors made them out to be but rather a constant open house where Lambert's friends gathered to drink dance and listen to country music.

Newsweek columnist Pete Axthelem, a regular at Lambert's when he was in Lexington, told Bean if someone started snorting cocaine at one of the gatherings, he would not be surprised but he had never seen it happen. Young women who worked in Lambert's discos were frequent guests in his home. From all indications, Becky Moore was part of the Old Dobbin Road crowd.

In 1979, Lambert and his friends joined to support the candidacy of John Y. Brown Jr., a Democrat, for governor in a race that pitted him against former Gov. Louie B. Nunn, (1967-1971) a Republican. During the campaign, *The Louisville Times* ran a series of articles linking Brown, a high stakes gambler, to Clifford and Stuart Perlman's Caesar's Palace, in Las Vegas, and revealing questionable activities at a Florida club Brown owned. There was mention of mysterious night cash withdrawals from a small Florida bank.

Nunn's efforts to tie Brown to the Perlmans' alleged involvement with the Myer Lansky and Carlo Gambino crime families and portray him as someone outside the mainstream of Kentucky politics were unsuccessful.

Brown insisted those rumors and others, such as his betting a million dollars on the Paul Hornung Golf Tournament at the Riviera Hotel in Las Vegas in 1976, were patently untrue. Brown won the election by unabashedly using the glitz surrounding his marriage to a former Miss America, Phyllis George Brown.

Hornung, a Louisville native, was part of Lambert and Brown's circle of high rollers. An All-American at Notre

Dame and Heisman Trophy winner in 1957, Hornung was suspended from the National Football League's Green Bay Packers in 1963 for gambling. A biography, *Golden Boy*, written by William F. Reed, stated that Hornung was a partner with Brown in four Arthur Treacher Seafood Restaurants and was a business partner of Louisville multi-millionaire Frank Metts, who headed the Kentucky Transportation Cabinet during Brown's administration. In the book, Hornung referred to Lambert as his good friend and talked about attending the 1970 Super Bowl with him.

It was understandable that Becky Moore's parents were worried about the company she was keeping. Sally Denton, in *The Bluegrass Conspiracy*, quoted Barbara Moore as saying, "My husband and I both believe that Becky know more about what was going on at Trumps than she should have known. Becky wasn't the type to go to the police and blow the whistle, so nobody had to worry about her being a threat. She was just a college kid."

With all these events occurring, Becky Moore's disappearance hardly caused a ripple in the December news cycle. Did Sgt. Ross and his crack KSP unit also have Lambert's cabin under surveillance at the same time they were watching his home? A remote cabin on the river would have been an ideal location for illegal drug activity.

The Futile Search

Christmas 1980 was a tragically sad holiday for John and Barbara Moore, their son James, other relatives and friends. The unspoken words that they might never again see Becky Moore alive must have permeated the atmosphere. One could only imagine their anguish both at their loss and those who may have been a part of such action.

After the Moore family had little success in getting Ohio and Kentucky authorities to look for their daughter, they asked a family friend, Peter Thielen, who had done some investigative work for a lawyer in Texas, to attempt to find Becky Moore a week after she disappeared.

Dr. John Moore, a veterinarian, and Thielen's father Dr. Albert E Thielen, a family practice physician, had been friends for thirty years. Moore treated all the Thielen pets at his Mt. Airy Pet Hospital, in Cincinnati. Dr. Thielen was one of the first physicians in the country to have a radio question and answer show and later moderated a live call-in television program.

Asking Peter Thielen to look into his daughter's disappearance was an indication Moore had lost all hope of an investigation by law enforcement. Yet, he was clinging to the idea that someone close to the family would execute a more diligent and effective search.

Thielen, in a series of interviews, described how he made sure the Moores knew he did not have a private investigator's license and, because of that, he might not receive any cooperation from law enforcement officials. The family assured him that was fine with them because they trusted him.

Thielen, a graduate of Ohio State University who now operates the well known private investigating firm of Ackerman, King and Associates, in Columbus, Ohio, said the Moores were quite certain, based on the people their daughter had been associating with, that foul play was involved in her disappearance. They gave Thielen an eight by ten color photograph of their daughter and a list of her friends and associates.

While keeping his case file on Becky Moore confidential, Thielen agreed to provide the author with a portion of his unpublished manuscript, *Tales of the King*, which described his efforts to find Becky Moore. Thielen changed only the names in the manuscript but it was clear who the principals were.

The details of his search were chilling.

After exhausting the list of contacts provided by Becky Moore's parents, with no success, Thielen turned to Lambert, since he was her employer as well as involved in a relationship with her. He called Lambert at Trumps and left a message for him. Thielen said when Lambert called him back he acknowledged his relationship with Becky Moore and said he wanted to find her as much as her family and friends. Much to Thielen's surprise, Lambert answered all of his questions without hesitation.

After compiling some background information, Thielen discovered the man owned a cabin on the Kentucky River.

According to Thielen's manuscript, Lambert, to whom he gave the name Tom Kirby, outlined his most recent association with the missing young woman: they drove to his cabin on the Kentucky River; went to an art gallery where he purchased, after soliciting Becky Moore's advice, a painting of a tiger for $1,800.000; went out to dinner where he spent another hundred dollars on food and wine; returned to the cabin; shared some wine before going to bed; when he awoke the next morning she was gone as was his black leather jacket with $1,100.00 in a pocket, he wrote.

The nightclub owner, Thielen wrote, said he thought she had taken the money and the jacket and gone to Florida because she was stressed out from college and wanted a vacation during the school holiday break but did not have the money to pay for travel.

Another young woman was missing but, not to worry, she had just gone to Florida.

Kirby (Lambert) according to Thielen, remained at the cabin for a few days waiting for Becky Moore to return but she never did. Thielen said Kirby (Lambert) told him he was alone at the cabin during that period, adding that not many people came down to the river during the winter months.

If the man truly believed Becky Moore had gone to Florida, why was he waiting for her return?

In the manuscript, Thielen said he asked Kirby (Lambert) why he failed to report the woman and his money missing. His reply was that he did not want her to be arrested but that he had spoken with a friend, who was a Lexington police detective, about the matter.

Becky Moore was reportedly last seen along the Kentucky River in Clark County, which adjoins Fayette County, which includes Lexington. The Clark County sheriff's office, not Lexington police, would have had jurisdiction over the case had Becky Moore's disappearance and the loss of money been reported.

Since the initial missing person report had been filed with the Richmond KSP post, the State Police, not Lexington detectives, had jurisdiction in Clark County.

Thielen's manuscript said Kirby (Lambert) gave the private investigator the address of his cabin, permission to search the premises and the Lexington detective's telephone number.

After consulting with John and Barbara Moore, the decision was made to extend Thielen's investigation of Becky Moore's disappearance to Lexington. Thielen called the detective who agreed to meet him at the Howard Johnson's Restaurant on North Broadway. A steady snow had been falling since Thielen crossed the Ohio River but detective Drexel Neal, referred to in the manuscript as Harold West, was at the restaurant to meet him.

Thielen found West (Neal) helpful in drawing him a map to the cabin but, he pointed out, the dirt road leading to the cabin would probably be covered with snow by the time he drove down to the Kentucky River.

When Thielen said he planned to leave immediately, he wrote that West (Neal) suggested he first take Becky Moore's photograph to Blue Grass Airport and ask airline ticket agents if anyone matching her description had purchased a ticket to Florida recently. According to the manuscript, the detective gave Thielen his business card with his direct number on the back and suggested that showing his card to airline personnel might encourage their cooperation.

There was that gone to Florida theory, again.

When shown her photograph, neither ticket agents, gate attendants nor anyone else at Blue Grass Airport remembered seeing a young woman, matching the picture, purchase a ticket to Florida or any place else.

Thielen, according to his manuscript, left the airport and drove toward cabin through the intensifying snowstorm with the sky was rapidly darkening. He missed a sign and drove about three miles out of his way, but finally found the dirt road in the darkness, leading to the cabin, which was indeed covered with a blanket of snow.

"Once I turned onto the one-lane road, all tire tracks ended, except for two sets," he wrote. "Who ever had driven on the road did not pull into the short driveway to the cabin. It was possible to see (where) the driver had backed up to turn around and double back to the road. There were no visible footprints around the cabin, which was about fifteen or twenty yards from the river." He added that the heavy snowfall would have rapidly filled any indentations made by someone walking.

There was no vehicle parked at or near the cabin.

Thielen said he knocked on the cabin's front door and it opened about four inches. He called out a couple of times; there was no response. He went inside and turned on a light. "The exterior was a rustic log cabin," he wrote, "but the inside was as modern as any home I had seen." He noticed two empty rifle mounts over the massive stone fireplace in the living room. Looking further, he said, he found the half-wrapped painting of the tiger leaning against a chair and wondered why the painting had not been hung.

He described the floor plan of the cabin: the living room and a small dining room; a kitchen to the rear with a stoop and a bedroom, larger than the combined living and dining room, with a small bath. After looking around in the bedroom, he wrote, he went into the kitchen and opened an interior door which led to a basement but the lights down there did not work.

"I leaned against the kitchen table and thought over this latest development and decided to get a flashlight from my van," he wrote.

The beam from his flashlight revealed no hidden attackers concealed in the basement. He found a workshop, in the basement, with tools strewn about on a table. In another basement room, there were more tools, a chest of drawers, some lanterns and an unattached door leaning against the front wall. Thielen wrote that he moved the door and found a smaller opening. "I would be lying, if I claimed my hands were not shaking," he said.

After opening the smaller door, his flashlight revealed a rolled-up carpet about seven feet long and about twenty-four inches in diameter. Assuming the obvious, Thielen rushed outside to get a breath of fresh air before returning.

"Even though I didn't want to," he wrote about returning to the small basement room, "I reached down and grabbed the end of the carpet and dragged it into the larger room. I unrolled the carpet and, with each turn, expected a head, a foot or a strand of hair to appear but they didn't. When I had the carpet unrolled enough to see there was no body inside, I put it back, left the basement, went back upstairs and outside to my van."

Despite the fact Moore's body was not in the rolled-up carpet, Thielen said the basement scene haunted his dreams for years.

Thielen wrote that he drove to the nearest restaurant and called Kirby (Lambert) telling him the cabin's front door was not only unlocked but open, there were no guns in the rack above the fireplace and complimented him on the painting of the tiger. He said Kirby (Lambert) appeared concerned about the front door being open and his hunting rifle missing. Thielen recalled that Kirby (Lambert) replied, in a calm voice, that he was hoped Becky Moore might be found in the cabin but that he guessed she was still somewhere in the south.

The idea that Becky Moore had gone to Florida was, indeed, ingrained.

In his manuscript, Thielen said Kirby (Lambert) asked him to fly to Miami to look for Becky Moore and he would pay all of the investigator's expenses and fees. It was a tempting offer but Thielen knew the likelihood of finding Becky Moore, even with all the assistance offered was futile.

He told Kirby (Lambert) first; he did not even know if she was in Miami; second, Miami was a large city in which to search for a missing young woman; third, he already had a client and taking him as a client would be a conflict of interest in his agreement with the Moores. However, he agreed to relay the offer to the Moores. Thielen wrote that Kirby (Lambert) replied, "I would think they would be glad to have me funding the search for their daughter."

Thielen said he also called West (Neal) reporting what he found and returned to the cabin to lock the front door. As he prepared to leave, Thielen noticed a neighbor nearby. He engaged him in conversation, showed the man Becky Moore's picture and asked if he recalled seeing her. The man said he saw her, wearing a black jacket, walking along the river and carrying a book of some kind a few days earlier. Thielen wrote the man added, "There aren't many people walking along the river her this time of the year and a girl that pretty, with that long blond hair, well, not hard to remember seeing her, if you know what I mean."

Thielen said he thought it was odd that the man would be out walking, near a river, in a blizzard during the hour of darkness.

After reporting his findings, such as they were, to Barbara and John Moore, Thielen said they agreed that he was correct in refusing the offer to fund a further search in Florida. He advised the Moores they should hire a licensed private investigator to follow up on the few leads he had uncovered.

Since neither Ohio or Kentucky law enforcement apparently had little interest in looking for the missing woman, Thielen felt his work in tracking Becky Moore to Lexington and then on to the Kentucky River cabin was more than anyone else had done.

In his manuscript, Thielen listed several things about his trip to the Kentucky River cabin that bothered him. Was the rifle stolen to make it appear that a robbery had occurred? Had Becky Moore's body been in the cabin prior to his trip there? If so, who moved it? Did someone else visit the cabin while he was at the airport that evening? Could her body have been dumped into the river that day? With a blizzard in process, it was not possible for Thielen to see if the river was frozen.

According to Sally Denton's account of the missing Becky Moore in her book, *The Bluegrass Conspiracy*, KSP Sgt. Ralph Ross' attention to the case came from Moore having been last seen in Lambert's company. When Ross learned of Moore's disappearance in mid-January, she wrote, he assigned a detective to trace the route she might have followed after leaving the cabin.

Apparently everybody knew Ross was watching Lambert's Lexington home, why was his unit not watching the cabin since he eventually raided both locations?

Quoting from a KSP detective's report, probably obtained from Ross, Denton wrote, "Assuming she tried to walk along the riverbank, she would have encountered approximately a half mile of steep earthen embankment followed by a half mile of sheer limestone cliffs. It appears impossible to travel by foot on the bank of the river in this area."

Moore's car was found at Lambert's home in Lexington, Denton wrote.

Retired KSP detective George Mayberry, of Winchester, said he was not called into the case until more than two weeks after Becky Moore was reported missing. In an August 8, 2007, interview, Mayberry said when he investigated Lambert's cabin and the surrounding area in mid-January, Moore's car was parked at the cabin on Upper Amster Grove Road, but he found none of her personal effects in either the vehicle or the cabin.

Apparently Moore's car traveled more than its owner after she was reported missing. Denton placed the car at Lambert's Old Dobbins Road home in Lexington. Thielen saw no vehicle around the cabin when he was there in December. Mayberry found her car at the cabin in January.

Mayberry not only questioned Lambert about Moore's disappearance but he gave him a polygraph examination. In the process of administering the polygraph, Mayberry said he received an unusual request from Lambert. "Lambert requested, prior to the (polygraph) test that I should also ask him about the disappearance of Melanie Flynn," Mayberry recalled. "He said he had been accused of being involved in her disappearance and he wanted to clear it up."

Denton wrote that Ross ordered Lambert to take the polygraph test and that created a problem between Gov. Brown and Neil Welch, a former FBI agent who helped set up ABSCAM—the organized crime and public corruption investigation, which garnered a U.S. Senator, six Congressmen and other public officials. Brown first appointed Welch as Secretary of the Justice Cabinet but later moved him to the Public Protection Cabinet.

An April 22, 1983, *Herald-Leader* article stated that Welch had warned Gov. Brown to end his association with Lambert.

According to Denton, Brown asked Welch for the results of Lambert's polygraph test. She wrote that Lambert had negative responses to a couple of questions.

Mayberry, who administered the polygraph, said Lambert's test results indicated no deception and showed he had no knowledge of Moore's death. The former detective said he did ask Lambert about Melanie Flynn's disappearance during the polygraph examination and the results showed that he had no knowledge of that missing woman either.

"I really don't think Jimmy had anything to do with Moore's disappearance," Mayberry said.

Mayberry's statements indicated the KSP had a file on the Moore case. An Open Records Act request to examine the Kentucky State Police's file on the Rebecca Anne Moore investigation produced surprising results. Mary Ann Scott, the KSP official record custodian, in August 2007, wrote, "A thorough search of Kentucky State Police records has been conducted and no records regarding the above referenced (Rebecca Ann Moore) has been found."

Without a doubt, the KSP once had a case file on Becky Moore. Denton quoted from the case file in her book. Mayberry clearly remembered his search of the Upper Amster Grove Road cabin and its environs, his interviews with Lambert and his administration of the polygraph examination. He would certainly have kept the appropriate records. Nor is there any reason to doubt Scott's statement that the case file no longer exists.

Mayberry said he had no idea why the KSP case file on Moore would be missing. But, missing it is.

When Becky Moore's body was pulled out of the Kentucky River, it was obvious to all concerned that she had not gone to Florida.

As the initial news spread that a young woman's body had been found in the river, the first public reaction was that Melanie Flynn had been found.

Recovery, Of A Sort

When George Hall, Sylvester Begley, Rocky Hall and Jerry Gilkerson, all commercial fishermen from Madison County, took their boat out on the Kentucky River on the evening of June 3, 1981, they never expected to have their work interrupted by the discovery of a putrefied body caught in tree limbs along the bank of the river.

In a September 11, 2007, interview, George Hall said they discovered Moore's body about 6:30 p.m. The river, Hall said, was going through what he called the June tide. "Due to a lot of spring rains," he explained, "the river level had gone down and then went back up." Hall, who lived on the river at Valley View, had spent thirty-five years fishing the stream for catfish, buffalo and perch and was well acquainted with its ever changing moods and levels.

Hall said he saw only the back of Moore's body, the black leather jacket and her skull as it was hanging over a tree limb. "There was a terrible odor coming from the body," he said.

He did not remember which law enforcement units responded but he clearly recalled a man from the coroner's office having to wade into the river to place the body in a black bag.

Much as Lexington authorities apparently had worked to avoid becoming involved in the Moore case, there was an irony in the fact that her body was found in Fayette County (Lexington), which was their jurisdiction and detectives had to deal with the case.

Hall placed the location where they found Moore's body as being halfway between Valley View and Clay's Ferry, near Jack's Creek Road on the west side of the river just below the apex on an inlet of Madison County land, which juts up into Fayette County. He said there was no doubt the body was found on the west side, or Fayette County area, of the river, which is the southern boundary between the two counties.

Had the body been found on the east, or Madison County, side of the river local authorities or the KSP would have been in charge of the investigation from that point.

As it was, investigators had difficulty placing the exact location where Moore's body was found. Detective John Bryant's report gave the location as being four miles south of the Clay's Ferry area. The coroner's report placed the recovery point as being five miles north of Clay's Ferry.

Hall's description matched that of Gwen Curtis, curator of the University of Kentucky Libraries' Map Collections. She found the distance, by river, from the Upper Amster Grove Road location, where Moore was last seen, to the spot where Hall and his crew found her, to be 6.5 miles. In an email to the author, Curtis wrote, "From Valley View to Clay's Ferry is about twelve miles, so halfway would be six miles, near Jack's Creek Road; from Clay's Ferry to Upper Amster Grove Road is 4-4.5 miles."

If there were questions about the exact location of the recovery of the body, investigators certainly had an extraordinary amount of personal information about Moore.

Detective Bryant's initialed, but undated, report stated, "The body is possible that of Rebecca Anne Moore F/W/2-25-56 ss#___-__-___, 5'4" blond hair, 130 lbs., missing 2-3 teeth lower left jaw and had a bridge. Subject reported missing to trooper Jasper White, KSP, Richmond on 12-18-80. Subject allegedly had a notebook and a man's leather jacket with $1100 in cash in the pocket. These items were recovered with the body. Dental records will be supplied by KSP. The address of the victim is 1777 Queen City, Cincinnati."

The color photograph of Moore's body in the case file provided nothing identifiable except for the black leather jacket. Her left jaw bone was disengaged and narrow layers of blue material, uniform in width, crossed through her open jaws.

Fayette County coroner Gary Ginn, in an August 24, 2007, interview said then deputy coroner William McCarney requested the state medical examiner to do the autopsy on Moore. Another coroner's office employee, Rolan Taylor, transported Moore's body to University Hospital, in Louisville, for state medical examiner, Dr. George Nichols III, to perform the post mortem.

Taylor, in a September 5, 2007, interview, talked about Moore being such a petit woman. He was at the Kentucky River recovery site and described how the body was caught up in tree limbs and how difficult it was to untangle the corpse. Taylor said the body was infested with maggots but did not remember the leather jacket or the material going through the jaws.

The jacket and the blue material had apparently been removed from the body before Taylor transported the remains to Louisville for the autopsy.

Assisted by Drs. Mark Alberhasky and L. C. McCloud, Nichols began the autopsy at 11:30 a.m., on June 6. From an initial examination, Nichols concluded the body was that of a female about 5'5". "There is total body decomposition and maggot infestation," his report read. "Examination reveals absence of the left hand, right foot and right forearm. There is an absence of soft tissue of the remaining lower extremities revealing intact skeletal members. Examination of the remaining soft tissue of the chest and posterior thorax reveal no evidence of blunt force injury."

Could Moore' missing right foot have been weighted down by a heavy object? Did her hands suffer a similar fate? There are some wild tales of excessively large catfish being seen in the Kentucky River.

"The mandible and cranial bones are intact," Nichols' report continued, "Removal of the breast plate reveals severely decomposed visceral organs. Examination of the internal chest wall reveals no skeletal fractures or pleural lacerations. The abdominal viscera exhibited marked putrefactive changes. The vermiform appendix is identified.

The uterus and bilateral fallopian tubes and ovaries are present. Removal of the cranial cap reveals no internal cranial fracture."

Nichols' report concluded, "No anatomic cause of death is determined in this case. Identification is by odontologic comparison." He was empathic that it was impossible to determine the cause of death. In a September 2007, letter he wrote, "The cause and manner of death in this case should both be undetermined."

Nichols carefully listed the article of clothing he found on Moore's body when it reached University Hospital. The list included, "A gold serpentine necklace; a pair of 'Gauchos' blue jeans; a pair of burgundy underpants, brand name 'Vanity Fair,' size 5; a blue slip-on sweater, size small, brand name 'Kidding;' a green three-button short sleeved sweater."

Lambert's black leather jacket and the blue material through the jaws were missing from Nichols' careful list of items removed from the body. What happened to these items? What happened to the $1,100?

In his September 2007, reply to those questions, Nichols wrote, "I did not see the leather jacket or I would have indicated its presence." He made no mention of the material in the jaws, as shown in the copy of the photograph sent him by the author nor did he respond to a second question about the tape-like material.

A police report, dated June 6, stated some cash money, presumably from Lambert's leather jacket, was found while the body was at Whitehall Funeral Home, where the coroner's office was then located. The report also confirmed that a notebook or sketchbook was found in one of the jacket's pockets at the mortuary.

Detective Bryant's June 7, 1982, report stated, "The parents have advised that they desire the remains to be cremated and returned to her father. Deputy (coroner) McCarney is ruling the death an accidental drowning based on the information supplied to his office at this time. The money will be turned over to Mr. Lambert unless the State Police desire to maintain it for their investigation."

Nichols completed the Moore autopsy the morning before Bryant's report was written and clearly stated no anatomic cause or manner of death could be determined due to excessive decomposition.

At some point, the coroner's final opinion as to the cause of Moore's death was changed from accidental drowning to undetermined, which matched Nichols' findings. Whether that decision was brought about from pressure from assistant state medical examiner Hamilton's charges the previous December or from Nichols' adamant conclusion of an undetermined cause of death was not known.

In Kentucky, when a difference of opinion occurs between the coroner and the medical examiner, who performed the autopsy, the coroner's decision prevails by law. Dan Able, executive director of the State Medical Examiner's office, said in an August 24, 2007, interview, "In all cases the coroner's opinion rules, even if reason is on the side of the medical examiner. We are only here to help the coroner in an advisory capacity."

The State Medical Examiner office should have had a case file on Moore's autopsy. An Open Records Act request brought this reply from Mandy Combest, the office's executive staff advisor, "We are unable to locate the autopsy report, photographs and any other data on Rebecca Anne Moore."

Two state agencies, The Kentucky State Police and the State Medical Examiner's office, whose record keeping and archival methods should have been above reproach, had no material relating to Rebecca Anne Moore's death, not even her autopsy report. The autopsy report was also missing from the police's case file. Fortunately, coroner Gary Ginn was able to locate the Moore autopsy report in his files.

Despite Nichols' conclusion that the cause of Moore's death could not be determined, there appeared to be evidence her death was not due to natural causes.

George Hall, the fisherman who found the body, made a rather valid point. "There was some talk at the scene," he said, "of her falling through the ice upriver during the winter." Hall said the previous December, when Moore was reported missing, ice on the Kentucky River, at his home in Valley View, was thick enough for him to walk out on it. He estimated the ice on the stream further north, at Upper Amster Grove Road, might have been thicker.

There was some logic to Hall's idea but there was no indication in the case files that his theory was given any consideration although the man knew the river like the back of his hand. It was possible Moore could have hit a thin spot on the ice and slid into the river. It was also possible someone could have chopped a hole in the ice and shoved Moore's body below the surface.

Then, there was the idea, advanced by a detective, that Moore might have committed suicide by taking a swan dive into the frozen river in the middle of December just to see if the water was cold.

Five days after Moore's body was recovered, detective John Bizzack sent a memo to detective John Bryant saying, "We have found evidence in the notebook taken from Moore's body that it has possibilities of being a suicide. I'll get with you later. Do not release this data."

Nothing else was found in the case file that mentioned suicide, which did not appear plausible.

It was never clear whether Moore had a notebook or sketchbook with her when she left Lambert's cabin. Could she have written or sketched something so devastating, so inflammatory that it could have been a factor in her death?

The question will never be answered because the notebook/sketchbook has vanished from police evidence.

Division of Police record custodians were unable to locate the notebook/sketchbook Bizzack described. Records custodian Karen Steed, in searching the Moore evidence folder, said, "Under Property Number 121839, Rebecca Moore is listed. On 6-9-81 Bizzack booked (11) parts of one hundred dollar bills as evidence. On 07-6-81, the evidence was released." Steed found no mention in the Moore evidence folder of a notebook or a sketchbook.

Although the black leather jacket was mentioned several times in the Moore case file, there were no references to that or the material which appeared in the photograph to be wound through her open jaws.

From all indications, the investigation of the death of Rebecca Anne Moore was intended to slither into oblivion.

Another of detective Bryant's undated reports concluded, "As no criminal offense has been reported or is known at this time, this compliant should be marked Unfounded." The report was approved by Bryant's supervisor, Sgt. Richey, on July 10, 1981, and was marked that no follow up investigation was needed in the case.

The Moore family was finally able to hold the last rites for their daughter and sister and mourn her passing. Complete closure was denied them in not knowing whether she was a victim of a homicide or died as a result of accidental drowning. If she was murdered, the family knew it was doubtful that her killer(s) would ever be brought to justice.

There are, however, degrees of closure, even if it is doled out in small particles.

When George Hall discovered Rebecca Anne Moore's body, the idea that she had somehow just irresponsibly gone to Florida, without telling her family and friends, was put to rest.

With the exception of the KSP investigation, which left many questions unanswered, of her disappearance, law enforcement appeared to have little interest in discovering what really happened to her. Peter Thielen did his best to follow a trail that, in many ways, was colder than the frozen Kentucky River.

The Moore family had little political clout in Kentucky and certainly nothing like that Lambert would later use when the FBI tightened the screws on him.

On April 21, 1983, the FBI raided Lambert's home in Lexington and his cabin on the Kentucky River and the home of Arnold Kirkpatrick, on Spendthrift Farm, where he was vice-president.

A former editor of *The Thoroughbred Record*, Kirkpatrick was also president of the Kentucky Jockey Club, which operated Latonia Race Course (now Turfway), near Cincinnati. The FBI and Lexington police, an April 22, 1983, *Herald-Leader* article stated, participated in the raid. Material seized in the raid was turned over to a federal grand jury in Lexington. The FBI's search warrants were signed by the US Magistrate's office.

The FBI's pursuit of Lambert became so intensive that a US Senator was prompted to intervene. Sen. Walter D. Huddleston, a Democrat from Elizabethtown, Kentucky, in September 1983, threatened to haul the Department of Justice before a Senate Committee to explain their handling of the FBI's investigation of Lambert. Huddleston suggested the FBI might have not followed their own guidelines on electronic surveillance in the Lambert investigation. Huddleston was not re-elected.

Just days before the raid, Gov. Brown fired Neil Welch, whom the governor had moved from the position of Secretary of the Justice Cabinet to Secretary of the Public Protection Cabinet. Whether Welch gave Brown the results of Lambert's polygraph test was not known. After Brown left office, Lambert was apparently on his own.

In October 1983, Lambert was fined $130 for driving under the influence of alcohol.

In January 1984, a federal grand jury, sitting in Lexington, indicted Lambert and one of his associates, Phillip Block, a nephew of former governor Julian Carroll, on sixty-seven counts of trafficking in illegal drugs. While the grand jury was considering the Lambert-Block indictments, another indictment was handed down. Arnold Kirkpatrick, the Spindletop Farm vice-president, was also indicted.

In 1984, Lambert, his good friend and stalwart protector horsewoman Anita Madden, whose Kentucky Derby parties were world famous, and three others were indicted for stealing 100 pages of carbon used in typing the grand jury's transcript, which was secret testimony. Charges were later dropped against Lambert and Madden, while Philip Ray Jeter, a former used furniture dealer also indicted, was tried and found guilty of obstruction of justice, conspiracy and theft of government property and sentenced to two years in federal prison. There was trial testimony that Jeter and Lambert were well acquainted with each other and, at some point, money had changed hands. Jeter had been previously sentence to a year in jail and fined $20,000, for unfair business practices.

Lambert and Block were allowed to plead guilty to one count of trafficking in illegal drugs in June 1984. Despite the two men's pleas for leniency, they were sentenced to five years each in federal prison. Lambert appealed his sentence to the Federal Court of Appeals in October 1985, and they refused to hear his case. Two months later, the Supreme Court declined to hear his case. Both Lambert and Block went to prison.

When they got out of prison, Lambert and Block opened a chain of successful jewelry stores, T & M Jewelry and The Castle.

Kirkpatrick pled guilty to possession of cocaine in the spring of 1984. A friendly federal judge, who said Kirkpatrick had been led to the use of the drug by friends, placed him on eighteen months probation instead of making him serve a six months jail sentence.

Dr. John Moore died never knowing whether his daughter was murdered or was the victim of an accidental drowning. His Mt. Airy Pet Hospital is still in operation.

Detective Drexel Neal's name never appeared in any of the case file, memos or reports on the investigation of Rebecca Anne Moore's death or the recovery of her body. Neal left the Division of Police and in 2008, he became the executive director of the Kentucky Community Preparedness Program, the commonwealth's Homeland Security initiative, located in Richmond, Kentucky.

Does anyone, with the exception of the Moore family and investigator Peter Thielen, have any remorse or regrets about the investigation of the death of Rebecca Anne Moore?

Cynthia

Carol

Baker

Harold

Daniel

Sheppard

The bloody bathroom, shown above, was where Cindy Baker and Danny Sheppard were killed. Note the bloody knife on the end of toilet tank. Neither the stack of soap nor the floral arrangements were disturbed in the small room where the violent deaths occurred. Baker's head, at an almost right angle, was at the end of the tub next to the commode. Sheppard was on top of her lower body at the other end of the tub.

Who Killed Whom?

The unusual circumstances surrounding the death of Rebecca Anne Moore were minute compared to those of the July 9, 1981, deaths of Lexington residents Cynthia "Cindy" Baker, 24, and Harold D. "Danny" Sheppard, 26. He sold gold jewelry at flea markets and she was a waitress. Some said they planned to get married. Others said an argument, which began the day before, would have led to their separation.

The two were described as low-level drug players and reputedly had connections to some of the people whose names cropped up in the Moore investigation. Sally Denton, in *The Bluegrass Conspiracy*, wrote, "The two were known drug couriers and had been identified by (KSP Sgt.) Ralph's (Ross) undercover men as regulars at (James P.) Lambert's house on Old Dobbin Road."

According to Denton, Baker and Sheppard became government informants against some of The Company members just prior to their deaths. In a July 9, memo to the case file, Sgt. John Bizzack acknowledged the residence where Baker and Sheppard lived, 1008 Molan Drive, had been under Division of Police surveillance.

Some of the same investigators in the Moore case, were also involved in the Baker-Sheppard case, which occurred just when detectives decided there was no further need to delve into Moore's death.

An effort to push the manner of Baker and Sheppard's deaths as a murder and a suicide, before the bodies were removed from their home gave an entirely new meaning to the phrase rapid response investigation. Both were stabbed in the chest: she had a single wound and he had three wounds.

Baker and Sheppard had shared the 1008 Moylan Drive residence, in a new southwest Lexington development near the Jessamine County line, with Douglas Ferguson and Carol Higdon for less than a month. Just how the quartet came to live together was not clear. Carol Higdon told detectives she only met Cindy Baker in April before they moved in together in June. Hidgon was the most elusive figure of the four housemates and very little background information was available about her.

Ferguson was the son of Ralph Ferguson, owner of Fayette Cigar Store, a long time fixture on Lexington's Main Street. The store was a relic of the past when tobacco stands and shops flourished. In 1910, local tobacco factories were producing 165,000 cigars per month. For years, the elder Ferguson fought successful battles with downtown developers and the local government to save his building, which now abuts a new court complex instead of being a part of it. The store once had a notorious back room for suggestive reading material.

According to the case file, Ferguson found the couple, Baker in her nightgown and Sheppard fully clothed, in the bathtub with the shower running after he returned home between 5:30 and 6:00 p.m.

Sheppard's body, clothed in a red-white nylon shirt and blue jeans, was partially atop the body of Baker, clad in a full-length white nightgown, in the tub in the blood-spattered bathroom. A Case brand "Sharktooth" lock-blade knife, smeared with blood and water, was found on the top of the commode water tank. Ferguson, according to the case file, attempted to rouse Sheppard, who was bleeding from chest wounds. With Sheppard's blood on his hands, Ferguson turned off the shower and shouted for two maintenance workers, there to repair their basement drywall, to call for an ambulance.

Unable to get the police on the telephone, Ferguson ran down the street where police officer Karl Hiten lived and told him about finding the bodies and asked him to call authorities.

Detective Bizzack, who had speculated that Rebecca Anne Moore might have killed herself, was head of the Special Investigative Unit of the Division of Police and took charge of the case as the lead detective.

Ferguson, Bizzack wrote in his July 9, memo to the case file, alleged that Baker and Sheppard's deaths were a possible homicide/suicide. That statement, the detective said, prompted deputy coroner William McCarney to call assistant state medical examiner Dr. David R. Dahlenburg, who was based at St. Joseph Hospital, in Lexington.

Bizzack described the scene as Ferguson led the Dire Department personnel and himself to the bathroom. "I observed Sheppard sitting on the edge of the bathtub and the head of Baker in a twisted position in the bathtub," he wrote. "It appeared from the doorway that Baker may have been decapitated due to the remainder of her body being concealed by the edge of the tub. As the first aid personnel entered the bathroom to examine both, I reviewed the other bedrooms, hallway and kitchen of the residence for the remaining portion of Baker's body or signs of blood."

The firemen informed Bizzack that both bodies in the bathtub were intact.

Bizzack described how officers removed Baker and Sheppard's bodies from the bathroom and placed them in the kitchen where Dahlenburg examined them. One can only imagine the bloody kitchen scene with bodies on the counters, table or floor.

Why was there such a rush to conduct a pre-autopsy at the scene instead of waiting for the post mortem conclusions the next day?

"Knife wounds were identified on each," Bizzack wrote, "and the opinion formed by the pathologist was that both had apparently stabbed each other or that Sheppard had attacked Baker and then committed suicide. The pathologist continued to review the bodies and then reviewed the bathroom blood spatters and pools which he said corroborated his view of the reconstruction of the incident."

Did Bizzack really believe Sheppard stabbed Baker,

then stabbed himself three times in the chest, placed the knife on top of the water closet before falling into the bathtub to die? If so, that conclusion was not found in Dahlenburg's autopsy reports.

Dahlenburg's autopsy reports, missing from the case file but found in the coroner's office, clearly stated that Baker and Sheppard died from stab wounds to the chest. The pathologist did not elaborate on who stabbed whom either in his final diagnoses or in his final reports on the post mortems. He estimated Baker's death occurred between 3:30-6:30 p.m., and Sheppard's between 4:00-6:00 p.m. on July 9.

Dahlenburg's final diagnosis and comments on Baker, who was 5'6" and weighed 110 pounds, were as follows. "Death in this young white female, who is shown to have used Quaalude recently before her death is attributed to a stab wound on the anterior chest with resultant hemopercardium (blood in the pericardial sac) and massive right hemothorax (accumulation of blood in the chest cavity).

"There is evidence of trauma to the head. The presence of Methaqualone in the individual's circulation at the time of her death may have dulled her ability to defend herself. Based on findings at the scene of her death, the most likely chain of events was trauma to the head, followed by stabbing and rather prompt exsanguinations (loss of blood). Subsequent immersion of the body in water most likely resulted in laryngosphasm (inability to breathe) and death."

Dahlenburg added that Baker had an area of discoloration in the bend of her left elbow. He found no abnormalities in her other body organs and determined she had not been raped.

The pathologist said there had been a struggle in the bathroom with the shower curtain and towel rack being found on the floor. "Spattered blood was on the right-hand wall of the room and only a small amount of blood mixed with water was found on the floor immediately adjacent to the tub," he wrote. "A long bladed knife with water diluted with blood was found on the most proximal (nearest) corner of the water closet compartment of the commode."

Nowhere in his autopsy report did Dahlenburg comment on who took Baker's life. Nor did his final diagnose match what Bizzack attributed to the pathologist in the detective's July 9 memo.

According to the detective's memo, Dahlenburg's post mortem examination of Baker "Revealed she had been stabbed twice in the chest, both through the same stab wound, which apparently was the first, entered the chest area and penetrated the right upper lobe of the heart. The second stab wound apparently thrusted toward the right lung area but did not touch the lung."

Dahlenburg attributed Baker's death a stab wound in the chest followed by her immediate drowning.

Dahlenburg's autopsy of the 5' 6", 180 pound Sheppard was as complete as that of Baker. "Death in this young male," the pathologist wrote, "who was found to have abused methaqualone and marijuana recently prior to his death, is attributed to stab wounds of the chest with penetrating wounds in the heart lacerating the tricuspid valve and leading to heropericardium, cardiac failure and cardiac tamponade.

"The level(s) of methaqualone reported are significant in that the deceased had recently used the drug. Level of tolerance to the drug, however, is difficult to appreciate. Frankly fatal levels of the drug, however, are not reported. The presence of Phencyclidine (PCP originally developed as an intravenous anesthetic later called "angel dust") stored in the brain, however, is not reported but there was apparently no recent use of this drug. The report also shows no alcohol to be found in either blood or urine."

Sheppard's chest wounds, Dahlenburg found, "Are present on the chest over the pericardium. The wounds through the bone, however, are much more vertical approximating perpendicular. There are no tears along the edges of any of the skin wounds or secondary cuts apparent.

"The three wounds are described according to the side of the body as follows: the right side wound is 2.2 x 0.7

cm and follows a track passing interiorly into the left-hand side of the body a distance of approximately 4 cm and extends 3.5 x 1.3 cm defect in the left outer edge of the sternum. A 0.2 cm hole is found on the deep surface of the sternum. This hole is of the same dimension on both sides of the sternum and extended into the pericardium and heart."

The medical examiner found Sheppard had a contusion on his right arm, a bruise on his right shin and old crusted lesions on his right hand.

Dahlenburg commented about the small amount of water and blood on the floor adjacent to the bathtub. Baker's face, he noted, was under water. Sheppard's body was on top of Baker's with his legs straddling the edge of the bathtub in a semi-supine (horizontal) position. The bathtub drain was at least partially blocked for water from the shower to accumulate the six to seven inches needed to cover Baker's face

If the bodies within the tub displaced just the small amount of water and blood Dahlenburg found on the floor, was it possible that Baker and Sheppard's deaths occurred only a short time before Ferguson found their bodies? Or, did water from the shower, since the curtain had been torn down, bounce off the bodies to produce blood and water Dahlenburg found on the floor?

Again, who turned the shower on was a pivotal question that was never answered.

Nowhere in his autopsy and reports did Dahlenburg comment on who administered the fatal wounds that killed Sheppard.

The Kentucky State Police laboratory examined blood evidence collected at the crime scene including blood found on the Chase knife, Baker's nightgown, Sheppard's shirt, blood spatters from the bathroom wall, finger marks' on the commode water closet top and blood spatters from the wall behind the commode. The lab found Baker's blood was Group O EPA A and Sheppard's O EPA BA.

"Examination tests were nonconclusive as to whether the blood was from those above areas were Baker's or

Sheppard's specifically but the blood was of their group," the lab report stated.

No fingernail scrapings were collected, according to the crime scene check list. Bizzack, in his memo, attributed the failure to get scrapings from under Baker's nails was that she chewed on her fingernails. Did Sheppard?

Both victims were fingerprinted.

Baker and Sheppard died in 1981, just as DNA was beginning to enter the field of criminal investigations. DNA evidence might have helped established whether or not there was a third, or perhaps, a fourth person in the bathroom with the victims.

Such a theory was possible, according to a medical panel the author asked to examine Dahlenburg's autopsy reports. A retired cardiologist, a cardiac care nursing supervisor and a nurse, who requested anonymity, were certain there was a third person in the bathroom when Baker and Sheppard died.

The medical panel found Bizzack's claim that Baker and Sheppard stabbed each other not only ludicrous but highly improbable. The first item that drew their attention was the center wound in Sheppard's chest where the knife penetrated the full thickness of the sternum. They said it was extremely doubtful that a woman of Baker's size and weight, already mortally wounded, could inflict such a blow with enough force that it would penetrate the broad, thick sternum.

Gary's Anatomy described the sternum, as being in the center of a cage containing and protecting the organs of respiration and circulation and having an average length of approximately 6.9 inches. The reference book pointed out that the sternum in an adult male is usually longer than that in an adult female.

The medical panel also doubted that Sheppard inflicted the third, fatal, wound on himself. If he had already stabbed himself twice in the chest, they said he would have been experiencing such respiratory distress that he would have probably lacked the necessary strength to inflict the fatal wound through the sternum. All three agreed there had to be another person in the bathroom at 1008 Moylan Drive when Baker and Sheppard died.

Bizzack, after his homicide/suicide and "they killed each other" theories, also entertained that possibility that a third person could have been present. In his July 10, memo, the detective wrote about finding Baker and Sheppard's bedroom being in disarray with items thrown about the room. "An examination of the drawers," he wrote, "showed some neatness to the items inside or possibly a third person involved in the death of the two persons in the bathroom."

Along with detective Farley Spencer, Bizzack searched the residence and made photographs. "After the photographs were made," Bizzack wrote, "I proceeded to process the items that could possibly relate to a third person. I processed the area in the bathroom around the vanity, lifted one latent (fingerprint) off that particular item. Also the shower stall, over the top of the victims was processed in the areas that were not wet and a partial palm print was lifted off one portion of that. There were also indications that where fingers had been streaked in the same area that the palm was lifted."

In the same memo, Bizzack said the knife, allegedly the death weapon, was not processed due to the large amount of blood on it. Dahlenburg said, in his autopsy reports, that the blood on the knife had been diluted with water. A report in the case file indicated that detective Farley processed the Case lock-blade knife into evidence.

"I went back to the bedroom occupied by Sheppard and Baker," Bizzack wrote, "and examined the dresser at the foot of the bed and found the case that was used to hold the knife. It was in the jewelry box on top of the dresser."

There was no mention in the case file of jewelry found in the house although Sheppard was buying, selling and trading gold jewelry. A memo, in the case file, from communication officer R. Crank to Bizzack asked the detective to call Sheppard's brother. According to the memo, Dale Sheppard, the Midland, Ohio, police chief, called the

Division of Police around midnight on July 9, and stated he could be the brother of Danny Sheppard. "He further states that Danny had a gold bracelet worth $16,000 and other valuable jewelry in his possession," Crank's memo read. "If at all possible contact him tonight at (telephone number blacked out)."

The only inventory found in the case file was made of the master bedroom. No jewelry was mentioned in that inventory. When, or if, Sheppard was contacted by detectives about his brother's death was not known. No statement from Dale Sheppard found in the case file.

Coroner Chester Hager ruled Baker and Sheppard's deaths were caused by stab wounds to their chests. The coroner's report, like Dahlenburg's, made no mention of who administered those wounds.

Attempts to locate Dahlenburg for an interview were futile.

The last medical license the author found for the pathologist was in Georgia for 2000. He had addresses, at one time, in Boynton Beach, Jacksonville Beach and Jacksonville, Florida. Letters sent to Dahlenburg at those addresses were all returned as undeliverable. Florida medical examiners' offices and libraries were unable to provide any information on him. The University of Louisville, where he graduated from medical school in 1971, listed a 1991, Lexington address for Dahlenburg in their alumni directory. However, Dahlenburg was not listed in their 2006 directory.

Bizzack took his double homicide theory to the media. The July 15, 1981, *Leader* quoted the detective as saying, "Ms. Baker had a single stab wound to the heart. But the autopsy indicated there had been two thursts of a four-inch knife in the same spot."

In the clinical summary of his autopsy report on Baker, Dahlenburg wrote, "The myocardium is found to have a 2.3 cm long wound in the anterior wall of the right ventricle at the base. This wound is 1.2 cm from the right coronary artery as it winds around the right hand edge of the heart." The medical examiner referenced a wound, not wounds.

The article continued to quote the detective, "Sheppard was cut three times in the struggle between the couple," Bizzack said. "Two of the wounds were superficial cuts to the chest, the third was a wound through the heart. We know they had been having arguments since the day before their deaths. And, we know that she intended to leave him." Bizzack said the knife used to kill the couple belonged to Baker.

"Based on our investigation at the house, the autopsies and interviews with people who knew them, we've have determined they (Baker and Sheppard) killed each other," Bizzack was quoted as saying.

Whether or not the reporter questioned the detective about his unusual description of how Baker and Sheppard's deaths occurred was not known.

Considerable experience dealing with the media enabled Bizzack to keep his statements short, to the point and lead reporters to accept his conclusion. Apparently, he gave little or no time for any follow up inquiries.

After he retired from the Division of Police, Bizzack wrote *Criminal Investigations; Managing the Results*, in which he listed twenty-three commandments for handling the media. They included: make only a brief statement; give reporters the impression you are earnestly trying to help them; do not believe in such things as 'off the record,' always be in charge by controlling the subject and the time frame of the interview or news conference, and refuse to be intimidated.

KSP Sgt. Ross, according to Sally Denton, was angry at the newspaper for the forum they provided Bizzack while never challenging the conclusion. Ross, Denton, wrote, "Tried to 'leak' tantalizing tidbits to individual news reporters, hinting that the state police, as well as the medical examiner, found the murder/suicide suicide explanation to be factually and physically implausible. But, his attempts to incite any investigative initiative fell on deaf ears."

Normally, when the coroner determined a death was a homicide, detectives investigated the crime. Baker and

Sheppard's homicides were apparently an exception. Detectives latched on to the coroner's ruling that both deaths were homicides as the easy way out with the double homicide conclusion.

An August 5, report by detective John Bryant effectively closed the investigation into Baker and Sheppard's deaths. Bryant wrote, "Based on investigation done by this office, detective Dan Gibbons and all members of SIU as well as information received from the Coroner's Office that the two subjects, Harold Danny Sheppard and Cynthia Carol Baker, died as a result of stab wounds received from each other.

"It is believed," his report continued, "that Ms. Baker first stabbed Mr. Sheppard and that he recovered the knife and stabbed her in return. Mr. Sheppard, reportedly, would have lived approximately twenty minutes after being stabbed and Ms. Baker about six minutes, although she would have lost consciousness almost immediately after being stabbed."

Bryant, like Bizzack, maintained the couple was breaking up, an argument ensued, Baker locked the bedroom door, Sheppard kicked the door open and the confrontation continued in the bathroom.

Bryant closed out the case saying, "Based on this information and the extensive investigation which has been conducted, which is outlined in the major case jacket and the ruling by the coroner that the subjects killed each other, this compliant should be cleared by exception."

The term Bryant used, cleared by exception, meant detectives working the case and their superiors were satisfied with the results of their investigation and no further efforts need be made.

The coroner ruled their deaths were homicides but did not say they killed each other. That was the solution chosen by detectives.

Did Bryant actually believe Sheppard lived for twenty minutes after killing Baker and stabbing himself twice in each side of the chest before administering the fatal wound to the heart, through his sternum?

The sternum is such a heavy, thick bone, medical examiners use saws or heavy, shrubbery cutters to cut through the sternum and open the chest. The medical panel, after reading Dahlenburg's autopsy reports, certainly failed to agree with the detectives' conclusions.

Did Bryant believe Sheppard jerked the knife out of his chest, after suffering the fatal wound to his heart, stabbed Baker, lay the knife on the top of the water closet before falling into the bathtub to die?

Where did Bryant get his timeline for how long Baker and Sheppard lived after receiving their wounds? There was no timeline in the case file from either the coroner or the medical examiner.

Dahlenburg's autopsy reports made no mention of how long they lived after being stabbed. He indicated Baker died soon after being stabbed. "Based on the findings at the scene of her death," Dahlenburg wrote, "the most likely chain of events was trauma to the head following by stabbing and rather prompt exsanguinations. Subsequent immersion of the body in water most likely resulted in laryngospasm and death." The medical examiner said nothing in his autopsy reports about how long Sheppard could have lived after being stabbed three times in the chest.

Bryant failed to mention Dahlenburg's autopsy findings, in his report, but did reference information provided by the coroner's office. The coroner's investigative report provided information about their birth/death dates, next of kin and manner of death, homicide. The report said nothing about who killed the couple.

The coroner's ruling of homicide gave detectives the opportunity to claim Baker and Sheppard killed other. The ruling allowed the detectives to quickly close the case without any further investigation.

Why were investigators in such a hurry to close the case? Was there a connection to the drug activities of Baker and Sheppard? Or, was there an effort to pad the detectives' cases solved statistics?

In his book, *Criminal Investigations: Managing for*

Results, written after he left the Division of Police, Bizzack wrote, "In managing to get results, there must be some mechanism by which progress can be measured. In private business this measure is in the profit and loss statement. You may want to consider records such as arrests and clearance statistics, community input, performance ratings or other means."

It seemed odd that the former detective was very careful in the book to make no references to the scores of Lexington murder cases he worked in the more than two decades he spent with the Division of Police.

Neighbors Knew Nothing

Cindy Baker and Danny Sheppard lived only a month on Moylan Drive and apparently were total strangers to their neighbors.

Detectives appeared to have spent much of their time interviewing the people who lived on the street and in the neighborhood. Those interviews were mostly unproductive. No accounts were found in the case file where detectives interviewed members of the Baker and Sheppard families or any of those connected to The Company.

Aside from the neighbors, only interviews with Doug Ferguson and Carol Higdon, Stephen Merritt and Kenneth Hahn, the two maintenance workers, and officer Karl Hiten were found in the case file.

Addresses of those interviewed were blacked out in case file copies provided the author. However, it was not difficult to find most of those addresses in the *1981 Lexington City Directory*.

Sally Powell, who lived at 1021 Moylan with her husband Mike, told detectives Drexel Neal and Dan Gibbons they did not know the residents at 1008 Moylan but did see construction workers in the neighborhood during the day of July 9. Sally Powell said she saw no cars at that house, no lights and no activity.

Mr. and Mrs. Robert W. Dowling, who lived at 1025 Moylan, saw nothing out of the ordinary on July 9, and did not know the victims.

Debbie Leonard, who lived at 1029 Moylan with her husband Bob, did not see anything unusual either.

Monica Hinkle, a resident of 1033 Moylan, told detectives she saw a boy, approximately three years old, standing in the door two days earlier. Presumably she meant the house at 1008 Moylan.

Mike Dinsmore, who lived at 1037 Moylan with his wife Carla, and Steve and Dianna Ham, who were not listed in the City directory, knew nothing that would shed any light on the case and did not know the victims.

The same was true with Bob and Laura Steinberg, who told detectives they had lived in the neighborhood for a year and seven months but did not know the victims. The Steinbergs were not in the City Directory.

Edward C. Alford, no address listed, saw nothing unusual when he was cutting his grass around 3:00 p.m., that day. He told detectives he and his wife Margaret had lived in the neighborhood for a year but did not know Baker and Sheppard.

Alijda and Del Vaught, of 1007 Moylan, had lived there for seven months. They knew nothing about the victims and did not see anything or anyone suspicious.

Tina Worden, no address available, told detectives she was out of her house only once that day, around 1:00 p.m., to call her children. She said she saw a barefoot man, with dark complexion and blond hair run past her house and down Moylan Drive. He was in a good mood, she said, and spoke to her. Worden thought he was a construction worker. He ran to the house on the left side of the street. She did not see him leave. She told detectives that her husband was not home and added that neither of them knew the victims.

Detectives did not identify the house on the left side of the street, in the case file. Was the blond haired, barefooted man one of the maintenance workers?

Jeffery H. West, of 1013 Moylan, also saw a man go down the street. He told detectives, "Today approximately between 3:00 and 3:10 p.m., I was mowing my grass when I saw a man walking very fast from 1008 and in about 10 to 15 minutes he came back to 1008 Moylan. He was about 6' with a little bit of a belly, with brown curly hair, beard and mustache, wearing blue jeans and no shirt; had a brownish looking t-shirt stuffed in his back pocket. I identified a photograph of Danny Sheppard as being the man I saw."

The Division of Police, by detective Bizzack's own admission, had Baker and Sheppard's residence under surveillance and their murders occurred right under their noses! Since they had the house under surveillance, they should have known where Sheppard went when he left his home and if anyone else entered the premises.

Detectives appeared to give Carol Higdon's signed statement a great deal of significance as it pertained to the demeanors of Baker and Sheppard that day. She said she left for work around 8:30 that morning and assumed Cindy Baker and Danny Sheppard were asleep. "Somewhere between 10:30 and 11:30 a.m., Cindy called me and wanted to know where my cigarettes were," her statement read. "She seemed in a real good mood before she hung up. I had no contact between (with) Danny or Cindy until around 2:00 or 3:00 p.m., when I received a call from Danny wanting to know where Doug (Ferguson) was.

"I told Danny Doug had gone to Louisville and that he would be home before I got home. Danny said Cindy had decided to move out and he wasn't for sure if he was going to move out. I asked Danny to wait until we all got home so we could talk before anyone moved out. About an hour after Danny hung up, I called him but did not get an answer. I then tried again about an hour later and Doug answered and we talked about Danny for a few minutes and then hung up."

When detectives asked Higdon what kind of a mood Sheppard was in when he hung up, she replied, "He seemed very depressed and seemed to be crying but he did not calm down any when I hung up."

In a statement to detective William Read about his activities on July 9, Doug Ferguson said he left 1008 Moylan around 10:30 that morning and returned about 5:30 that afternoon. When he entered the basement from the garage, he said he heard the shower running.

Ferguson placed his arrival time as corresponding to when M.A.S.H., the television program, was ending. "I came in and picked up the TV Guide to see what else was on," he said. "The phone rang, it was Carol. She talked about Danny calling her earlier at work, upset over Cindy leaving. After I talked to her for a few minutes, I hung up and watched TV for about 10 minutes. The doorbell rang; it was the maintenance men. They came in and we went downstairs, we talked for a minute or two. Then I went back up (stairs) to tell Danny that they were here so he would know."

"That's when I saw the bodies in the bathroom," he said. "I opened the door and saw Cindy's head laying under water and Danny was lying in the position he is in. I shook Danny; he was cold to the touch."

Before he called for assistance, there was something Ferguson had to do. "I knew what was in the bag he had in the house, so I got it and put it in my company car," he told detective Read. In his July 9 report on the case, detective Bizzack wrote, "Ferguson, during this period, made the admission to Det. Read that he had gone through the residence and collected drugs before the police arrived. He turned over those drugs, a small quantity of Quaaludes, marijuana and paraphernalia to Det. Root. Det. Root and I booked those items into property."

The ID Bureau's evidence examination report, which listed the drugs, made no mention of any paraphernalia. The report contained this interesting statement at the bottom of the page, "The enclosed items were recovered at the scene of the double homicide on July 9, 1981. Charges are pending on other occupants of the residence where the homicides occurred." Detective John Bryant's name was on the form, which was dated 7-21-81.

Nothing was found in the case file to indicate Ferguson or Higdon were ever charged in connection with the drugs or Baker and Sheppard's deaths.

Ferguson, in his statement, explained his actions after placing the drugs in his car. "I came in and dialed 0 and it didn't ring the operator," he said. "I yelled at the maintenance men (in the basement) to call an ambulance. I ran down to where the policeman is three doors down and told him there was 2 dead people and he said he would make the calls."

In response to detectives' questions, Ferguson said he did not know of Baker and Sheppard being in trouble with anyone recently. When asked it they had a problem with each other recently, he said, "We went to the lake yesterday, they got into an argument and weren't talking. My girlfriend's sister had made a statement to the effect that she wanted to go out with Danny and Cindy had gotten mad over it."

Karl Hiten, the police officer who lived at 1020 Moylan, said he was feeding his baby daughter when Ferguson knocked on his front door and told him he had found two of his friends dead in their house. "I told him that I would call the police by phone for additional help because he told me he had already called an ambulance," his statement read. "I then went up to the house where I found the 2 men that had just left my house where they were doing some repair work. They had just gone up to 1008 Moylan to finish some work up there"

Hiten, when he got to the house, said he was informed that a man and woman were in the bathroom dead. "At that point," he said, "I told the guy, (Ferguson) to get that dog 'out of here' and for everyone to either stay in the living room or go outside. I then ran down to my cruiser where I told the dispatcher to go ahead and start ID, detectives and commander."

The dog Hiten was referring to was a Doberman Pincher belonging to Sheppard. Bizzack, in his July 9, report, wrote that the Doberman was being trained as a guard dog.

Stephen Merritt and Kenneth L. Hahn were the maintenance workers doing repairs on Hiten's house and the one at 1008 Moylan. Since both men were working on different houses in the development, both buildings may have belonged to the same company/person.

Merritt, in his statement to detectives, said that Ferguson took them to the basement where the repairs were to be made and went back upstairs. "Doug came back to the entrance at the top of the stairs and yelled, 'you need to get an ambulance right way; they have been fighting.' I picked up the downstairs phone and called the operator and she connected me with the fire department. I advised the fire department that there was an emergency and gave the address."

He and Hahn then went back upstairs and tried to calm Ferguson down and give him some water, he said. "He seemed upset and didn't know what to do," Merritt continued. "He (Doug) said, 'they had been fighting last night.' We told Doug he ought to go down and get in touch with Carl (Karl) Hiten and find out what to do. Ken and I stood outside on the front stoop while Doug ran down to Carl's. Doug then came back; he walked back in first and we followed him back in. We asked him if he needed water or anything and we came back outside. At that time an ambulance and a brown car arrived in front of the house."

Merritt said, while Ferguson was gone, he opened the bathroom door and saw the girl in the water, closed the door and left.

Hahn recalled events a bit differently. He said when Ferguson came to the top of the stairs to ask them to call the ambulance, he kept repeating, "I think they're dead, I think they're dead." Hahn said he ran up the stairs and asked Ferguson were the bodies were and he pointed to the bathroom. "I saw a female and a male," he said. "The female was in the water and the male hanging over the tub." Hahn said Ferguson said Baker and Sheppard had been fighting and kept repeating, "I didn't think it would come to this."

Hiten concluded his statement by saying, "I know nothing further about this case because I really never met anyone that lived in that house."

Bizzack, in his July 9, report, said he was called to the scene by officer Pat Murray, who lived at 1012 Moylan, because Murray knew the residence at 1008 Moylan was under SIU surveillance.

It was interesting that officer Murray lived at 1012 Moylan, officer Hiten lived at 1020 Moylan and the residence at 1008 Moylan was under police surveillance and detectives appeared to know nothing about the activities of Baker and Sheppard on the day of their deaths.

They Planned to Get Married and Everything

How could Cindy Baker and Danny Sheppard's three-year relationship, which began at a Lexington party in 1978, have ended so tragically in the bloodstained bathroom of their home?

There had been a series of separations and reconciliations but nothing to indicate either was capable of the brutal and vicious acts, which took their lives.

Dale Sheppard maintained his brother and Cindy Baler were in love, planned to get married and return to Midland, Ohio, to operate a jewelry store. Others, including detectives, said Baker wanted out of the relationship.

Sheppard told reporters Jennifer Hewlett and Jim Warren in the July 12 *Herald*, that he questioned the possibility of the couple breaking up. "I never saw two people that cared for each other the way they did," he said. Sheppard acknowledged the couple separated around Christmas but did not know when they patched up their differences. Cindy Baker and his brother had lived together in Midland and Sheppard became acquainted with her there.

Obviously, Dale Sheppard came to Lexington as he told reporters about a note found in the Moylan house after the couple died. "It said something to the effect of 'I love you. There'll never be any other.' The note also said something to the effect that, you know, I couldn't live without you," he said. Shepard also said his brother and Baker sometimes pouted with each other but he had never seen any violence between them. "I never saw two people that cared for each other the way they did," Sheppard added.

No note, such as Dale Sheppard described, was found in the case file. An inventory of items found in the master bedroom listed several notes, composition books, receipts, checks and telephone numbers.

The attractive, petite Baker was described by her sister, Judi Baker Hall, as being a people oriented person. Hall told reporters her sister was a good person, outgoing, liked music and loved to dance and go camping.

A Lexington native, Cindy Baker was the daughter of Ernest and Louise Baker. Along with her parents, a sister and a brother, she moved to California when she was thirteen, according to the July 13, *Herald*. Later, the family returned to Lexington. The coroner's investigative report listed her father as living in Jacksonville, Florida.

Cindy Baker dropped out of Henry Clay High School in her senior year, according to the article and worked in various department stores. At some point, she apparently received a General Education Diploma since she enrolled in Lexington Technical Institute to study nursing. At the time of her death, she was a waitress at Mr. George's, a restaurant on South Broadway. She had worked there two months.

Bob Joseph, Baker's boss at Mr. George's, told reporters that, in addition to being attractive, she was well mannered and competent. "She really looked younger than 24," he said. "But, I really didn't know her at all outside of work. She didn't sit around and talk too much."

However, Joseph was observant and knew quite a bit about Baker's social life. He told reporters that, in late May or early June, a tall, dark-haired man picked her up several times after her shift ended. The man would not have been Sheppard, who was only 5' 6", the same height as Baker. "But," the article continued, "he said that about two weeks ago Ms. Baker had dinner at the restaurant with another man. The waitress who served the couple, described Baker's companion as having brownish hair and a beard, a description which matched Sheppard's appearance."

Joseph said he never saw Baker again after she and Sheppard had dinner there.

Baker and Sheppard's bodies were found on July 9. Joseph told reporters, on July 12, that detectives had not interviewed him. No interview with Joseph was found in the case file.

Danny Sheppard grew up, with two brothers and two sisters, in Midland, Ohio, where his father was a jeweler. "He was kind of an average individual," Dale Sheppard told reporters. "He was never cross or anything like that. I never saw Danny have any kind of violent outbreaks." Sheppard said his brother, who had previously been married, liked to ride motorcycles, play racquetball, lift weights and had once worked for a private detective agency in northern Kentucky.

Although reporters spoke extensively with Dale Sheppard, no interview by detectives was found in the case file. Efforts to located Dale Sheppard in Ohio were futile. An employee in the Clinton County (Ohio) sheriff's department remembered when Sheppard was Midland's police chief but had no current information about him.

Danny Sheppard had a police record.

According to newspaper accounts, Danny Sheppard was charged in March 1981, with public intoxication, criminal trespassing and resisting arrest. The charges were later merged and he paid a fine of $25.00 plus court costs. The same month he was charged with two counts of trafficking in drugs, both misdemeanors. One count was dropped, he was convicted on the second and placed on six months probation.

Baker worked as a waitress. Sheppard was buying, selling and trading in gold jewelry at flea markets. Along with Doug Ferguson and Carol Higdon, Baker and Sheppard had leased, with an option to buy, a newly built three-bedroom home in Lexington, near the Jessamine County line in June 1981.

From all indications, Baker and Sheppard had an active social life going to parties and taking trips to the lake. Where did the money come from for those activities and to pay their share of the $450.00 monthly lease for their house? Baker, Sheppard, Ferguson and Higdon leased the house from S. Jay Congleton. According to the case file, Congleton purchased the house at 1008 Moylan from Sullivan Enterprises in February 1980.

What was the source of their income? Baker could

not have earned that much as a waitress and Sheppard's income from flea markets had to be unreliable. Did some of Sheppard's income come from the sale of illegal drugs? Did his drugs come from the shipments imported into the commonwealth by The Company?

Prior to Baker and Sheppard's deaths, law enforcement was closing in on notorious members of The Company, which was headed by Lexington native Bradley Bryant and associates that included former detectives Andrew Thornton, William Canan, Steve Oliver and Jack Hillard.

State and federal officials were testifying before a Fresno, California, grand jury during the summer of 1981, about The Company's involvement in drug smuggling, illegal arm sales and the theft of military hardware and equipment from the China Lake Naval Warfare Station, in the desert near, Inyokern, California. Larry Bryant, Bradley Bryant's brother, had security clearance as a China Lake employee.

China Lake, in a sparsely populated desert setting, began as a research, development and testing facility for World War II weapons, according to the November 4, 1993, issue of *The Rocketeer*. In the 1950s, torpedoes, underwater ordinances and missiles were tested there. During the next two decades, China Lake was involved in the development of guided missiles, avionic software, optical and laser systems and anti-radiation guidance research.

Before Baker and Sheppard were killed, China Lake had moved on to missile interceptors and a parachute escape system for the space shuttle. China Lake was touted by the government as being theft proof. Yet, Larry Bryant was reportedly able to steal a remote controlled helicopter, a radar receiver from a sidewinder missile, 150 rounds of .31 caliber tracer ammo, a low level television.

The weather, in the summer of 1981, was not the only heat experienced by the far-flung empire of The Company. It was entirely possible Baker and Sheppard were caught in the rapidly tightening net being played out by federal officers to rein in The Company. The failure to investigate that area of their deaths left a gapping hole in the case.

On June 19, three weeks before Baker and Sheppard died, the federal grand jury in Fresno handed down a twenty-page indictment charging Bryant and Andrew Thornton, The Company's co-founders; Jack Hillard, a former police captain who lived in Versailles; Steve Oliver, a former narcotics officer who lived on Larkspur Drive, in Lexington, and fifteen others with conspiracy to import large quantities of marijuana from Central and South America into the United States.

Bradley Bryant, when the California indictments were handed down, was being held in the Kane County (Illinois) Correctional Center in lieu of $11 million in bond. He was caught in Chicago on May 20, 1981, attempting to sell 800 pounds of marijuana to an undercover detective. The marijuana was estimated to have a street value of $354,000, one of the largest seizures made in the Chicago area at that time.

In January 1979, according to the Lexington newspaper, a mysterious DC-4 landed at Blue Grass Airport and dropped off a huge shipment of marijuana. After the marijuana was downloaded, the plane was cleaned and flown to Bowman Field, in Louisville, where it was abandoned. The indictment charged Oliver as being the pilot of the DC-4. Oliver, employed by the Division of Police for less than two years, was described as spending his time with the social crowd and local jet setters. He came to Lexington from the Savannah, Georgia, police force.

The Fresno grand jury reached deep into Kentucky's political world tapping Dan Chandler, who worked for Caesar's World Casino in Lake Tahoe, Nevada, as an unindicted co-conspirator. Chandler was the son of former governor and Major League Baseball commissioner, A. B. "Happy" Chandler and was once married to Bradley Bryant's younger sister, Lynn. Chandler was also a member of the college crowd along with John Y. Brown, Jr., and James Lambert. Others named in the Fresno indictments with

Kentucky connections were Alvin Snapper and Roger Dale Barnard of Harrodsburg. Snapper, a prolific inventor, was credited with developing the special paint used on Stealth bomber and fighter planes.

Wallace "Mike" Kelly was arrested at his home on Mt Tabor Road, in Lexington, and charged with being a fugitive. Kelly, who grew up working in his father's wholesale pharmaceutical company, was charged with attempting to smuggle $13 million in marijuana in a 72-foot shrimp boat on Florida's west coast. Another of The Company members, Kelly came from an affluent Lexington family and grew up knowing Bryant and Thornton.

Like Cindy Baker, Kelly attended Henry Clay High School. Perhaps they knew each other there. Unlike Bryant and Thornton, Kelly bypassed college to engage in manufacturing and altering firearms and was a licensed firearms and ammunition dealer. He also manufactured alarm systems, some of which were reputed to be in judges' homes. Kelly's wife, Bonnie Gee, would later go to prison for the assassination of Florida prosecutor Eugene Berry, whose work set the stage for Kelly's prison conviction.

The whirlpool of criminal events, which transpired before Baker and Sheppard died, possibly had some connection with their deaths. If they had agreed to snitch on The Company for Ross' KSP unit and/or federal agents, then they could have been killed by any number of people. Nothing was found in the case file that indicated an investigation was pursued along that line.

Those and other puzzling questions were left unanswered by detectives' apparent efforts to close the Baker-Sheppard case as quickly as possible. With the handy homicide death designations, it was easy to make the leap to the double homicide theory, which enabled them to quickly close the case.

In his book, *Criminal Investigations: Managing for Results*, Bizzack wrote, "Perhaps law enforcement in this society is like other larger bureaucracies such as the army; no one individual from within is likely to alter its course, correct it deficiencies and move it swiftly toward the organization it is supposed to be."

As far as Cindy Baker and Danny Sheppard were concerned, it appeared the bureaucracy, Bizzack wrote about, made little effort to either investigate their deaths or correct the case's deficiencies. Without a doubt, the case did move swiftly.

For Baker and Sheppard, regardless of who they were and what they did, and their families, justice was both delayed and denied in a most appalling manner.

Jean Michel Gambet

Jean Michel Gambet's burned BMW.
(Lexington Division of Police)

"Couldn't Get a Job as a Hotwalker"

The French horseman, Jean Michel Gambet, was incinerated on December 13, 1982, in his blazing BMW, on Redd Road in rural Fayette County, after receiving a fatal bullet wound to his head.

His death left a trail of high living, a shattered family, disgruntled business associates, an impending ouster from the Thoroughbred world he so highly valued, a difficult estate without a final accounting, and medical examiners at odds with police investigators over the cause of his death.

Twenty-six years later, two official causes of death are still listed concerning the demise of Jean Michel Gambet.

Gambet's death had implications beyond Lexington and Fayette County, when coroner Chester Hager, following a March 1983 inquest jury's decision, ruled that Jean Michel Gambet's was murdered by person(s) unknown.

Lexington Division of Police detectives considered evidence supporting the verdict of the coroner's inquest jury flawed and continue to classify, for internal reporting purposes, Gambet's death as a suicide.

Gambet died twenty-one years after the confusing, and also unsolved, death of Betty Gail Brown. In the intervening years, state laws governing coroners' investigations of wrongful deaths changed, making the office even more powerful. Previously, local funeral directors were often elected as coroner, without training in or access to forensic pathology, simply because of their profession. They were ill equipped to handle complicated death cases. When Gambet died coroners, if they chose, had assistance from the newly established Kentucky Medical Examiner's Office in determining if a wrongful death had occurred and deciding on the cause of the death.

In 1968, seven years after the bumbling investigation into Betty Gail Brown's death, David Jones, a Georgetown funeral home director, and Al Austin, a deputy commissioner of the Kentucky Department of Health, began laying the ground work, using federal grants, to establish a chief medical examiner' office in the commonwealth.

After the Kentucky judicial reorganization of 1975, coroners and their deputies had the authority of peace officers while retaining the sole responsibility for establishing the cause and manner of death. If they chose, coroners could call for assistance from forensic professionals.

Eventually, Kentucky's medical examiners' program became one of the best in the nation. The problem was, and is, Kentucky's archaic coroners' statutes, which allow those officials, some of which are still not well trained, to supercede medical examiners' expert opinions at will.

Hager, knowing he as coroner had the last word on Gambet's death, appeared content to await the outcome of medical examiners' forensic battle with detectives over whether the horseman was killed or committed suicide.

During the investigation, detectives sifted through Gambet's life and death as well as some of the unseemly sides of the Thoroughbred world. Gambet appeared to operate in the upper realms of that world where he participated as more than a minor player but without the financial resources to reach the inner circles.

Gambet used the established reputation of his father-in-law Harry B. Scott to enter the Thoroughbred business. "Harry Scott was a respected horseman who did deals on a handshake; his word was his bond," former Lexington police detective Philip Vogel said in a January 2007, interview. Gambet, Vogel said, plunged into that world on "Scott's coat tails" and accumulated more debts than he could possibly repay.

Gambet, if he had lived, was finished in the horse business, Vogel said. "He wouldn't have been able to get a job as a 'hot walker.'"

Did Gambet make the difficult decision to commit suicide, knowing he would never again see his wife and two young daughters, by setting his car on fire and then shooting himself? His recent depression, excessive debts and questionable attempts to make authorities believe that he was being stalked convinced detectives he committed suicide. In addition, his life insurance policies were worth double the insured amount if he died an accidental or homicidal death but paid only face value if he killed himself.

Did all of Gambet's carefully laid plans to make his death look like a homicide, strangely coincided with his actually being murdered, shot in the eye, on that isolated country road? Was his death "an eye for an eye" type of retributive justice going back to the Code of Hammurabi, one of the earliest sets of law enacted in 1780 BC in Mesopotamia, which now covers Iraq, eastern Syria and southeastern Turkey?

Regardless of the unanswered questions and disagreements, all those involved in investigating the death agreed on one thing, the horseman was dead. The battle lines were drawn over whether he killed himself or was murdered.

Gambet's life, which ended so tragically, began on a high note when he came to Kentucky in 1972, with his dashing good looks, French charm, high powered connections and intense ambitions to be part of the select world of Thoroughbred horses. A graduate of the Institute Agricole de Monteburg, in Monteburg, France, he became interested in horses while working for Daniel Weilderstein, a prominent Parisian art dealer and horse owner who specialized in the paintings of Claude Monet and compiled a four-volume biography/catalogue of the artist's works.

Working as a pedigree writer at the Jockey Club, in Lexington, gave Gambet an opportunity to study Thoroughbred breeding lines. The Jockey Club maintains a register, description and sales transactions of all Thoroughbred horses. He also worked as an assistant farm manager at Faraway Farm on Huffman Mill Pike.

Faraway Farm was home to one of the greatest Thoroughbreds, Man O' War, during his racing career. "Big Red," as he was known was buried at Faraway after his death in 1947, and remained there, beneath a life-size statue, until he was disinterred in 1977, and reburied at the Kentucky Horse Park. His statue was also moved.

Gambet's August 24, 1974, marriage to Vella "Cissy" Karrick Wise Scott, daughter of Harry Burgoyne Scott II, and Vella Wise Scott, owners of Shandon Farm, on Russell Cave Pike, gave him entrée to the equine business and social set with memberships in the Keendland Club, Idle Hour Country Club, Thoroughbred Club of America and the Lexington Club.

The Scott family's connections were deep in the Kentucky Thoroughbred world. The 200-acre Shandon Farm, on Russell Cave Pike, was purchased by his father Harrie (Harry) B. Scott for an estimated $65,000.00 in 1939. That year Shandon Farm's consignment of young horses sold for the highest average price paid at the Saratoga Thoroughbred Yearling Sales. The 1934 Kentucky Derby winner Cavalcade, owned by Isabella Dodge, was standing stud at Shandon Farm when he died of shipping fever. Hannibal, bred by the elder Scott, ran eighth to the winner, Hill Gail, in the 1952 Kentucky Derby.

Scott and his wife Vella continued the operation of Shandon Farm while the Gambets, after their marriage, lived on Sycamore Valley Farm, on Versailles Road. Sycamore Valley Farm was purchased in 1938, by banker Harry B. Wise and his wife, the former Vella Karrick, who were Vella Wise Scott's parents. Gambet and his father-in-law operated the Euro-American Bloodstock Agency out of the Sycamore Valley Farm.

After Harry B. Wise's death in 1960, his widow Vella K. Wise, Cissy Gambet's grandmother, continued to operate Sycamore Valley Farm, took care of the family's other business interests and kept a tight rein on their purse strings until she died in 1993, at ninety-six.

An heiress to a large block of food chain Winn-Dixie Estate stock, Vella Karrick Wise was a member of the National Society of Magna Charta Dames and Barons, which required a fifteen-generation background check for membership. Organized in 1909, according to their Internet site, the Society perpetuated the memories of the English Barons who worked to secure the Magna Charta and promoted fellowship "Among descendants of those who compelled King John to grant the Magna Charta."

The Frenchman Gambet fitted very well into the Anglophile family, at least in the beginning. He lived on Kentucky horse farm in a relatively new home, drove the best cars and had all the right social and business connections.

The Gambet's housekeeper, Mabel Jones, told detective Philip Vogel in a December 1982, interview that she thought Mrs. Wise had given Cissy Gambet the large home, built around an original log cabin on the Sycamore Valley Farm. Jones said the family spent lavishly renovating and building an addition for the Gambets. The house and farm are located opposite the Versailles Road (US 60) and Parker's Mill Road intersection.

"It wasn't his place but it was his wife's," Jones told Vogel. "You know and he was doing all he could." Jones said Gambet told her he had bought a farm in France, which was much nicer than the Versailles Road farm. "You can't help this farm none," she quoted him as saying, "there's too much to do here."

Gambet's farm, in the Basse-Normandie region of France, was where he kept mares and weanlings. Basse-Normandie included sites of the D-Day invasion of France in June 1944, during World War II.

His father Claude Gambet managed that farm, leasing a portion to American horseman William DuPont. At the time of his death, according to the estate's probate file, horses on the farm were valued at 3,346,650, in French Francs or $508,609 in American Dollars. However, not all the horses there belonged to Gambet.

Living The High Life

The young Frenchman appeared to be living out his dreams of being a player in the Thoroughbred world. He traveled within the correct Lexington social set where neophytes, with plenty of money but little knowledge of the intricacies of the Thoroughbred business, were plentiful.

Jean Michel and Cissy Gambet's older daughter attended a private school, The Lexington School. The Gambets had an active social life, at least in the beginning, with their attendance at private parties, country club events and entertaining his business clients.

Gambet made telephone calls to Europe as if they were local calls. Sometimes his telephone bill was more than $9,000 a month.

Detectives, investigating his death, concluded he had made some money in the buying and selling of Thoroughbreds, at least in the beginning. Apparently, the money Gambet made he spent lavishly. Some of that money went for expensive furnishings for their newly renovated house. There was no indication, in the available records that his wife participated in selecting the furnishings but she may have.

Gambet, according to his estate's probate file, purchased seven Queen Ann walnut side chairs, circa 1740-1760, from New York antique dealer Israel Sack, Inc., for $65,000 in 1981; that was $9,286 per chair. He still owed $34,000 on them when he died.

Through London art dealers, Frost and Reed, he paid $52,000 for a Sir Alfred Munnings painting, "The Rough Common." Munnings, a famous nineteenth century English equine artist, also painted Aristides, the first winner of the Kentucky Derby, and other early famous American Thoroughbreds. Gambet owned other equine paintings, including one by another English artist, John F. Herring, as well as bronzes by Bureadu and Lexington artist George Claxton.

Gambet's antique gun collection included 1851 Colt Navy and 1860 Colt Army revolvers and an 1842 Springfield rifle. The horseman had knowledge of and was familiar with firearms.

He had an extensive array of still and movie cameras with complete accessories. Other items in his tangible personal property inventory included Oriental carpets, an English partners' desk and other period furniture.

He owned a 1977 Peugeot sedan. His automobile insurance paid his estate $17,500, for the burned BMW. The items mentioned above, and numerous other articles, far exceeded the $50,000 estimate of personal property listed in his estate's probate file in Fayette District Court.

Gambet's case file, assembled by Lexington police detectives, revealed another side of his life beyond the expensive furnishings and high-flying lifestyle. That side of his life was filled with dark and threatening financial realities, which endangered not only his future but that of his family and business associates.

The probate file of his estate mirrored, to some the extent, the debts he incurred in an effort to continue his lavish lifestyle, which investigators uncovered.

Those critical monetary problems, requiring immediate attention, continually hovered over Gambet driving him, detectives concluded, to take his own life. The case file gave no indications that his wife, who knew about some of their monetary problems, appealed to her family, especially her grandmother, for financial assistance. Harry B. Scott, who was also Gambet's bloodstock agency partner, gave detectives the impression he was unaware of his son-in-law's impending financial disaster.

The Wrong Road Taken

Cissy Gambet knew something was seriously wrong with her spouse. She told detectives her husband had been depressed for a month. "He wouldn't shave or bathe and wore his pajamas for days at a time," detective Vogel recalled. The detective said she told him their marital relations had suffered in recent weeks before his death.

Mabel Jones, the Gambets' housekeeper, also told Vogel that Gambet had been depressed for some time. She said he did not talk to her about his problems but did discuss them with Joe Manypenny, a Sycamore Valley Farm employee.

Gambet often left the telephone off the hook to avoid calls about his fiscal problems.

He went to extraordinary means, both legal and otherwise, to meet those obligations. Some of Gambet's fiscal problems appeared to stem from his inability to get any money out of France after President Francois Mitterrand nationalized the banks following his election in 1981.

A November 11, 1982, letter he received from Credit Commercial de France stated, "We gave you credit for the $230,000.00 which you had transferred to your account from the account of the CCF agency in Caen. But we were reprimanded by the Bank of France at the end of the month's closing. We were, therefore, obligated to debit your account until we were authorized by the Bank of France to transfer to a foreign account in France from a foreign account overseas."

The letter said Gambet's Lexington bank, as well as a Mr. Schmidt's bank, had been advised of the action. There was no further identification of who Schmidt was or his connection to Gambet other than the two men obviously did business together.

As of that date, Gambet's account at the Caen's bank was credited with 2,253,231 francs, which, using the 1982 rate of exchange, was $342,436.32 in American dollars. The bank's letter expressed regret for the problem they had caused Gambet and added they were available to apologize "To the people to whom the checks were returned."

Apologies would hardly help the horseman straighten out his money problems.

Gambet had a $35,000 payment due on a loan of more than $200,000 at the Bank of Commerce and Trust, in Lexington, past due accounts from American Express, other pressing debts, disgruntled business partners, a maze of questionable Thoroughbred transactions and he was probably going to be late in making a payment on a half-million dollar loan to a New Orleans bank.

On August 8, 1982, Gambet, who owned no real property in Fayette County, obtained a $500,000 unsecured loan from the American Bank and Trust Company in New Orleans. The note was cosigned by Georgetown horseman Don Sucher, 57, owner of Echo Valley Horse Farm.

Gambet's willingness to pay a staggering twenty percent interest rate on a loan from a Louisiana bank of questionable reputation indicated the depths of his financial morass. According to the *Survey of Current Business*, published in 2000 by the Bureau of Economic Analysis of the US Department of Commerce, the prime interest rate in July 1982, was twelve percent per annum and home mortgage rates were in fourteen percent range.

Perhaps Gambet intended to repay the loan from a pending deal. The horseman, according to his estate's probate file, was to sell seven mares to James L. Tinder III, for $950,000 in a deal to be concluded on or before January 1, 1983. There was no indication in the probate file that the transaction occurred.

Gambet came from generations of sturdy French ancestors but his fate seemed determined by Irish concept of Murphy's Law: if it was possible for anything to go wrong it usually did. That, coupled with financial incompetence, contributed to his downfall. His fiscal situation led to numerous theories, on both sides of the ocean, about his death ranging from suicide to a Mafia hit.

David Gordon, in a May 2003, article in the *Belfast Telegraph* about the kidnapping of the Aga Khan's great stallion, "Shegar," speculated that, "The Mafia was suspected of killing Gambet for not repaying a loan he had taken out to buy an interest in the Champion Stakes winner, Vayrann, from the Aga Kahn."

That was the $500,000 loan from the New Orleans bank.

The current Aga Kahn, a direct descendent of the Prophet Mohammad and the Imam of millions of Shia Ismaili Muslims, was chosen by his late grandfather as his successor instead of his wayward father Prince Aly Khan. Aly Khan and Englishwoman Joan Guinness, parents of the Aga Khan, were divorced. Aly Khan later married the American actress, Rita Hayworth.

Lucille Wright Markey, matriarch of Lexington's famed Calumet Farm, named the stable's last great horse, Alydar, for Aly Kahn. She said the name meant, "Aly darling." Alydar ran second to Affirmed in all three 1978 Triple Crown races, the Kentucky Derby, Preakness and Blemont Stakes. Aly Kahn attended several Kentucky Derbies.

The Aga Khan had Thoroughbred farms in Ireland and France and was reputed to be a man in the horse world one did not want to cross.

On August 2, 1982, Gambet wrote the Aga Khan a check for $166,000 for a ten percent interest in his three-year-old Irish stallion, Vayrann, who in eight starts had four graded stakes victories and placed in three other races. The check was written by Gambet on his Bank of Commerce and Trust's Sycamore Valley Farm account.

According to an October 29, 1982, audit of American Bank and Trust Company of New Orleans, by J. K. Byrne & Company, New Orleans, Certified Public Accountants, Gambet and Sucher signed the $500,000 note on August 8,

1982, six days after Gambet wrote the check for an interest in the stallion.

It was obvious that the Aga Khan's bank received the horseman's check. The copy of Gambet's $166,000 check, in the case file, made out to S. A. Aga Khan, had been deposited in a Paris, France, bank and was stamped, "Insufficient funds."

An American Bank and Trust Company reminder notice stating the note plus interest, $523,013.70, was due on December 1, 1982, was sent to Gambet and Sucher in care of Wayne H. Goodwin at First Security National Bank and Trust Company in Lexington.

On December 1, Gambet made two telephone calls to the American Bank and Trust Company number in New Orleans. The first was only for one minute and the second lasted ten minutes. Whether Gambet was arranging to pay only the interest on the note or a portion of the principal was not known.

Detective John Thurston's December 14, interview with Gambet's personal attorney, Don Sturgill, revealed it was possible Gambet had money to make a payment on the loan. Thurston quoted Sturgill as saying, "Mr. Gambet had a $500,000 note due, that he had put a down payment on and that another client of Mr. Sturgill's had co-signed the note from his bank for Gambet for a horse deal between Europe and the United States. Evidently, the deal never developed and Mr. Sturgill's client may be held responsible for the $500,000."

What happened to the $500,000 Gambet and Sucher borrowed and exactly when the transaction took place were only partially cleared up after the Frenchman's death. The money Gambet had to make a payment on the loan, that Thurston quoted from Sturgill's interview, remained a mystery.

Gambet's wife appeared to be unaware of the $500,000 note other than knowing her husband had some financial transactions with the New Orleans bank, according to detectives' memos in the case file. She knew her husband had some dealings with the Aga Kahn. However, Cissy Gambet, 31, appeared to know quite a lot about some of her husband's other financial problems in Lexington.

According to Thurston's memo, she told authorities that her husband, in addition to the cash flow problems, had some difficulties with two local individuals concerning financial matters.

Thurston's memo stated, "The first one is Al Stilz, Jr., at the Bank of Commerce. This will be in reference to money matters and the lack of a cash flow he has been having of late." Stilz, a bank official, had asked Gambet, on the day he died, to make a $35,000 payment on his $200,000 loan.

The second person Cissy Gambet mentioned to the detective was Robert Green and a transaction involving one of the biggest names in the Thoroughbred business. Multimillionaire philanthropist W. T. Young was in the process of building a successful breeding and racing operation, Overbrook Farm, on Delong Road in Lexington.

Gambet appeared to play only a minor role in events surrounding Young's purchase of a horse but Thurston, for some reason, devoted a half page of his four-page memo to the situation.

"Next was Robert Green, whose son, Chris Green, owns Mint Lane Farm, where a horse is standing at stud at that location and this has a short story with it," Thurston wrote. "Green had advised Mr. W. T. Young to buy a certain horse. The horse did not do well, so Mr. Green advised Mr. Young to sell the horse. The horse was sold at much less than the purchase price. At that point, another trainer of Green purchased the horse and, all of a sudden, it began winning. The horse is now standing stud at a considerable profit and believed to be syndicated thus far. The two different trainers that Green has now share an interest in the horse.

"A Mario Ruspoli is the son-in-law of W. T. Young, and asked the alleged victim, Mr. Gambet, to check on some telephone numbers for him about the horse. Gambet had told the Young son-in-law to call Frezig (Fasig) Tipton in New York to check on some things about the horse."

Young, according to his obituary in the January 14, 2004, *Courier-Journal*, turned to others for advice about buying horses. He employed trainer D. Wayne Lucas in 1982, to train his horses and advise him on Thoroughbred purchases.

The situations Thurston described in his memo were indicative of how some deals were made in the Thoroughbred industry in the 1980s. The underlying tone of the memo pointed to the industry's preference to operate in a closed environment, much like a private fraternity. Gambet, from all indication, was not only a member in good standing but also a player and a fast learner in an arena where Thoroughbreds were bought and sold without checking Jockey Club ownership certificates.

A man who worked with Gambet shortly after he came to Kentucky said the Frenchman had a limited knowledge of horses at that time but he learned quickly. The man, who preferred to remain anonymous, spoke of Gambet to the December 16, *Lexington Leader*, saying "He had a strong ego and I don't necessarily mean that in a negative way. He was willing to do and learn things."

Some of the things Gambet learned about the business may not have served him well. In a December 16 memo, detective Vogel related how Gambet attempted to delay paying some of his debts. Gambet apparently copied the Bank of Commerce's letterhead on a blank sheet of paper. A typed letter, using the bank's letterhead, stated that Gambet's bank account had been frozen and was being audited by the Internal Revenue Service (IRS). The name and signature on the letter was that of Malcolm Roberts, whom detectives were told by Henry Alvin Stilz III, a bank officer, had never been associated with the Bank of Commerce.

Detectives Vogel and Thurston contacted the IRS, and learned there was no audit but were told Gambet failed to file federal tax returns for 1980 and 1981. Obviously,

Gambet had filed previous tax returns. After his death, the IRS filed a $277,632 tax claim against Gambet's estate.

Captain Phil Kitchen's August 1, 1982, memo stated there was "Some evidence of fraudulent business deals with close associates of Mr. Gambet. This was found due to the fact several horses listed in limited partnership agreements did not exist and/or liens were found on horses and their foals."

As the financial noose was tightening, Gambet appeared to be planning to take his own life by carefully laying down a trail to make his death look like a homicide.

At 8:38 a.m., on the day he died, Gambet called the Lexington Police Department to report threatening telephone calls. A record of his call contained this conversation: "Good morning, sir. My name is Jean Michel Gambet and, uh, I've been getting about now four phone calls telling me that, us,...well 'I'll get you, you bastard,' and I just, you know, would like to find out what it is all about if that possible. I just don't know who can call me this way because I can't remember doing anything to anybody."

The communication officer, who took Gambet's call, suggested he have the telephone company put a trap on his line where he could keep a record of all such calls or change his telephone number.

In her interview with detective Vogel, Mabel Jones, the Gambet's housekeeper, seemed certain that he was not receiving any threatening telephone calls at his home or office. Jones said, "If he was getting obscene phone calls, I would have got some too, because I answer both phones sometimes (when) both of them's gone."

The financial strain was taking it toll on Gambet. Joe Nickell and John F. Fischer, authors of *Mysterious Realms*, included a chapter on the Gambet case in their book. "Two of his closest friends stated that he was extremely upset and worried over his credibility and standing in the horse community," they wrote.

Nickell and Fischer quoted Gambet as remarking to a close friend, "My God, the way things are going, sometimes

I think—the pressure of this business—if it wasn't for my wife and children, sometimes I feel like I'd blow my head off."

Gambet picked up his older daughter, Emma, age four, and a neighbors' daughter from the Lexington School about 11:45 a.m., on December 13. Also waiting for his daughter was Henry Alvin Stilz III, a Bank of Commerce and Trust officer. Stilz, whose father was the bank's president, told detective Thruston that he walked over and got into Gambet's BMW to talk with him about his overdue loan payment. The banker, according to his interview with detectives, told Gambet that a $35,000 installment, on his $200,000 loan, was past due and should be paid that day because the bank's board of directors was meeting and would question the delinquent payment.

"He stated that he would pay it soon because he had sold some horses in France for $500,000, and the money was on the way," detectives quoted Stilz as saying. Detective Thurston later discovered those horses had not sold while Gambet was in France because none of the bids reached the reserve prices he set. There was nothing in Stilz's statement to investigators to indicate Gambet mentioned he was being followed that morning or was receiving threatening telephone calls.

Nickell and Fischer pointed out, in their book, that when Gambet dropped of the neighbor's child, he had picked up at the Lexington School, he told the mother about receiving anonymous telephone calls saying that he was being watched and followed.

"She looked but saw no car that might be following him," they wrote. "During the twenty minutes or so that she talked with him in the driveway, she thought he appeared 'upset,' even somewhat 'distraught.' She suggested that he call the police and he said he would, while neglecting to tell her he already had."

Former detective Vogel called attention to a fallacy in Gambet's claim that he was being watched from a location across from his farm and was being followed. Lexington detectives and officers who lived outside of Lexington, in Woodford, Franklin and Anderson counties, parked their marked and unmarked cars, which they were not allowed to take out of Fayette County, at the Keene Motor Lodge, which was directly across US 60 from Gambet's home.

"There were officers coming and going to and from in their police units and civilian cars 24/7 at that location," Vogel said. "In all the years I can remember, the (nearby) convenience store was never robbed nor burglarized because of the high police presence a that location. This, in my mind, dispels Gambet's ruse that he was being watched by people across the street from his home under the nose of Lexington officers coming and going all hours of the day and night."

In addition, Vogel said the license plates of motel patrons were constantly checked for criminal activity and the convenience store owners reported they had not observed any suspicious or unusual activity around their property.

The description Stilz gave detectives that Gambet was unshaven, his hair and clothes were messed up and his conversation was garbled confirmed what Cissy Gambet told investigators. She said her husband had not shaved that morning after his bath but added that he was a very meticulous in personal grooming. Others commented on his appearance that day since he was usually such a careful and neat dresser.

Gambet, after returning from the school, left his wife a note saying, "I have been followed all morning by a black 1981 or '82 Chevrolet. I am going to the police station and to your father's and to Don Sucher's." Sucher was the co-signer on Gambet's half-million-dollar note with the New Orleans bank.

If he was planning suicide or was actually receiving threatening telephone calls, Gambet must have been in abject agony knowing he would never again see his wife, his daughter Emma nor her sister Elizabeth, age one. He would not be around to enjoy the pleasures of their growing up, getting married and having his grandchildren. Whatever, his business shortcomings were, Gambet appeared to value his family and was apparently prepared to sacrifice his life to protect his wife and children and insure their financial future.

Mabel Jones talked about how sad he looked when he brought his older daughter home from school and she gave him his telephone messages. Jones said he went into his office to return the calls. The case file's telephone log indicated Gambet made calls to two different numbers in France. The first call, at 12:12 p.m., lasted twelve minutes; the second, at 12:24 p.m., was only four minutes. He had called both numbers earlier in the day. The telephone log indicated Gambet made 188 calls to France from November 14th to December 13th. His telephone bill that month was $9,012.70. The telephone log, in the case file, contained only outgoing calls, not incoming messages, for the bloodstock agency number.

Jones, the housekeeper, provided the best insight investigators had into the Gambets' life style. "Why, I knew more about his wife than he did," she said. "He'd come in the kitchen and say, 'Mabel, where's Cissy' or 'How long has she been gone' or 'Do you know which way she's gone?'" The housekeeper described Gambet as a quiet but awfully nice man. She said when her washing machine stopped working Gambet bought her a new one the previous Christmas.

"I was the last one to talk to him," she told Vogel, "right here in this kitchen. He was here a quarter to one and just thinking when I went home, he was dead and I didn't even know it until later that night (when) I talked to you."

Gambet finished his telephone calls, told his daughters goodbye and prepared to leave his home for the last time around 12:30-12:45 p.m. Jones asked him, "You want me to tell them that you'll be back later on this afternoon, late this afternoon? He said yes. Got in his car and left."

"He did look kindly sad," Jones recalled. "You, know, he looked kindly confused like (he was) worried about something."

The End Brings No Closure

Gambet's movements from the time he left his home on Versailles Road until his death a few hours later were not entirely clear.

Detective Drexel Neal, according to his February 3, 1983, memo attempted to track the source of the can, containing kerosene, found in Gambet's car. A year earlier, Gambet had purchased two five gallon cans of kerosene from Rainbow Oil and Coal Company, in Versailles, for space heaters used while their home was under renovation and construction and to thaw out Cissy Gambet's Mercedes station wagon the previous winter.

Joe Manypenny, the farm maintenance man, told detectives Gambet had taken him to the Versailles firm to buy kerosene because they were the nearest business that sold the clear fuel he preferred to use.

Steve Hogg, the Rainbow Oil owner, identified both Gambet and his car but, according to Neal, was unable to remember if he purchased the can and kerosene on December 13th. The store's register tape for that date indicated a purchase of $4.25, the price of the can, was made but there was no time stamp on the tape or identification of the product sold.

A Rainbow Oil employee, Steve Poole, told Neal that Gambet had purchased some gas or diesel conditioner, a one-gallon metal container and one gallon of kerosene sometime before December 13 and identified Gambet's white BMW. Poole remembered towing his wife's Mercedes station wagon in for repairs the previous winter when he worked at Bluegrass Parkway Gulf, near the Sycamore Valley Farm.

Neal retraced Gambet's probable routes from his home to Redd Road, where his body was found in the burning BMW. "The route is US 60 to Mt. Pisgah," Neal's memo said, "Pisgah Road north to Payne's Mill Road, east on Payne Mill's Road to Redd Road and then turning right on Redd Road to the pull-off at the Kentucky Utilities Transformer Station. The distance is 8.2 miles and takes approximately 13 minute to travel." If Gambet left his home to go to Rainbow Oil to buy the kerosene, another ten to fifteen minutes could be added to the time frame.

Vogel pointed out that if Gambet did not buy the kerosene at Rainbow Oil, he would have had to drive back into Lexington to find that type of fuel. "To the best of my memory," Vogel said, "that particular brand/model of can was distinct to Rainbow Oil and Gas. No other hardware or feed store in Versailles sold that brand/model." However, he said, it was possible that Southern States, in Lexington, might have sold the same style of can.

Using Neal's estimated time frame, Gambet, if he did not drive into Lexington or make any other stops, arrived at Redd Road in twenty to thirty minutes after leaving his home around 12:45 p.m. What did Gambet do from approximately 1:15 p.m., until he died? Fire Department Engine 12 was not dispatched to his automobile fire until 3:58 p.m.

Did Gambet once again weigh his options, to live or die? If he chose to live, he alone knew the depth of his financial problems and the scandal they would bring not only to his family but to friends and associates. Would his marriage into a socially prominent family survive? If he chose to die, he could avoid the financial embarrassment and disgrace for himself and probably leave his family with enough money, after his debts were paid, to sustain them while they dealt with all the problems connected to his demise. The weighty issues Gambet faced affected people in France as well as in Lexington, Louisville, Georgetown and Woodford County.

How long he sat in his car at the Redd Road location was not known. Neither was it known if he came in contact with anyone at the remote area before he was shot and the fire started. If he was actually being followed, why would he choose to park in such an isolated site?

While pondering his decisions, the black Chevrolet, which he said had been following him that morning, or another vehicle, might have arrived on the scene. Hired assassins, if indeed that was what they were, or someone with a deep and consuming grudge against Gambet, may have felt comfortable in carrying out an assassination in such remote area. If that was the case, they could have shot the Frenchman with his own .38 Smith and Wesson to make his death look like suicide, collected the shell casing, tossed the pistol aside, torched the car and body and left the scene.

Was his death an "Eye for an eye" type of retributive justice begun by Hammurabi?

Those who believed the horseman was murdered theorized that the killers were probably on their way out of the state by the time the fire department arrived at the scene. It was not known if scheduled commercial flight manifests or general aviation charters were checked at Blue Grass Airport for that afternoon. The black Chevrolet, he reported was following him, could or could not have been a part of the mystery.

Although Redd Road was located in a remote area of Fayette County, several cars were observed at or near where Gambet parked his car. According to Capt. Kitchen, investigators were unable to identify any of the vehicles or their occupants.

What ever the time frame, theories or circumstances, everything ended for Gambet that windy, winter afternoon near the Woodford County line as the fire's flames, consuming the man and the car, flashed vividly into the cloudy winter sky.

Walter Ernest, who lived nearby, told Thurston he came upon the fire and heard "pinging" sounds like a .22 being fired. Ernest also reported seeing a vehicle, possibly a maroon Opel, a 1978 or 1979 model, with two white men in it sitting near the scene of the burning car. He described them as being possible seventeen or eighteen years old and wearing black jackets. Ernest said he followed the vehicle, which made no attempts to escape notice, as they continued down Redd Road to Elkchester Pike after Ernest turned into his driveway.

Phil Bach told Thurston he saw the flames and smoke from his house, two miles away, drove to the scene, returned home, called the fire department but saw no other vehicles in the vicinity.

Detectives, investigating the case, believed Gambet doused the car's interior and himself with kerosene, lit the fire and then shot himself in the head. Vogel estimated, if Gambet doused himself and the car with kerosene, he would have had several seconds to shoot himself before the flames reached him. The conflagration burned slowly but intensely. The bituminous pavement under the vehicle was melted down to the gravel roadbed. The BMW's wheel covers melted down onto the pavement, Vogel said.

In his request to the Kentucky State Police (KSP) Crime Laboratory, in Frankfort, for forensic tests, detective Drexel Neal estimated Gambet's body was subjected to heat of 2,000 to 2,700 degrees Fahrenheit for more than twenty-five minutes. In Lexington, where the elevation was approximately 1,000 feet, water boiled at 210 degrees Fahrenheit. The automobile fire generated more than ten times the heat required to boil water.

Smoke from the fire was so thick that the Lexington Fire Department Engine 12 crew, responding Bach's call, was unable to see the body until the flames were almost extinguished. "After partially knocking down the flames, I reached inside the car to pull the hood latch," Lt. Remious Day wrote in his report. "The driver's door was already open. Smoke was still so heavy you could hardly see the auto. After extinguishing the flames under the hood, we found the body which was partly in the car and partly out on the driver's side front seat." Firemen were at the scene for almost four hours.

Officer Y. S. Davis, the first investigator to reach the scene and the officer of report, gave a description of the position of the body matching that of Day's. In her report, Davis described the victim's body as lying in a prone position across the driver's seat with the left leg fully extended outside the vehicle. "Victim's right leg was bent and partially outside of vehicle," she wrote. "Victim's right foot (detached from the leg) was lying on the ground near the rear wheel." She noted a gun was found near the detached foot.

When detective Thurston and other investigators arrived at the scene, they examined the .38 caliber handgun on the pavement near the car's left rear door. The nickel-plated Smith and Wesson, a six-shot revolver with a four-inch barrel, was chambered on an empty casing which bore a firing pin indentation. Three shells in the cylinder were intact and two had damaged primers. The pistol's wooden grips were burned away.

"The area (pavement) around the gun showed no traces of burned residue from the grips indicating that the gun had probably been moved from its original location, possibly by firefighters," detective Leroy Richardson wrote in his report. As the BMW's front passenger door was closed, the pressure from the firemen's hoses could have easily backwashed the gun out of the car. If that was the case, the residue from the revolver's grips was gone.

An important piece of evidence, the spent .38 caliber bullet, was never found. If Gambet was murdered, the assailant(s) could have fired the gun, left it on the pavement, in an effort to make the death look like suicide. Consequently, that shell casing could have been anywhere but at the crime scene. Or, the shell could have melted in the intense heat after Gambet killed himself.

Investigators located the open, empty kerosene can in the car's right front floorboard area. The can's cap was found under Gambet's body in the driver's seat.

Vogel said the location of the cap from the kerosene can, while an under-appreciated piece of evidence, was extremely important. "The location of that fuel (can) cap," he explained, "lends itself to the probability that it was thrown down on the (driver's) seat before the contents of the can had been emptied; the can thrown on the passenger side of the floorboard; ignition of the kerosene mix; the gunshot to the front of the head; the body falling forward into the flames and on top of the fuel can (cap); weapon falling from the hand of Mr. Gambet, as he fell forward onto the seat on top of the fuel can cap."

Vogel said he and detective Thurston reproduced what they believed to be Gambet's physical movements immediately prior to his death, without using a flammable liquid, several times and came to the same conclusion. "No other weapon was involved in the scene of the homicide, other than the weapon Mr. Gambet had in his possession," he said.

Officers and detectives assisted deputy coroner Gary Ginn in removing the body from the car. Gambet's remains crumbled as they were placed in a black body bag. The skull, officer Davis said, shattered into ashes when touched. At some point the skull remnants were placed in a separate plastic bag. After the body was removed, investigators continued to search the area for several hours looking for evidence. Gambet's personal possessions, found in the vehicle, were logged into evidence and later returned to his wife. They included a bag of coins, a ring, silver bracelet, belt buckle and keeper and a Cartier watch. Boxes of burned catalogues, books and papers, as well as a charred television set, were found in the BMW's back seat.

Investigators returned to the fire scene the next day but their search failed to yield any sign of the spent bullet. Detectives spent two more days tearing apart the burned BMW, which had been taken to Williams Wrecker Service, in Lexington, looking for an indentation, which might have been caused by a bullet. None was found. Deputy coroner Ginn, in his report, said he assisted in the continued investigation of the burned vehicle and found bone fragments from Gambet's right hand, which he placed with the rest of the remains.

Gambet's body was taken to the University of Louisville to be autopsied by Kentucky's chief medical examiner Dr. George R. Nichols III and Dr. Mark Bernstein, a forensic dentist. After Gambet was identified as the owner of the burned 1977, white BMW, detectives went to his home on Versailles Road and informed his wife and father-in-law that a body had been found in his vehicle on Redd Road a few hours earlier.

When detective Thurston asked Cissy Gambet if her husband owned a gun, she said he did. She went to a bedroom closet, where the gun was kept, and found an empty box. The pistol, found at the death scene, was a gift to Gambet from Patrice E. Nudd Mitchell, according to Thurston's December 12 memo. Gambet had been issued a permit for the pistol on November 17, 1977.

Vogel disagreed and said that Gambet, a French citizen, had purchased the gun from Phillip Gall's, a Lexington firm dealing in sporting goods and firearms. The Smith and Wesson revolver, Vogel said, had been reported stolen but later reappeared. Gambet's wife could give detectives no explanation for the missing gun on the day of her husband's death.

Cissy Gambet, a former bank teller, acknowledged that her husband had financial problems. She thought they were serious but told detectives the most pressing problem was getting money out of France. She told investigators about a letter from the French bank's New York office stating Gambet could not transfer money to Lexington banks because of that nation's new banking rules.

When questioned by Vogel and Thurston about her husband's business schedule, Cissy Gambet replied that he had no set schedule since his office was located at their residence. "He would leave the house day or night with no regular pattern to conduct business," she told the detectives.

At the detectives' request, Cissy Gambet recounted her husband's activities since his return from France on December 7. That was the date, she said, when he told her the threatening telephone calls began. Gambet, she recalled, did not recognize the male voice on the telephone and told her he was having a trap put on their line.

Since it was almost a week later, December 13, when Gambet talked with police about having a trap put on his telephone lines he evidently did not consider the calls, if they actually occurred, a pressing problem. According to investigators, nobody but Gambet heard the alleged calls.

On December 11, she continued, her husband showed horse farms to a client from Atlanta and that evening they went out to dinner. Gambet's telephone log indicated he made six calls to an Atlanta number, determined by investigators to be that of John Candler's, on November 22, December 3, and December 11. There was nothing further in the case file to indicate whether Candler was a member of the wealthy and influential Atlanta family that owned and developed Coca-Cola from 1889 until 1923.

Another call to Atlanta, on December 11, was to Tiffany's. Perhaps Gambet ordered a surprise gift for his wife, with whom he shared a birthday on December 22.

The next day, December 12, Cissy Gambet told detectives her husband had a meeting with Lexington horseman Tom Moler about a horse deal. Moler owned some horses in partnership with Gambet.

In accounting for her whereabouts the afternoon of December 13, she told Vogel and Thurston she did not see her husband after he picked up their older daughter from school as she returned home around 3:00 p.m. She found the note he had left her about his being followed and list of his appointments. She checked with her father and Don Sucher, to see if her husband kept his appointments with them. He had not. Then, she took their daughters and left. There was no indication, in the case file, of where Cissy Gambet went. Vogel's memo stated she returned home around 5:30 p.m.

She told Vogel her husband was a Roman Catholic but did not attend church regularly as he was not impressed with the manner in which mass was conducted in Lexington. The December 16, *Leader* reported the couple was married at Christ Church Episcopal and attended services there. "She believed that her husband did have strong personal religious beliefs and that he had a very strong belief in the family unit," Vogel wrote.

After leaving the fire scene, detective Neal went to the Gambet residence. Neal, with the family's permission, took Gambet's briefcase for evidence. In the brief case was a $27,000, ninety-day overdue bill from American Express, plus numerous other bills and duns from creditors.

Detectives later spent two hours, according to Thurston's December 16 memo, in a candid conversation with Harry B. Scott, Gambet's father-in-law and bloodstock agency partner, about the victim's financial situation. They showed him the fake bank letter and other information investigators had gathered about Gambet's financial dealings.

"Mr. Scott, although not admitting wholeheartedly that his son-in-law could have committed suicide, we believe now realizes the financial condition that his son-in-law was in and the thought of suicide is not beyond the realm of probability," Thurston wrote.

Whether or not detectives showed him the paperwork dealing with the $500,000 loan from the bank in New Orleans was not known. However, it was puzzling that Scott, not only Gambet's partner but his wife's father, would not have known something about the depth of his son-in-law's financial crisis.

Vella Scott flatly refused to believe their son-in-law committed suicide. Mabel Jones, the housekeeper, said Vella Scott asked her, the day after Gambet's death, who could have killed him? Jones said she replied, "I said, uh, have you ever stopped to think that he might have killed himself?" Jones said Vella Scott refused to accept the idea of suicide saying, "Oh no, he's happy and he's got two lovely children and a wife and everything."

Vella Scott's remarks underscored the cultural differences relating to suicide between the United States and France, Vogel pointed out. "Remember this was 1982," he said, "suicide was not generally accepted in the US and thought of suicide were repugnant and often thought of as a symptom of mental illness. While, on the other hand, in French society, it was not thought of disdainfully and there were even 'societies' and much written about the acceptance of suicide and differing methods of accomplishing suicide.

"Suicide by someone troubled with (a) mental defect or disease is one thing," he continued, "but the planning of suicide to enhance the financial gains of his heirs requires a fool proof plan to deflect an investigation of suicide."

Jean Michel Gambet was nobody's fool.

While detectives continued their investigation, the battle over how Gambet's life ended began.

Entrance and Exit Wounds or Fractures?

Chief deputy coroner Gary Ginn, in his case file report, said he and deputy coroner Rolan Taylor carefully removed Gambet's remains into a pouch and took them to the coroner's office in Whitehall Funeral Home, which was owned by coroner Chester Hager and his family.

Having secured Gambet's remains, Ginn notified the chief medical examiner, Dr. George Nichols III, in Louisville and made arrangement for him to autopsy the remains as soon as possible.

"On December 14th, early a.m., the remains were transported to Louisville by Deputy Coroner Rolan Taylor for the autopsy," Ginn wrote.

Nichols, who became Kentucky's first state medical examiner in 1977, had an impressive professional resume. He was an assistant clinical professor of pathology and director of forensic pathology training at the University of Louisville, as well as an instructor at the National College of District Attorneys in Houston, Texas. Both Nichols' undergraduate degree in American history and his Doctor of Medicine degree came from the University of Louisville.

Dr. Nichols' autopsy report stated, "Death in this case is due to a penetrating gunshot wound to the head. The decedent was alive during the conflagration." Nichols said the carbon monoxide saturation in Gambet's body was twenty-six percent. His post mortem examination notes revealed the only skin left on the body was in the left abdominal quadrant, the arms were amputated at the elbows by the thermal effects of the fire and the right foot was missing at the ankle.

"Since the body was in the condition that it was, that is, massively incinerated," Nicholas later said, "and since any physical touching of the body caused the bony structure of the body to be dissolvable, just literally fragments with touching, an examination of the head was not performed other than just looking at it that particular day and x-raying it particular day."

Nichols, said Dr. Mark Bernstein, the forensic dentist on this staff, removed the jaws to compare the teeth with dental records. "Dr. Bernstein," Nicholas said, "concluded the identity of Mr. Gambet was positive quite early on."

When a positive identification was made from his dental work, Ginn went to the Sycamore Valley Farm residence on Versailles Road on December 14, to officially notified Mrs. Gambet of her husband's death. Death notifications are the responsibility of coroners and their deputies.

"On December 15th," Ginn's report continued, "Deputy Coroner Rolan Taylor returned to Louisville to pick up the remains of Jean Michel Gambet which had been left in Louisville on December 12, 1982, at the request of the Medical Examiner Dr. Nichols." When the remains were returned to the coroner's office, Ginn examined them and found that the head had not been returned.

"I immediately called Dr. George Nichols and informed him that he had not returned Mr. Gambet's head. He assured me the remains were intact. I told him I would examine the remains again to make sure I was correct. I did examine the remains and the head was not there."

Ginn said he again called Nichols about the missing body part and the medical examiner told him he would consult with Dr. David Wolf, the forensic anthropologist, and Dr. Mark Bernstein, the forensic dentist, to see if they had retained the head. "He (Nichols) called me later and stated that their office had found the head in the freezer and we could pick it up whenever we wanted it," Ginn wrote.

Lexington detectives wanted a second opinion and asked that another medical examiner check Gambet's skull.

"On Dec. 17, 1982," Ginn continued, "Detective John Bryant picked up Mr. Gambet's head and transported it to the Cuyahoga County coroner's office in Cleveland, Ohio, for examination so they could render an opinion in the case. The rest of Mr. Gambet's remains were taken to the University of Kentucky Anatomy Dept. for storage until the investigation by the Cuyohaga County coroner's could be completed."

Meanwhile, Cissy Gambet wanted to bury her husband. But, Gambet's body parts were in three locations in two states. His head was in Cleveland, Ohio, his jaws and teeth were in Louisville, Kentucky, and the rest of his body parts were Lexington.

Graveside services were conducted for Gambet on December 17, in the Lexington Cemetery, according to the *Herald-Leader*. Survivors included his wife; two daughters, Emma Karrick Scott Gambet and Elizabeth LeCarpentier Gambet; and his parents Claude and Ginnette Gambet, of Mathieu, France. The newspaper described Gambet as "A well established figure in the Bluegrass thoroughbred industry."

On December 18, Ginn requested the following evidentiary materials be returned to the coroner's office. Those remains included: "Burned and partly carbonized resected upper jaw; massively incinerated and shed resected lower jaw specimen; cortical plate of left body of mandibular bone; completely ashed remains of right posterior mandible and ramus containing carbonized tooth # 32 (third molar) loosely within socket; eight separate carbonized dental roots and thirteen fragments representing portion of dental crowns, the largest of which contains an amalgam restoration."

The deputy coroner's report stated that the dental remains were extremely fragile. "The slight movement or touching in transport will likely cause irreparable damages."

Ginn's report concluded, "On Jan. (day left blank) 1983, the head was returned to the Fayette County coroner's office by the Lexington Fayette Co. Police Dept. I then went to the University of Kentucky Anatomy Dept. and picked up Mr. Gambet's remains and the remains were released to Milward Funeral Directors intact."

Gambet's remains were united weeks after his graveside service.

Nichols' autopsy report of his examination of the remains and Wolf's alleged reconstruction of the skull became pivotal issues in their determination of the weapon used in Gambet's death. The medical examiner said he found "A hemorrhagic wound tract (that) is identified within the left superior parietal area within the thermally damaged brain tissue. Measurement of the entry wound in the right supraorbital plate is 0.25" maximally." His next sentence became the central issue in determining the cause of Gambet's death. "A fragment of the left parietal bone reveals a semi-circular outwardly beveled defect measuring maximally 0.45". This mark is located at a point 1.5" from the sagittal suture of the left parietal bone."

In other words, the bullet, according to Nichols, had entered Gambet's head in or near his right eye and exited above the left ear. Nicholas said he had never heard of a suicide victim shooting himself in the eye.

Wolf, the forensic anthropologist, set out to prove the entrance and exit wounds in Gambet's skull were made with a smaller caliber pistol than the one found at the fire site. The anthropologist's undergraduate degree came from Kansas University, he had a master degree in anthropology and human genetics from the University of North Carolina and a Ph.D. in anthropology and archeology from the University of Arizona. Wolf was a UK professor before joining Nichols' staff on a full time basis.

From the beginning, Wolf appeared determined to proved the entrance and exit wounds in Gambet's skull came from a smaller caliber pistol than the .38 caliber found at the fire site.

Wolf claimed he reconstructed Gambet's skull from pieces collected at the fire scene. He later testified the skull was fifty percent intact and another third had been recovered.

The skull had been handled by a number of people: deputy coroner Ginn, his assistant, the forensic anthropologist, the medical examiner, the forensic dentist, investigators and an Ohio medical examiner. Gambet's skull had been transported from Lexington to Louisville to Cleveland and back to Lexington. The forensic dentist had resected the upper and lower jaw bones and parts of the mandible to examine the dental work, which would have caused further damage.

Officer Davis said the skull crumbled at a touch and she doubted if there was enough of it left to indicate a bullet entrance or exit wound, let alone enough for a reconstruction. Yet, Wolf, who had made some colossal blunders in other investigations, later told a coroner's inquest jury that approximately fifty percent of Gambet's skull survived the fire.

Not even Nichols went that far. The medical examiner, in describing what happened when water from the firemen's hose hit Gambet's body, appeared to contradict Wolf. "This is not unusual at all in cases of human beings that are massively incinerated because the bone quite frequently will actually explode when water is sprayed onto the heated bone. It will literally explode, plus the fact that the incinerated bone, every time it is moved or touched, will crumble and fall apart."

However, this did not deter Nichols from agreeing with Wolf that Gambet had been shot with a .22 or .25 caliber pistol, not the .38 found at the scene. They argued that what they determined to be the entrance and exit wounds were too small to have been made by the .38 caliber bullet. No other weapon was found at the scene and the one bullet fired out of Gambet's Smith and Wesson revolver was never found.

At this point in the investigation, the detectives were convinced Gambet committed suicide. Nichols and Wolf were equally convinced he was murdered. The only thing all agreed on was the most vital piece of evidence, which could have settled the issue, the spent bullet, was never found. Numerous conferences were held by detectives and the medical examiner in attempts to reach a mutual agreement.

Seemingly contradicting to Wolf's theory that Gambet was killed with a .22 or .25 caliber bullet which he said entered and exited the skull, was a January 26, 1983, report from the Kentucky State Police Crime Lab. Technicians had examined a bone fragment from the right orbital area of Gambet's skull. Their report revealed no appreciable lead was found around what Wolf said was the entrance wound in the skull bone. Technicians could draw no conclusions from the beveling around the edge of what Wolf called the exit wound. The beveling there was called slight and inconclusive.

If detectives were depending on the findings of the Cugahoga (Ohio) County coroner's examination of Gambet's skull to refute Wolf's assertions as to the caliber of the bullet's entrance and exit wounds, they were disappointed. Dr. Lester Alderson, chief deputy coroner and professor of forensic pathology at Case Western Reserve University in Cleveland, said he and his staff were unable to render an opinion on the question.

"Unfortunately, but understandably, the skull, the critical structure, has undergone extreme fragmentation as a result of three factors," Alderson wrote in January 1983, "gunshot injury, sufficiently prolonged exposure to extreme heat as to result in incineration and postmortem examination and manipulation."

"As a result of the foregoing triad of destructive forces, much of the skull was not (and could not) be made available to us for our examination," he concluded.

Yet, Wolf would later not only testify at a coroner's inquest jury he was able to reconstruct approximately sixty-five percent of Gambet's skull but convinced jurors to accept his conclusion on the caliber of the bullet.

Investigators Not Convinced

As the winter months passed, little changed in determining the size of the bullet that entered Gambet's head. Nichols and Wolf insisted that he was shot with a .22 or .25 caliber pistol. Detectives maintained Gambet killed himself with his .38 caliber Smith and Wesson revolver.

On January 28, 1983, Phil Kitchen, captain of the Lexington Police's criminal investigation section, wrote coroner Hager saying he had been involved in Gambet's death investigation from the beginning and that he had difficulty drawing a firm conclusion of whether suicide or homicide was the cause of death. "Pending the revelation of some new evidence and/or facts I am leaning toward suicide," Kitchen wrote.

Kitchen enclosed a memo Lt. Drexel Neal had prepared for the upcoming coroner's inquest into Gambet's death. Neal pointed out the Lexington police's investigation, based on interviews with witnesses, autopsy findings, scientific examinations and case detectives' observations into Gambet's death was continuing.

In the absence of an eye-witness, Neal said investigators had to rely on circumstantial evidence and expert opinions. "As with any investigation involving the opinion of several experts, we could not always get conclusive findings and we have experienced some conflicts in opinions," he wrote.

"Since conflicts cannot be resolved, it is the opinion of myself and the investigators that our only source of determination is weighing all the evidence, statements, expert opinions and tests against one another. Depending on which of the above one places the most credence and confidence in, obviously affects the conclusions one draws.

In essence, my point is that depending upon whose expert opinion you rely on determines which way the scale will tip," he continued.

Neal, who headed the investigation, said that from the beginning he had instructed his investigators to be as open-minded and objective as possible. He said they approached Gambet's death to determine if he died from natural causes, an accident, suicide or murder. "From our initial contact, it was obvious the death was not accidental and that it also was not due to natural causes. This left only suicide or murder," he wrote.

The problem of determining suicide or homicide, Neal acknowledged, was difficult. "Since most injuries can be found in either of these occurrences, the successful solution to the problem must depend to a great extent on the investigator's opinion, observation and the amount of information he is able to obtain," he said.

Gambet's wound, Neal said, could indicate either suicide or homicide but the Frenchman's gun found at the scene indicated a high probability he took his own life. The detective addressed Wolf's opinion that the entrance and exit wounds were too small to be made by a .38 caliber pistol saying, "The small fracture that Doctor Wolf is calling an entrance wound is, in fact, a fracture caused due to the extreme heat." Neal said Wolf's only evidence of the so-called entrance wound was based only on the measurement of the opening taken during the autopsy and skull reconstruction.

Neal said the skull, that ordinarily would have provided conclusive evidence, was too heavily damaged by the intense heat of the fire. "This caused the skull to have a very large number of heat induced fractures. It also resulted in some of the skull being lost upon removal from the vehicle and also the inability of the pathologist to make a complete examination of the bullet entrance and exit wounds and projectile travel through the brain," he said.

Gambet, according to Neal's letter, discussed the alleged threatening telephone calls with several people he talked to on December 13, and asked one person if he thought he should start carrying his gun. Gambet's erratic behavior along with his business problems, debts and insurance policies led investigators to believe he committed suicide.

"It is our opinion," Neal wrote, "that Mr. Gambet was aware that if his death appeared to be a homicide, his family would be in a position to collect over a million dollars in insurance. This amount would possibly cover all his outstanding debts and assure his family would not be financially ruined by the debts he had incurred. It is also noted that he was observed approximately thirty minutes before the fire started sitting alone in his vehicle on Redd Road."

Neal also listed several indicators that Gambet's death could have been a homicide. "Mr. Gambet was heavily in debt on several horse deals. These debts were in the form of non-contractual agreements with friends and customers. It is believed that several of these people had become upset over the fact they were unable to retrieve their money from the horse deals they had invested in, either with Gambet or at his advice. Although there are no indications, there is the possibility that some of these people have become upset enough to harm Mr. Gambet."

Former detective Vogel disagreed. "No evidence or witnesses placed anyone with Mr. Gambet," he said. "If one is a 'history buff' and looks into the deaths of Central Kentucky horsemen, I'm sure none have ever been murdered over a bad horse deal. After all, when your reputation had been tarnished as was Mr. Gambet's, he was as good as dead in the horse business in Kentucky."

Unlimited time, money and manpower for the investigation, Neal said, would have been unlikely to result in any more information than investigators had already collected.

Lexington police went outside their own investigators to hire experts. The March 3, *Herald-Leader* quoted nationally known arson specialist Barker Davies, from Fort Worth, Indiana, as saying that he initially believed Gambet was murdered but changed his mind after further investigation. Davies' report, which was not in the case file or the coroner's files, reportedly indicated that he supported detectives' theory that Gambet committed suicide.

By March, neither the medical examiners nor the detectives seemed willing to change their respective conclusions on the size of the bullet that resulted in Gambet's death. With no possibility of solving the impasse, coroner Chester Hager convened a coroner's inquest.

Coroner's Inquest

On March 1, 1983, coroner Chester Hager, assisted by county attorney Cecil Dunn, convened a coroner's inquest and impounded a jury to consider evidence in deciding whether Jean Michel Gambet died as a result of murder or suicide. Jurors were Dale S. Kearns, Richard J. Martin, Donald Yates, Delmer L. Dalton, Donald G. Hartman and Diana Tutt, all of Lexington.

Nickell and Fischer, in their book *Mysterious Realms*, wrote that Dunn explained to the jurors, "Because the inquest was a 'non-adversary type hearing,' the police did not cross-examine the expert(s) nor present an expert of their own for rebuttal."

Cissy Gambet testified that her husband's debts were $1.5 million and his assets were about $400,000.

A check with the Fayette County clerk's office on September 6, 2006, revealed the horseman died without a will. Apparently, some accounting work had been done prior to her testimony or she could not have given those figures.

According to the March 2, 1983, *Herald-Leader*, most of Gambet's assets involved his property in France, horses he owned, there and in Lexington, outright or with others and the bloodstock agency he operated with his father-in-law out of his wife's Versailles Road home. Nothing was found to indicate if the bloodstock agency was profitable. His debts included the $500,000 loan from the New Orleans bank, the $200,000 loan from a Lexington bank and a myriad of other obligations.

The jury learned of three Northwestern Mutual Life Insurance Company policies that named his wife as the beneficiary. Those policies were paid up to date, according to the case file, and would pay double indemnity, $1.26 million, for an accidental or homicidal death. If Gambet committed suicide, the policies only paid face value, $630,000.

Gambet had a fourth insurance policy, with the same company, for $250,000, which named the Bank of France as the beneficiary. This policy was intended to cover the mortgage on his farm in France. The farm policy, less than a year old, did not cover suicide but would also pay double indemnity, $500,000, for an accidental or homicidal death.

A legal ruling on whether the horseman was murdered or committed suicide would have an enormous impact not only on Gambet's wife and children but his business associates in Kentucky and in France. If the coroner ruled his death was a suicide, Gambet's family would be mired in financial difficulties and his associates, many of them prominent Lexingtonians, could lose a great deal of money. If the coroner decided Gambet's death was a homicide, the fiscal picture for the family, his partners and the Bank of France brightened considerably.

It was assumed Northwest Mutual eventually paid Gambet's estate the double indemnity claim of $1.26 million.

Gambet's remains provided clues to the cause and manner of his death but it was left up to the inquest jury, the medical examiner and the coroner for interpretation.

Nichols' inquest testimony described Gambet's body as being "Massively incinerated, and since any physical touching of the body caused bony structure of the body to be dissolvable, just literally fragments with touching." His description of the burned remains matched that of officer Davis, who said the remains, especially the skull, crumbled at a touch. Blood from the heart was analyzed, the medical examiner said, and indicated a twenty-six percent saturation of carbon monoxide, meaning Gambet was alive after the fire started, as detectives Thurston and Vogel had surmised.

Toxicology analysis, according to the coroner's records, indicted no salicylates or drugs were found in Gambet's body.

Nichols told jurors he did not examine the skull the first day of the autopsy other than having it x-rayed but carefully examined and dissected the body, below the chin, to determine if Gambet received any trauma to his vital organs, had been beaten, strangled, stabbed or shot in those areas. He had not.

Wolf, the state's forensic anthropologist, was called in by Nichols to look at the results of the autopsy. The next day the two men examined the skull fragments, kept in the separate pouch from the rest of the body, and found no evidence of a bullet within the remains. Leaving Wolf with Gambet's remains, Nichols said he began another autopsy. A few hours later, he said he received a call from Wolf saying he had found a gunshot exit wound in the skull.

"At this point I removed the incinerated and thermally damaged brain of the deceased from the body to allow Dr. Wolf access to the base of the skull so that we could see if there's a wound coming upward through the base of the skull that would have produced the exit wound as we found it," Nichols testified. He added that the brain, due to the intense heat, had shrunken and hardened as the result of the incineration.

Nichols said they found the entry wound in the right orbital plate, a portion of the right frontal bone, which measured 0.25 inches in diameter. Nichols said, in his nearly six years as medical examiner for the commonwealth, he had never seen a suicide wound through an eye.

He pointed out the brain had shrunk by fifty to sixty percent, due to thermal damage. However, he said the bullet track was still visible but not the same size or same diameter as it would have been if incineration had not occurred. Consequently, the bullet track provided little accurate information on the caliber of the bullet.

In describing other damage to the skull, Nichols said the top of the skull had literally exploded when water, from the firemen's hose, was sprayed on the body. Every time the skull was touched or moved, he said, it would crumble and fall apart.

When asked by Dunn to examine the portion of the skull that Wolf determined contained the exit wound, Nicholas stated, "Let's say that this has been somewhat tampered (with) or somewhat changed because of the nature of the bone from the time that I saw this, because it was much clearer in its vicinity circular; the nature and beveling was much more obvious than what your have just shown me."

Nicholas was asked to explain the term beveling. "If you take a B.B. gun and shoot it through a pane of glass," he said, "the hole on the entry side is smaller than the hole on the passage side. The same thing occurs with bone. So that if a projectile passes outward, as it does in this case, the hole on the outside of the skull compared with the hole on the inside of the skull will be bigger. That's called beveling."

The Kentucky State Police lab found no conclusive evidence of beveling when they tested the same portion of the skull.

Nichols engaged in a testy exchange with jurors 352, 353 and 361 over the size of the weapon whose bullet made the holes in Gambet's skull.

Juror 352 asked Nichols, "Are you saying that the entry hole is not consistent with the type of projectile that would come out of that handgun (Gambet's .38 caliber) ?"

"Yes sir," Nichols replied.

Juror 353 asked, "In your opinion do you believe that it was a self inflicted gunshot wound?"

Nichols, relying on his years of experience, said he had never seen a self-inflicted gunshot wound to the eye. "Plus, if the entry would as we believe it is, the diameter of the bony defect excludes a .38 or .357 from being the weapon involved. Does that answer your question?"

The medical examiner's answer failed to satisfy juror 361, who asked, "You are saying that that gun (Gambet's) did not produce the hole in the skull?"

Nichols replied, "I said that gun did not produce the entry wound that we believe to be the entry wound in the right orbital plate. I do not know—heat will literally shrink bone. I know it will cause bone to lose water, but bone, unlike other human tissue has a structural integrity that will prevent it from shrinking as in a similar analogy."

Juror 352 asked, "So, if the part of the skull in the rear, if it was shot with a .38, would that be consistent with the size of the remains you had or would it be larger?"

"The exit wound could be of that size," Nichols replied. "The exit wound could be of that size if it's a .38 caliber round." He explained that there are several variables in exit wounds. "If the round changes in size, if it becomes distorted, if it mushroomed, if it turns so that the—rather the front edge of the projectile strikes the bone, the edge will," he added.

After a few more questions, Dunn closed out Nichols' examination and Wolf was sworn in to testify. The forensic anthropologist said, judging from the photographs taken at the fire scene, "The cranium was pretty much intact, with the exception of one post-mortem defect caused by either the burning or the treatment after the fire.

"When I viewed the cranium, the skull, part of it was still attached to the neck, the remainder of it was in a plastic bag containing soft tissue of the brain, some of the external muscle and miscellaneous bone fragments that had been broken either during recovery or transit to Louisville."

The anthropologist was adamant that fifty percent of the skull was intact. "Probably another third of it was recovered," he continued. "I would imagine the rest of it remained at the scene in the vehicle."

Early in the inquest, Wolf began to lay blame for missing evidence on local investigators. "Frequently this happens when people are not trained in the recovery of these kinds of bodies," he said. "They leave precisely those parts behind because they don't recognize them as parts of a burn victim."

If, as Wolf claimed, he was able to reconstruct that much of the skull, those who worked the fire scene must have been rather proficient in recovering body parts.

He said he suggested to chief deputy coroner Gary Ginn that the remainder of the skull fragments were likely still in the vehicle. "I did not examine the vehicle," Wolf continued, "I was not called to the scene and so I really don't know the events that followed."

Wolf said Ginn told him some additional body parts had been recovered from the car but said he had not seen that material. Ginn clearly stated that the bones he recovered, when examining the burned BMW the day after the fire, were from Gambet's right hand and they had been placed with other body parts. Gambet's skull, not his hand bones, was in question.

Dunn asked Wolf to look at some photographs and inquired if he was supplied those pictures before examining Gambet's remains. Apparently, Dunn was inferring Wolf was not present when the pictures were taken of Gambet's body after it arrived in Louisville for the autopsy.

Wolf admitted pieces were missing from the skull and, not having been at the scene, he knew what happened. "This is a post-mortem defect," he said, "caused by the fire and/or the putting out of the fire and extinguishing the body. That's typical when bodies are found in a burning structure or vehicle. If they are not extinguished in the proper manner, the cold water hitting them will cause that kind of defect and that is typical of that type of defect."

Keep in mind the first responders all reported that Gambet's skull crumbled at a touch and the skull had been transported from Lexington to Louisville and on to Cleveland before being returned to Lexington. It was amazing that there was anything left to examine at the coroner's inquest.

What Wolf determined was an exit wound in the skull measured .45 of an inch, could have well been fracture damage from the fire as investigators pointed out.

Wolf referenced the KSP Crime Lab report, prepared by Lawrence W. King only to verify his original measurements of what he termed the entrance wound. He neglected to say that the Crime Lab was sent only the bone fragment from the right orbital area of the skull, which he determined to be the entrance wound. Nor did he tell jurors that King's report stated, "No appreciable lead was found around the hole and beveling around the edge was very slight and inconclusive."

Instead Wolf told jurors, "It's more likely that lead particles would be present from the flattened projectile on the exit wound than on the entrance wound because the location of the entrance wound provided very little resistance to the projectile. The thin bone on the upper part of the eye orbit was not of sufficient thickness to provide a resistance that would deform the bullet and likely to cause small deposits of lead and so forth to be deposited in the bone, which is typical of an exit wound or passage through a very large bone, such as an arm or leg bone. So, to my knowledge that analysis has not been performed."

Wolf further explained, "I talked with Lt. Neal, explained to him that the caliber of the entrance and exit wound(s) could not have been (made by) a .38. It had to have been a smaller caliber handgun."

Wolf, like Nichols, was showed the piece of skull bone, which contained, what he called, the entrance wound. "It's similar. It appears to--it--is it--appears to be the original bone but the entrance wound itself seems to have been, again, deformed somewhat since the time I saw it."

The anthropologist differed with Nichols' exploding skull theory. "The condition of the skull in this case, at least the parts that I saw that had been recovered, did not indicate that it was of such a nature that it would have been destroyed and crumbly and vaporized as a result of the burning." Wolf appeared to be the only person connected with the case to believe the skull was not severely damaged by the intense heat of the automobile fire. What was even more astounding was most of the inquest jurors actually believed his testimony.

Dunn asked Wolf, "Does the fire ever react and make the bones brittle and break up and powdery?"

The anthropologist said that it did.

The attorney had another question, "And in this particular case, what was the skull, what was the consistency of it?"

"The consistency of the skull was not of the degree of incineration to cause that type of destruction," Wolf replied. "The feet, I could not speak to because I did not see those, apparently those were not recovered."

Evidently, the anthropologist failed to read the case report or even Nichols' autopsy findings.

No copy of Wolf's written report on the Gambet case was found either in the police or coroner's case files. Nichols admitted to the jurors that he had never received a report on the case from the anthropologist, though Wolf said he sent him a report.

Did Wolf even make a report on his reconstruction of Gambet's skull? If so, where was evidence to support his theories?

Wolf and Nichols agreed the weapon used to make, what they determined were entrance and exit wounds in Gambet's head was either a .22 or .25 caliber pistol. Wolf said if Gambet shot himself with the .38 found at the scene, "He (would have had to) shoot himself, switch hands and pitch it out the window, it is highly unlikely that those series of events would have occurred." He admitted that he did not know if Gambet was right handed or left handed.

"If indeed, Mr. Gambet had shot himself in the right eyeball," Wolf continued, "we do not have that information—shooting himself in the right eyeball, the gun would have fallen down in the middle of the car, in the middle area or to the right side, the passenger side."

Wolf's gaffe about Gambet pitching the gun out the car window was allowed by county Attorney Cecil Dunn to stand. There was no need for Gambet to even attempt to toss the gun out the window since the driver's side door was open. Wolf apparently did not read the firemen and detectives' reports saying the gun had probably been flushed out of the car by the power of the high pressure firemen's hoses. He was not asked nor or did he address the lack of residue, from the burned pistol's grip, where the gun was found indicating it did not burn on the ground.

In answering questions about whether Gambet was shot inside or outside the car, Wolf waffled with his reply. "It was difficult to say for sure whether he was totally inside or outside the car, but from the position of the body, at least when it was photographed, it was lying forward and into the middle of the car, face forward with the head down. And if in fact he was shot in the car you would expect to find it there."

Juror 352 asked Wolf if Gambet could have been shot outside the vehicle and if the position of the body indicated someone had picked him up and laid him across the seat without taking time to put his legs in the car. Wolf again refused to provide a definitive answer. "That is a reconstructible scenario," he replied.

The juror persisted, "His body was in such a position that that could have taken place?"

The anthropologist replied, "Yes sir. It appears from the information that I saw, which was limited to a few photographs of the scene."

Despite Wolf's admitted limited knowledge of the position of the body at the death scene, he continued to spin his own case scenario for the jury.

Wolf literally bombarded the coroner's inquest jury with slide presentations. He brought in sample skulls to illustrate the difference in bullet wounds' exit and entrance sizes to prove a gun, of a smaller caliber than the revolver Gambet owned, was used. He utilized an old, empty skull, shot through with a .22 caliber bullet, to demonstrate the size differences between that shell and a .38 caliber bullet.

On it face, it was compelling evidence.

Wolf was not questioned by either Dunn or the jurors concerning different results obtained by firing a bullet through an empty skull and one traveling through a skull filled with brains and tissue and covered with hair and skin.

The anthropologist said he disagreed with the conclusions of arson expert Baker Davies and detectives Neal,

Vogel and Thurston that Gambet saturated his body with the accelerant before starting the fire and shooting himself. Wolf also questioned the length of time investigators said the automobile burned and temperature being in excess of 2,000 degrees, although he had no concrete proof to support his opinions.

There was a vast chasm in what Wolf actually knew and the assumptions he broadly made without any supporting evidence.

Only the inquest testimonies of the forensic physicians, Nichols, Wolf and Benrstein appeared to have survived. Consequently, no testimony of the other inquest witnesses was available for comparison. On the coroner's witness list, arson expert Barker Davies was scheduled to testify before the three forensic specialists but his testimony, which supported suicide as the cause of death, was not in the coroner's or detectives' case files.

Attempting to locate the remaining Gambet inquest testimony was still another mystery connected to the puzzling case.

An Open Records Act (ORA) request of Fayette County coroner Gary Ginn's office produced none of the testimony of the thirty-two other witnesses who were subpoenaed to appear before the inquest jury. The coroner's office did not even have the seventy-three pages of testimony from Nichols, Wolf and Bernstein, which came from the police case file. The author provided her copy for the coroner to replicate for his case file.

A September 6, 2006, telephone call to Jerry Carlton, in Frankfort at the Kentucky Department of Libraries and Archives (KDLA), where state documents are housed, provided a clue to the mystery of the missing testimony from the Gambet inquest.

When coroner Chester Hager retired, Carlton explained, "We had to go to court to get Chester Hager's files; he wanted to take some of his files with him." Carlton added that the KDLA took the matter of custody of the coroner's records, which belonged to the office not an individual, to the Fayette County Attorney's office. Carlton said, "The county attorney persuaded Chester to return the records."

However, the Archives had none of the coroner's case records in Gambet's death.

Another ORA request to current Fayette County attorney Larry Roberts provided no further information. Roberts, in a September 13, 2006, letter, said his office had no records of the KDLA's request concerning the coroner's documents. "We have inquired of my successor in office and understand that no such records were in the care, custody or control of this office during her term of office from 1993 to 2006."

Yet, another ORA request, concerning the inquest testimony, was made to former coroner Chester Hager in an effort to locate the records from his tenure as coroner. Hager chose not to reply to the request and was not required by law to do so since he no longer held the office.

The coroner's case file included the names of jurors and witnesses called to testify. Would the testimony of detectives Drexel Neal, John Thurston, Philip Vogel, William Allen, Leroy Richardson; firemen Remious Day, Tommy Hayes and Robert Work; arson expert Barker Davies, and others have refuted the questionable testimony of Dr. David Wolf? How much importance would the jurors have given to the testimony of the first responders who worked the death scene, if they heard them?

Officer Y. S. Davis, who was the officer of report in the Gambet case, was not subpoenaed to testify before the inquest jury. Her testimony that Gambet's skull crumbled into ashes at a touch would have refuted Wolf's claim that he was able to reconstruct almost two-thirds of the skull.

Testimony of Gambet's family, farm employees and those he did business with could have provided interesting information. The testimony of his housekeeper, Mabel Jones, would have been most enlightening. The inquest testimony of Joe Manypenny, who was subpoenaed, would have provided an insight into the dark world Jean Michel Gambet inhabited in the days before his death.

Others, who owned an interest in Thoroughbreds with Gambet, included Elizabeth McAshan, of Troy; W. L. Wilson and Frank F. Wilson II, of Lexington; John O. McKinstry III and Lucy J. McKinstry, of Lexington; William R. B. "Berry" Potter, and Guy Bradley, of Lexington, and John W. Phillips, of Columbus, Ohio, were not subpoenaed for the coroner's inquest. McAshan and the McKinstrys had extensive dealings with Gambet.

Coroner Chester Hager and county attorney Cecil Dunn controlled the decisions on who was subpoenaed and which witnesses would appear before the coroner's inquest jury.

With the investigators' and first responders' testimony unavailable, Neal's January 28, 1983, letter to Hager, provided a revealing look at the rapid fraying relationship between detectives, the coroner and the county attorney.

Neal said the arson expert, Davies, staged a reenactment of the scene using a similar model BMW. "It is our theory that after dousing the interior of the vehicle with kerosene, which he had already obtained in the container found in the car, he also doused himself with the liquid. At this point, we theorize he ignited the kerosene somewhere within the car after throwing the can over into the right floorboard. Since kerosene and gasoline mixed is a slow burning flammable liquid, it is feasible that after he ignited the liquid he still had enough time to commit the suicide act."

According to Neal's theory, Gambet shot himself, dropped the gun, fell into the driver's seat and continued to have vital signs since carbon monoxide and soot particles were found within his body.

The position of Gambet's body, Neal explained was only slighted altered due to the intense heat of the vehicle fire. "In severe burning of the victim's bodies, the body will experience what is commonly called 'the pugilistic attitude.' This causes the arms to assume a position similar to what a boxer would use in his defense stance. It also causes the legs to draw up."

Neal solved the question of whether Gambet was right or left handed. The head wound was consistent, he pointed out, with one inflicted with the right hand and he established that the horseman was right handed. He said all the BMW's doors were locked except for the driver's side door.

Based on the reconstruction, Neal said, the bullet would have traveled upward and out from the vehicle or it possibly struck the driver's door. "Since that area of the car experienced the most extreme heat, any projectile would have melted and probably vaporized," he added.

The coroner's inquest jurors deliberated six hours and five minutes before deciding that Gambet's death resulted from a homicide. The five men voted for homicide but Diana Tutt abstained. Jurors Don Hartman and Dale Kearns, according to the March 3, 1983, *Herald-Leader*, were impressed by the testimony of Nichols and Wolf. "I felt it was the most hard evidence we had and it did not fit the suicide scenario," Hartman was quoted as saying. Mrs. Tutt declined to comment on the verdict.

Upon hearing Hager read the jurors' decision, the newspaper reported Cissy Gambet, sitting with friends and her brother Harry B. Scott III, an Episcopal bishop who lived in Virginia, exclaimed, "It's over, it's over!"

Unfortunately for the Gambet family, the controversial case was far from over but a vast financial burden had been lifted from their shoulders.

Hager's signature on Gambet's death certificate enabled his beneficiaries to collect $1.26 million in insurance policies. The $500,000 insurance payment from the fourth policy presumably took care of the mortgage on his farm in France. Who inherited the farm was not known.

Investigators strongly disagreed with the results of the coroner's inquest jury. Capt. Phil Kitchen, in a memo to the files, wrote, "It is the opinion of the case investigators that the unresolved and conflicting opinions of Dr. Wolf was the reason the coroner's jury voted for murder as the cause of death at the inquest. The jury was not aware of all the case information and several points were not brought out or (not) brought out completely or stressed to the jury. The jury was not made aware of Dr. Wolf's previous mistakes in identifying human remains and some errors in his testimony were not challenged."

Wolf was a man with a trail of dreadful forensic decisions but the coroner's inquest jury was not made aware of that fact. There were a number of reasons to doubt his veracity.

Kitchen's reference was to a case where Wolf incorrectly identified animal remains as being human. Five years earlier, Wolf made an even worse blunder in a Louisville case.

The August 12, 2004, *Courier-Journal* reported Wolf identified bones found in Louisville's Villa Ana subdivision, in 1977, as those of an African-American girl, murdered by a blow to the head, and buried ten to fifteen years earlier. The slivers of wood found with the remains, Wolf said, were debris from sewer construction, which occurred at the location at the time of her death.

In 2004, Dr. Emily Craig, the state's forensic anthropologist who succeeded Wolf, was asked to re-examine the Villa Ana case. The results, according to the newspaper, were astounding. Dr. Craig determined the remains were those of a young female adult buried in the mid to late 1880s and the hole in the skull was typical bone deterioration. What Wolf called construction debris turned out to be pieces of wood from the woman's coffin, according to Craig.

Craig said she was unable to explain Wolf's findings. "Mistakes happen, that's all I know how to say it," she told the newspaper. "It's good that it's been cleared up. It's unfortunate that the agency had to carry it as an unsolved homicide for all these years."

The mistakes Wolf made in the Gambet case are not likely to be corrected.

Detectives turned to another forensic pathologist in January 1983, six weeks before the coroner's inquest was convened. Dr. Lester Adelson, professor of forensic pathology at Case Western Reserve University Medical School and chief deputy coroner of Cuyahoga County, (Cleveland) Ohio, was asked by detective Thurston to examine portions of Gambet's skull, which he said were inadequate to provide any conclusions on the caliber of the bullet which killed the horseman due to extreme fragmentation.

The list of coroner's inquest witnesses did not include Dr. Adelson, whose January 20, 2983, letter, with the results of his examination, would have directly refuted Wolf's testimony.

However, detectives were not willing to give up on the investigation.

In August 1983, detectives called in Baltimore forensic pathologist Dr. Rudiger Breitenecker to examine their investigatory practices, case file and conclusions. His medical degree came from the University of Vienna (Austria) and, while doing a pathology residency at Cleveland's Metropolitan General Hospital, he taught at Case Western Reserve University. A former medical examiner, Breitenecker had taught forensic pathology at the University of Maryland, John Hopkins Medical School and the University of Louisville's Southern Police Institute. After two other pathologists failed to determine the cause of the 1978 death of Rev. Jim Jones in Jonestown, Guyana, Breitenecker was retained by the Department of State to examine the body and found the cause of death. He also performed autopsies on Jonestown's poisoning victims.

Due to the incineration of Gambet's body, Breitenecker, like Adelson, found problems with the autopsy due to loss of much of the skull and partial obliteration of the bullet wound track. His notes, in the case file, pointed out no metal fragments were found in the skull x-rays and expressed doubt the 0.25" opening was the entrance wound. "Extensive burning, fracturing and missing bone fragments from that region (skull) cast serious doubt upon its exact significance," he wrote. "If it actually was the entry wound," he added, "it represents only an incomplete fractured portion of the wound unsuitable for definite statements as to the caliber of the bullet involved." Breitenecker said he had consulted with medical examiners from Maryland and Texas and none recalled an instance where a .22 caliber bullet exited the thickest part of the skull as described in the Gambet autopsy report.

"The exhibit at the hearing (coroner's inquest) of an old skull shot through by a .22 ca. bullet is totally misleading and irrelevant to this case," he said. "A head with skin and brains simply cannot be compared with an empty skull."

He countered Nichols and Wolf's argument that suicide victims did not shoot themselves in the eye by saying the weapon could have discharged prematurely because of the intense heat. "The position of the body with potential interference of the right arm by the driver's seat lends some credence to this thought," Breitenecker said.

Neal sent a copy of the Baltimore pathologist's report to coroner Chester Hager and county attorney Cecil Dunn. In a June 6, 1983, letter to Kitchen, Neal pointed out the Bietenecker's report, which was in direct conflict with Nichols and Wolf's opinions, should be considered new and very significant evidence. "The Coroner's Jury Verdict," he told Kitchen, "is only advisory to the coroner. Its decision is in no way a mandate to a law enforcement agency nor does it have any force of law."

Neal found himself caught in a 'dog and pony' show between the country attorney and the coroner. "The oral report which was given to me by Coroner Hager was that the County Attorney was not sure what he could do in the matter," Neal told Kitchen. "My previous conversation with Cecil Dunn led me to believe there were only two options: (1) call for a new coroner's jury and inquest or (2) Chester Hager could amend the death certificate and notify Frankfort of the change. Mr. Dunn further stated that his recommendation would the latter."

"He (Dunn) further added," Neal wrote, "that he would recommend that if Chester chose the second option he would recommend that he hold a news conference and release new evidence and answer questions by the media. We both agreed that Chester would have great difficulty doing either of the two options."

"I was later advised by Chester," Neal continued, "that Cecil (Dunn) did not know what could be done. Chester then asked me to get an opinion from the Attorney General's Office in regards to the options." When Neal asked the Attorney General's office for an opinion, he was told the request had to come from the coroner.

Neal pressed for the conflict be resolved in one of three ways: officially request a new coroner's inquest; officially ask for an amended death certificate or, if neither of those steps were taken, for the police to officially change the manner of death to suicide for their internal reporting purposes and call a news conference to make the announcement.

Before the police could schedule their news conference, Nichols stoutly defended his and Wolf's conclusions. According to the September 25, 1983, *Herald-Leader*, Nichols, in a speech to a medical technology group in Lexington, again declared Gambet's death was a homicide. "The police department, for reasons known only to the investigating officers, has sacrificed the truth," he was quoted as saying. Neither did Breitenecker escape his scorn. Nichols called him a scientist past his prime. He said if Breitenecker could not find conclusive evidence of the .22 or .25 caliber bullet wound it was because the bone fragments from Gambet's skull had been "Handled, mishandled or damaged since the autopsy."

On September 30, 1983, the Lexington Division of Police released a lengthy statement, which concluded, "The death of Jean Michel Gambet is being officially classified as suicide for internal police reporting purposes." The statement was even-handed and listed reasons why homicide or suicide could be considered the cause of death. The detectives faulted the evidence presented to the coroner's inquest jury. Their statement made it clear the case would be re-opened if new and credible evidence was found.

That was unlikely to happen. Still, the Gambet family's trials continued.

Business Maze

After the coroner Chester Hager ruled Gambet's death was a homicide and signed the death certificate, Cissy Gambet was cleared to receive the insurance money from her husband's policies. Problems for his family, however, continued. His wife and father-in-law became enmeshed in efforts to straighten out his personal assets and ownership of eighteen Thoroughbred broodmares, nine yearlings and seven foals.

Declining to administer her husband's estate, Cissy Gambet asked her father to do it instead. Harry B. Scott II, was appointed estate administrator by Fayette District Court on March 3, 1983, the day after the coroner signed the death certificate. Scott posted a surety bond of $150,000 surety bond as the estate administrator.

Retired detective Vogel considered it peculiar that Gambet's business partner in the bloodstock agency would be appointed to settle his estate. He considered it a possible conflict of interest.

Cissy Gambet's request that $7,500 be set aside for her use was granted by the court according to probate file, No. 83-f-136, in Fayette District Court.

Gambet's only real property, the farm in France, was, according to the probate file, worth $200,000, and the value of horses on the farm was estimated to be 3346,650 in French Francs or $508,609 in American Dollars. However, not all of the horses belonged to Gambet.

His interests in Thoroughbred horses, in Kentucky, was set at $100,000, including those he owned outright and in various partnerships. His tangible personal property was estimated to be $50,000.

Although these were only estimates, a number of individual items far exceeded the tangible personal property estimate. The Munnings painting had cost Gambet $52,000. The seven Queen Ann side chairs, circa 1740-1760, were purchased by the horseman for $65,000. Other equine paintings and bronzes, furniture, Oriental carpets and his antique gun and camera collections were estimated to be worth much more than $50,000.

For more than two centuries, those who estimated the worth of Kentucky estates often leaned toward either a lower estimate or a higher figure, whichever one was the most advantageous for the deceased's family.

Israel Sack Inc., the New York antique dealer, agreed to take back the antique walnut chairs, according to the probate file, and paid the estate the $31,000 Gambet had paid on them.

There was no indication in the probate file, which lacked a final accounting or settlement, of what the disposition was of his farm in France and his interests in the Thoroughbreds there.

A deputy clerk in the Fayette District Court probate office, when asked why there was no final accounting of the estate settlement, replied that, unless someone asked for it, such a settlement was not required.

Scott, Gambet's partner in the Euro-American Bloodstock Agency and now administrator of his estate, discovered his late son-in-law kept practically no records of any type in his personal business. Scott, who kept the books for their bloodstock business, stated in the probate file that he had to reconstruct records and review bank accounts since Gambet failed to even keep stubs from the checks he had written.

It was possible that some of Gambet's personal business records burned up in the car with him. Detective Leroy Richardson mentioned boxes of burned books and catalogues found in the back seat of the car. Gambet possibly had some of his records in those boxes. Ownership records of horses Gambet owned himself or had an interest in, when Scott finally pieced most of them back together, placed the Frenchman in a most unfavorable light, which could explain his failure to keep adequate accounts or his possible intent to destroy what records he did keep.

Three weeks after being appointed administrator of his son-in-law's estate, Scott was sued by Don Sucher for $600,000. Don Sturgill, Gambet's former attorney, filed the suit in Fayette Circuit Court on behalf of Sucher. The amount, according to the March 25, 1983, *Herald*, included the $500,000 note, on which Sucher said he had paid $100,000 plus interest the previous December, plus $98,600 for stud fees, which Sucher said he advanced Gambet, but the horseman never paid to the stallions' owners. The action also asked that Sucher's interests in horses he owned with Gambet be protected.

The court case file included a record of three checks Sucher had given Gambet. A December 16, 1981, check to Gambet for $67,230.00 was for a half-interest in "Moon Trip" and "Afleet." An August 9, 1982, check for $34,503.00, that Sucher gave Gambet, was for stud fees, boarding and vet bills. A certified check made out to Gambet for $20,000.00 went to the First National Bank.

Sturgill, according to his October 2002, obituary in *Texas Horsemen*, was one of the nation's foremost equine attorneys specializing in syndication, simulcasting and was considered an expert on the Interstate Horse Racing Act of 1978. A political activist who worked in the presidential campaigns of Lyndon B. Johnson and John F. Kennedy, he had been general counsel for the National Horsemen's Benevolent and Protective Association and formerly owned Beaconsfield Farm, in Lexington, with his brother Thomas C. Sturgill.

Don Sturgill, according to detective John Thurston's December 14, 1982, memo in the case file, stated that Gambet had the money to make a payment on the New Orleans bank loan. "Mr. Sturgill did relate to me," Thurston wrote, "that on December 1, Mr. Gambet had a $500,000 note due, that he had put a down payment on..."

What happened to the money Sturgill said Gambet had for the loan payment was another mystery. Had Gambet diverted those funds to other ventures? Or, did he actually make the payment? His business affairs were in such disarray it was impossible to determine.

Scott's co-defendants in the lawsuit were partners with Gambet on various horse deals. The included Guy Bradley, assistant vice-president of Kentucky Mortgage Company; Steven Parrish, with Mutual of New York; William R. B. "Berry" Potter, who headed Coleman Smith Heating and Air Conditioning; John and Lucy McKinstry, childhood friends of Cissy Gambet's who owned Montrose Farm on Bryan Station Pike, and Elizabeth McAshan, who lived in Troy in Woodford County.

According to Scott's May 26, 1983, deposition concerning horse ownerships, Bradley, Parrish, Potter and Gambet each had a quarter interest in "Doubling Time," "Cezana" and "Spyboat." Potter and Gambet each had a half interest in "East Dancer." Four of the horses in Gambet's possession, "Knightside," "My Red Devil," "Marie Galante" and "Indian Satin," were owned entirely by Parrish, according to Scott.

Sucher, in his April 1, 1983, deposition, said he had been in the horse business for seventeen years and met Gambet seven years earlier when he was the agent for "Princess Mistletoe" when the plaintiff purchased the horse. Sucher testified that he had finalized forty or fifty previous horse deals where he did not require Jockey Club ownership certificates prior to the sales. In his deposition, he described the buying and selling of Thoroughbreds as a, "Trust type business."

Sucher, according to his deposition, had paid Gambet $67,230 for half interest in two mares, "Afleen" and "Moon Gem," who were on the farm in France. Sucher said he did not ask Gambet to produce Jockey Club ownership certificates for those horses.

There were further twists concerning the $500,000 loan. Sucher, in his deposition, said he agreed not only to co-sign the note but made arrangements with Louis Roussel III, an officer with the American Bank and Trust Company in

New Orleans, to lend Gambet the money for a deposit on a stallion he wanted to purchase from the Aga Kahn and syndicate.

That was the first time syndication was mention in connection with Vayrann. Did Gambet intend to sell his tenth interest in the stallion, use it for collateral to borrow money or did he have an agreement to purchase the remaining ninety percent of the stallion?

There was no mention of the stallion, Vayrann, in his estate's probate file.

Sucher's testimony indicated that he had a more than casual relationship with Roussel, the New Orleans banker. The Scott County horseman said he called Roussel to make arrangements for the note only a couple of days before the loan was signed at a Lexington bank. Sucher, revealed in his deposition, that he advised Roussel on purchases of horses and boarded some of the Louisiana man's Thoroughbreds at his Echo Valley Horse Farm.

Roussel, according to former *Times-Picayune* reporter Tyler Bridges' book, *Bad Bet on the Bayou*, was known as "Little Louie" in New Orleans to distinguish him from his father who established the family fortune from banking, oil and gas, gaming and politics. During the 1980s, the Roussels owned Fairgrounds Race Course, in New Orleans, the third oldest continuous operating track in America. Roussel later purchased "Risen Star" from Bourbon County Thoroughbred breeder Arthur B. Hancock III, and the horse won the 1987 Preakness and Belmont.

In the investigation of the gaming scandal, that sent Louisiana Governor Edwin Edwards to prison in 1996, "Little Louie" Roussel had sacks of money, $2,500 for favored senators and $1,000 for representatives, distributed by the leaders on the legislative floors, according to Bridges.

From all indications, Gambet was far out of his league with men like Roussel.

In return for his arranging the $500,000 loan from Roussel, Sucher said in his deposition, Gambet promised to give him first refusal on any horse, stallion shares or seasons he handled on a reduced or no commission basis. Sucher also required Gambet to put up collateral to guarantee the loan.

It was interesting that Sucher, the middleman, not the lender, Roussel's bank, required collateral for the loan.

Gambet pledged five horses to Sucher as security for the loan. Those horses included "Doubling Time," in which, according to Scott's deposition, Gambet had only a quarter interest; "Katie Mae, in which he had a half interest;" "Sally," in which he owned no interest and his half interests in "Afleen" and "Moon Gem." Sucher said, in his deposition, that he was with Gambert at Keeneland in September 1980, when he purchased "Doubling Time" and was unaware Parrish also owned an interest in the horse.

Cissy Gambet, in her August 11, 1983 deposition, said her husband had told her that Potter, Parrish and Bradley each owned a quarter interest in "Doubling Time." She also said her husband planned to give their daughters a half interest in "Sally."

Sucher admitted, in his April 21, 1983 deposition, that he did not ask Gambet if he was the sole owner of the horses he pledged to guarantee the half-million-dollar loan.

Scott, in a June 21, 1983 deposition, said when Gambet brought "Doubling Time" to his Shandon Farm to board he told him he owned a quarter interest in the horse along with Parrish, Potter and Bradley. However, Scott said he was unable to find any partnership documents or agreements concerning the horse after Gambet's death.

The bank note, Sucher testified, was executed at the First Security Bank and Trust Company's Gardenside branch on September 15, 1982, because it was more convenient for all involved and "Little" Louie Roussel was more than willing to make the trip from New Orleans to Lexington. After much confusion and dithering by the witness and his attorneys, according to Sucher's deposition, they finally agreed the note was signed September 8, 1982.

They were mistaken.

When asked by Jod D. Turner III, attorney for Stephen Parrish, if he was aware Gambet actually borrowed the money prior to September 15th, Sucher appeared rather confused. There was no mistaking the date the note was signed. Both the copy of the New Orleans bank's signed promissory note and their bank's audit, from the police case file, dated the loan as being executed on August 8, 1982.

"Are you saying other monies, prior, to or, I, I'm not sure I'm quite, you're wording is coming across?" Sucher asked. Turning to Sturgill, Sucher said, "I'm not sure what he means."

Sucher and his counsel, according to his deposition, discussed whether or not the loan was a sixty-day note and whether it was signed on September 1st, 8th or 15th. "I'm not taking time to read all my notes, I guess," Sucher said. Apparently, Sucher and his attorneys were not reading their own exhibits filed in the case, either.

Exhibit # 1, from the court case file, was a copy of the American Bank and Trust Company bank note signed by Gambet and Sucher, in the lawsuit against Gambet's estate clearly stated the note was executed on August 8, 1982, and the period of time for repayment was "A year of 365 days." Was the September 8, 1982, date simply a mistake or were there two loans? Why was there so much confusion over the date the note for the bank loan was signed?

Actually, the question of the various loan signing dates corresponded with other events surrounding Gambet's life and death, most of which appeared to be confusing, convoluted and often contradicting.

Sucher, in his examination by Turner, said he intended to co-sign the loan as owner of Echo Valley Horse Farm, not as Donald Sucher individually. "It should have been Echo Valley Horse Farm and at a later date after the execution of the note it was discovered I believe while my wife was filing them away that my name was on them and not the farm." Sucher said that his attorney in Detroit, Irving Keene, drew up a September 24, 1982, Assignment, Exhibit #2 in the lawsuit file, which transferred the note to Echo Valley Horse Farm.

There was no indication of why Sucher, already represented in Lexington by Don Sturgill, noted for his equine legal talents, also employed a Detroit, Michigan, lawyer to handle legal matters for his farm, which he described as containing less than seventy-two acres.

The Assignment Keene executed for Sucher, transferring the note to the farm, stated the date the $500,000 loan and security agreement documents were signed was September 8, 1982.

Apparently, for some reason, September 8, 1982 was the date Sucher and his attorneys were determined to use and the court did not blink an eye.

In his June 21, 1983, deposition, Scott answered, for the most part, the question of how Gambet used the $500,000 he borrowed. According to Scott's reconstructed records of Gambet's finances: $22,500 went to Ecurie Fourty; $158,000 was transferred to Gambet's bank in France; $21,000 went to Haras Vu Victode; $13,150 was paid for a season to "Mr. Leader;" Guy Bradley received $57,000; $20,000 was paid on the Bank of Commerce loan plus $6,680 in interest; $7,340 went to Ropar Development Company; $2,000 paid a bill to General Telephone Company; $340 was used for horse insurance; $1,650 was used to reduce his American Express account; $1,600 went to a French company for a video of his farm and operations in Basse-Normandie, and $166,000 was paid to the Aga Khan for the tenth interest in Vayrann.

The payment to the Aga Kahn, Scott cited, opened up even more questions.

The copy of Gambet's August 2, 1982, check to the S. H. Aga Kahn for $166,000, from the police case file, was clearly marked insufficient funds and had been returned from a Paris, France, bank. Perhaps, Scott found another bank transaction confirming that another check was issued or the August 2nd check cleared on a second deposit. The check was for a tenth interest in the Aga Kahn's stallion, Vayrann. There was no mention in Gambet's estate probate file concerning an interest in the stallion. As Gambet left no will, there was no record of what happened to his property in France, the horses he owned there or his interest in Vayrann.

Scott, according to the probate file, spent nearly 12,000 hours attempting to straighten out Gambet's business affairs and the Thoroughbreds his son-in-law owned both individually and in partnerships with various investors. He managed to reconstruct the ownership of most of the horses in Gambet's possession. Establishing ownership of "Melantha" and her foal proved difficult. Scott said he believed that John W. Phillips, from Columbus, Ohio, paid Gambet for a half interest in the two horses but he lacked "Sufficient information to form an opinion or belief as to the actual ownership of this mare, or her 1983 progeny."

Fayette Circuit Judge Armand Angelucci, who had been the county attorney during the Betty Gail Brown murder investigation, had moved up to the bench. Angelucci apparently used the records reconstructed by Scott, as set out in his fourteen-page deposition, and testimony provided by the investors to determine ownership of the horses.

Angelucci ruled that Echo Valley Horse Farm owned a half interest in "Afleet" and "Moon Gem," plus the estate's interests in "Doubling Time," "Katie Mae" and "Sally." Scott's May 26, 1983 deposition clearly stated that "Sally" was jointly owned by Elizabeth McAshan and the McKinstrys. "Sally" produced a filly, according to Scott, before Gambet sold his half interest in the mare to McAshan and Scott said that the filly was jointly owned by the estate and the McKinstrys.

Tom Moller testified, according to the court case file, that he paid Gambet $50,000 for a half interest in "Minifer" and also owned a half interest in her two foals for whom he paid the stud fees and mortality insurance. The other half interest in the three horse, Scott found belonged to Gambet's estate. Jill Moller verified, in her testimony, her husband's statements. Another mare, "Noua," Scott said was owned entirely by Moller.

The judge also ruled that Sucher was due the $98,600 he paid to Gambet for stud fees and $30,000 from the sale of

"Doubling Time." The estate, he ruled, was liable for the $500,000 New Orleans bank loan.

All of Scott's co-defendants had to pay their own attorneys and court costs.

Scott was paid $40,000 for his work as estate administrator, according to the probate file. The Bank of Commerce and Trust, one of Gambet's creditors, objected saying he was only entitled to the normal rate of five percent. However, District Court judge John Adams ruled Scott was entitled to that amount due to the extraordinary and unusual condition of the estate.

Adams' ruling, that the estate was extraordinary and unusual, mirrored the confusing events that followed Gambet in life and death.

Cissy Gambet, according to the October 11, 1987, *Herald-Leader*, married Harry Collins, who was associated with the Frankfort, Kentucky, real estate firm of Chenault and Hoge, Inc. She was married in the same church where she wed Jean Michel Gambet thirteen years earlier.

Whether he killed himself or was murdered, Gambet's death had a lingering effect on a lot of lives and questions about his demise remain unanswered. The coroner's decision, despite the work of detectives, that the cause of his death was murder, by person or persons unknown, remains on the death certificate.

Lexington's Division of Police continue to maintain, for their internal reporting records, that Gambet's cause of death was suicide resulting from a head wound inflicted with his own weapon after he started the fire that cremated his body.

Neither Chester Hager, nor any coroner since he left office in 1989, has seen fit to open another inquiry into Gambet's death.

A small, but vocal, group still contends that Gambet was killed by the Mafia or hired assassins but lack any evidence to back up those theories. There is a theory that an exceedingly wealthy person or persons, with a deep, consuming loathing of the Frenchman could have jetted into the Lexington airport, killed Gambet and were long gone before the smoke from the burning BMW was ever reported.

Philip Vogel maintains that the cause of Gambet's death was so unique there was no other conclusion than suicide.

"I am as convinced today," he said in a January 2007, interview, "as I was back then that Jean Michel Gambet sought a honorable way to spare his wife and children and the Scott family the indignation of being labeled untrustworthy, a scoundrel and financially indigent."

Regardless of the legal haggling over whether Gambet was shot with a .22, .25 or .38 caliber revolver or if he killed himself or was murdered, the final resolution was certainly justice delayed and justice denied.

About the Author

Justice Delayed, Justice Denied is the fourth book by former journalist Betty Boles Ellison. Her previous books were *Kentucky's Domain of Power, Greed and Corruption*, about a century of athletic scandals at the University of Kentucky; *Illegal Odyssey, 200 Years of Kentucky Moonshine*, which included interviews with moonshiners and the revenue agents who pursued and sometimes caught them, and *A Man Seen But Once*, a biography of Cassius Marcellus Clay, one of the nation's most dynamic nineteenth century politicians who was President Abraham Lincoln's minister to Russia.

Mrs. Ellison attended Centre College, Danville, Kentucky, has a Bachelor of Arts degree in American history and a Master of Arts degree in Kentucky History from the University of Kentucky, plus thirty-two post-baccalaureate hours of graduate history seminar work.

She edited the *History of the Daniel Boone National Forest* for the U.S. Forest Service; researched a book for Kentucky's historian laureate Thomas D. Clark; was a research consultant for David Grubin Production's PBS documentary on Mary Todd and Abraham Lincoln; did research for and was interviewed on the 2002 CBS Sports Special about the 1966 UK-Texas Western NCAA championship basketball game.

For eleven years, Mrs. Ellison sat on the board of the Kentucky Mansions Preservation Foundation, which restored and operates the Mary Todd Lincoln House, in Lexington, the first shrine in America to honor a former First Lady. She was also involved in the restoration of White Hall, the ancestral home of Cassius Marcellus Clay.

Current projects include a biography of Mary Todd Lincoln and the history and management of stock car racing in the United States.